# The Hip Girl's Handbook

## for Home, Car, & Money Stuff

# The Hip Girl's Handbook

## for Home, Car, & Money Stuff

Jennifer Musselman
Patty DeGregori

WILDCAT CANYON PRESS
A Division of Circulus Publishing Group, Inc.
Berkeley, California

Copyeditor: Jean Blomquist
Proofreader: Lara Deans Lowe
Cover Design: Mary Beth Salmon
Cover Illustrations: Sheryl Dickert
Some Interior Illustrations: Sheryl Dickert and Judy Gray
Art Direction: Leyza Yardley
Interior Design & Typesetting: Margaret Copeland/Terragrafix
Typographic Specifications: Text in Palatino 11/16, headings in Girls Are Weird.

Printed in the United States of America

Library of Congress Cataloging-in-Publication Data

Musselman, Jennifer, 1973–
    The hip girl's handbook for home, car, & money stuff / Jennifer Musselman & Patricia DeGregori
        p. cm.
    Includes bibliographical references.
    ISBN 1-885171-67-6
    1. Dwellings—Maintenance and repair—Amateurs' manuals. 2. Automobiles—Maintenance and repair—Amateurs' manuals. 3. Finance, Personal. 4. Do-it-yourself work. I. DeGregori, Patricia, 1975– II. Title.

TH148 .M87 2002
643'.7—dc21

2002027005


10 9 8 7 6 5 4 3

To *Ben and Jerry's:*
The two consistent men in our lives.

# Table of Contents

## Household Hijinks

## Automotive Antics

# Financial Fun

# Acknowledgments

## Jennifer Musselman

For the profound and eclectic experiences that have shaped my life, I want to thank God, for life and everything right in it (but especially for forgiveness every time I mess it up!); Mom, for her tumultuous relationship experiences and adult conversations filled with unconditional love; Dad, for spiritual guidance and making me finance my own college education; Jan and Will Zabel, for lattice-top apple pies, coaching "little league," and the gift of dance; all my sisters and brothers, for unfair pillow fights (and for knocking me down every time I got back up) and for each of your own personal adversities, from which I learned a lot; G'ma, for white powdered donuts and your tenacity; sacred friendships (and you know who you are), for clearing my dance space, holding back my hair while praying to the porcelain god, and telling me when my clothes are getting too tight; *Fox News/KTTV*, for the "sink or swim among sharks" opportunities; and for Linda Kicak, my boss-turned-confidante (who knew then your encouraging inscription in a thesaurus would actually predict this book?); *MTV Networks/Nickelodeon*, for corporate politics, strategic business and publicity know-how, and fulfilling childhood fantasies; *Marshall Fields*, for your support (especially you, Jackie Schutty!); and of course Patty, my co-author and dear friend, for late-night walks and igniting the torch.

## Patty DeGregori

Oh my goodness where do I begin? To my friends and co-workers, at both Franklin and Hermosa Valley School, I am extremely grateful for your support. Thank you for letting me bounce ideas off you and helping me brainstorm. Most of all, thank you for believing in me and making me realize this book was something that I could do.

Hugs and kisses to my Mom and Dad! Thank you for funding my college career. It was during those years at Chico State that I began to learn how to solve problems on my own. (But, not without error of course!) Dad, a special thanks to you, for keeping a level head through all of my panic-stricken phone calls. Your years of financial and fix-it wisdom have helped me tremendously in writing this book.

Most importantly, I want to thank my co-author and beloved friend, Jennifer Musselman. Without her immense love and motivation for writing, along with her keen sense of business, none of this book would have been possible. Thank you, Jennifer, for helping me develop a passion for writing and guiding me through the whole whirlwind process. This teacher could have not turned writer, without you. For that alone, I am grateful.

For their diligence, creative inspiration and guidance, both authors would like to thank:

All the Hip Girls who allowed us to use their disaster stories for this book (your sisterhood in sacrifice can now serve not just as good drinking stories, but as life lessons to learn from); our genius of an attorney David Brown; art-inspired guru Judy Gray; Mary Filar for stepping up to the plate; photographer extraordinaire Greg Hunter; Farmer's Insurance agents Greg[2], and our very own handy fact checker John DeGregori. And a special thanks to the brilliant team at Wildcat Canyon Press... Tamara Traeder, Leyza Yardley, and Patsy Barich. We appreciate your unwavering dedication to making this book the best it could be. Lastly, a heartfelt recognition to Roy M. Carlisle for your faith, continued support, and genuine interest in making our dreams come to fruition.

# Authors' Note

The Hip Girl's Handbook is meant to simply introduce you to future first-time experiences (much like your parents' "birds and bees" conversations) or to ease those scenarios where you might feel out of your element. While we hope that we've done our job and you feel more informed after reading this book, please keep in mind that the instructions are general and that your situation may require a slightly different approach. Therefore, this book shouldn't be viewed as a definitive guide for home rental and care, car buying and maintenance, or financial well-being. Rather, it's a handbook for gettin' the "dialogue" going.

Specifically, the "Automotive Antics" section covers a plethora of information for the basics of buying and maintaining a car. While this section will get you started (so to speak), please remember this *most* important tip when reading the car maintenance sections: All car brands and models are a bit different from each other, and some information in this section may or may not apply to your ride. (Just because that pair of Lucky Jeans looks hot on the model, there's no guarantee it's going to work just as well on your figure. Get the picture?) We can't guarantee that each of the instructions in this book applies to your specific vehicle. How do you make sure? Cross-reference our suggestions with the instructions from your car manufacturer's owner's manual before doing any maintenance or repair to your car.

Also of note, the same is true when reading the "Financial Fun" section: While we try to help navigate you through some basic personal finance examples, it should be taken as general information only—we are not giving financial advice! (Girl, you earn your money, you decide how to spend it!) Everyone's financial situation and needs are different, so let reading this book be the first step you take for investigating other resources that can offer you more personalized financial choices or investment wisdom.

If you'd like more in-depth facts about some of the issues we cover in this book, check out some of the resources in our bibliography. They're all great sources of information. And once you get the basics here, you can supersize your Hip Girl knowledge using those resources.

We encourage you Hip Girls to find out how to manage things on your own. That's what this book is all about, after all. (Well, that and for a good laugh every time you mess up. Take comfort in knowing that between our mishaps and that of our friends, chances are your mistakes ain't half as bad.) But if the instructions in this book are not clear to you for any situation, or they don't seem to apply to your particular circumstances, get some help! Then you can learn from someone else how to take care of the problem next time. Hip Girls aren't afraid to ask for advice, too. Otherwise, why else would we need to run in packs when going to the restroom?

# Honing Your Hipness

$A$s SINGLE, INDEPENDENT WOMEN, we were both mortified and amused when we reminisced about our years of successfully surviving (sometimes just barely) the everyday challenges faced by a girl on her own. Whether it was managing a car overheating in the desert while moving to college halfway across the country, or simply understanding smart money management, we marveled at how unprepared we were. We found our way through trial and error (which often included costly or even potentially life-threatening mistakes), or we relied on the kindness and knowledge of our parents, brothers, sisters, boyfriends, girlfriends, or complete strangers. Yikes! This revelation, believe it or not, shocked us. We are, after all, two, smart Hip Girls. Why, then, did we leave it to chance or others to manage our crises instead of figuring out the solutions for ourselves? After all, we'd never dream of letting someone else choose our wardrobe for us—unless, of course, it was a world-renowned fashion stylist.

Whether you're newly independent, going off to college, or your boyfriend or husband is not the fix-it type, *The Hip Girl's Handbook for Home, Car, & Money Stuff* is a must-have for commanding emergencies and everyday life with flair, ease, and a sense of pride. The book's step-by-step instructions for the basics of independent living empowers you in areas that are often overwhelming or simply scary. But don't expect this book to read like some boring manual or college text written with such industry-specific complexity that you're better off paying for expensive help. Heck no! We're busy gals—balancing our careers, family, social engagements, friends, and volunteer projects. We don't have time for information overload. In this book, we bring the info into our world, the life of a Hip Girl, who accomplishes her goals with fun and style. Our girlfriends were kind enough to recount their own mishaps so you too could learn from their comical (and sometimes painful) mistakes of inexperience. (Some even reveled in stories of their roommates', boyfriends' and husbands' lack of how-to knowledge.) Because no matter how we try to conceal it, most of us weren't born hip, we grew into it (just look at old school photos for proof)! From fashion and culture to body-image confidence and business stature, becoming hip and self-assured takes careful nurturing. So, too, is the case with conquering everyday living challenges with grace.

Don't misunderstand us. We usually prefer (and recommend) taking the easiest route when fixing or educating one's self on home, car or money troubles. (Let's face it, male or female, most people would rather be socializing with friends or reading a good book than hassling with a time-consuming problem.) So if you have 24/7 access to trustworthy, inexpensive help for conquering certain day-to-day living circumstances, utilize it! Appreciate it! But more important, learn from the person taking care of the situation so that if he or she isn't around the next time the same issue arises, you can handle it yourself—like the strong, independent woman you are! This book is for those times when it's up to you to maneuver through the treacherous mountains of uncertainty and confusion. Whether you create a new path, or follow the footsteps of someone before you, we think you'll find the "hike" to self-sufficiency a rewarding experience.

So help yourself get with it: Stash a copy of this book in the glove box of your car, in your desk drawer at home, or in your Prada bag or Eddie Bauer backpack. And embrace the adventures of the wondrous journey as a Hip Girl with confidence and style. Soon enough, you too will proudly relish your own bold achievements for beating life's little disasters on your own!

# Household Hijinks

With independence comes kitchen and bathroom duty (and yep, that means the toilet too). So whether you're a Suzy Homemaker or a Household Hazard, get ready to roll up your sleeves and get dirty because this section's going to school you in the joys and agony of dorm, apartment, and home living. From clogged garbage disposals to overflowing toilets, we've got you covered for all the best and worst adventures of living in the space you proudly call home.

# Moving Makeover:

## Scopin' Out a New Place and Getting All Your Stuff There

—◦◦◦—

"Sophomore year of college, I was so excited about moving into my first apartment. The only thing that I was more excited about was the brown leather couch that my aunt donated to me. I loaded the couch into the pickup and hit the open road for my new home. About halfway to my destination I stopped off the freeway to get a bite to eat, where I noticed something missing. Somewhere in the last sixty miles I'd lost the middle cushion. Replacing that one cushion sure made a free couch awfully expensive."

—Kris, 20

## Where Do I Start In Finding The Right Home?

WHETHER YOU'RE RELOCATING TO TAKE A NEW JOB or just starting college, moving is exciting and overwhelming all rolled into one.

But seize the opportunity to make a fresh start by exploring your options for just the right home. Read on for tips:

◆ **Pick your location.** Check out different neighborhoods to see if you'd like to live there. Where you decide to live will definitely affect your quality of life. Pay close attention to the neighborhood, including surrounding buildings and streets. Skip your kickboxing class and put your walking shoes on. Tour the neighborhood. Are there abandoned buildings? Does it appear to be a safe environment?

◆ **What can you afford?** Some neighborhoods just may be too far out of reach price wise. Find out what typical rents are—although you may want to live at the beach, it may not be in the cards yet. Weed out the too-expensive neighborhoods.

◆ **Keep your eyes open!** One of the easiest ways to locate a house or apartment is to cruise the neighborhood where you want to live. Look for "For Rent" signs. Most signs will list phone numbers to contact for information. It's best to have a pen and pad ready to jot down the numbers and any important notes—like an apartment's proximity to your favorite hangout. Better yet, if you have a cell phone, call right on the spot and try to have a showing right then.

◆ **Grab the paper.** Although the newspaper is packed full of everything from the daily news to upcoming sales, it's also useful for finding a place to live. Turn to the classified sections. Grab a highlighter and circle the places in your chosen neighborhoods that sound appealing. Ocean views, fireplaces, or dishwashers can be deal makers!

◆ **Browse the phone book.** Real estate agencies often carry rental properties in their "inventory." Simply call the agency and ask if they have any rental properties available in the area you've chosen.

◆ **Surf the Net.** If you are trying to rent a place in a larger city, there are many places on the Internet that can help you locate a place to live.

A few good sites are: rent.net, homestore.com, springstreet.com, apartment.com, craigslist.org

## Narrowing the Search

*The Neighborhood*

See something you love? Before you sign any lease, visit the neighborhood again.

◆ **Use your nose and ears.** Visit when you would most likely be at home—perhaps on weekend days and at night. Listen to the noise. Smell the air. Does the environment seem livable (or will the constant smell of trash scare a date from ever coming back to your pad)?

◆ **Transportation.** Can you easily and safely get to your neighborhood? How about getting from there to where you'll need to go, like work or school? If you have a car, is there street parking? Does it feel safe? Can your friends find it?

◆ **Errand time.** Nothing is more annoying than running all over town just to do your errands (especially in the event your car is broken down). Take a moment to find out where the nearest grocery store is. Are there any other businesses such as a bank, hardware store, nail salon, shoe repair, dry cleaners, or drugstore nearby? Is there a post office in the neighborhood? Is the rental conveniently located near restaurants or the happening coffee shop or pub?

◆ **What is the crime history in the neighborhood?** Talk to the public relations department of your local police station; they can give you an idea of the types and frequency of crimes in a neighborhood.

◆ **What happens in the dark?** When you're there at night, see what happens in the neighborhood. Although it may sound strange, who knows? Maybe the restaurant across the street turns into a late night dance club. Although your first reaction may be excitement, we doubt you would feel the same way when you need to study for a final or get to work early in the morning. So check the nightly routines of the area. How do you feel? Nearby bars that have police called on a nightly basis could cut into your sense of safety (not to mention your precious beauty rest).

◆ **Where do your friends live?** It's comforting to know that there is someone nearby whom you know. If you think you might feel isolated in a neighborhood, you might want to find somewhere else.

## The Living Space

Now that you've done your neighborhood research, it's time to look closely within. (We know it's tempting to look inside first, but spare yourself the pain of falling in love with a place that ultimately is in the wrong neighborhood!)

◆ **Is the place clean?** Look around. Does the property seem to be kept up well? If people are currently living in the apartment or house, keep that in mind. Just because they're messy doesn't mean the place always has to be.

◆ **How is the light in the apartment?** Try to look at the place in the daytime. Is it appealing?

◆ **Mailboxes, doors, and windows.** Do the doors feel sturdy and have deadbolt locks? Is there a peephole in the front door? Can you open and lock the windows securely? Is your mailbox locked?—because having your mail stolen may become a big problem. See the *Stolen Identity* chapter.

◆ **Open closets.** Do they open smoothly, and more importantly, are they big enough to support your shopping habit?

◆ **Is there hot water?** Run each tap to make sure. How's the pressure?

◆ **Examine.** Look around for mildew and mold. Are the tiles or linoleum in the bathroom or kitchen loose? These signs may mean there's a plumbing leak.

◆ **How's the security in the building?** Do all exterior doors automatically lock when closed? Are there bright lights around entrances, in common areas, and where you park your car?

◆ **Do you see temperature controls?** If not, that may mean that the heat and air conditioning (if any) are set by someone else.

◆ **Ask questions.**

□ Are utilities included in the rent, such as water, electricity, cable, and garbage pickup? What can you expect to pay for utilities not covered in the lease?

□ How long is the lease? Is it a one-year rental agreement? Or is it a month-to-month lease? With a month-to-month lease, you are not required to live in a rental for more than one month at a time, nor is the landlord required to let you live there for more than one month at a time.

□ How much is the security deposit? A security deposit is the amount of money the landlord requires from you up front to cover cleaning and any damages you do to the property. Deposits vary in amounts from nothing (good luck finding that!) to two times the monthly rent amount or more. Deposits typically are used to pay for apartment or house repairs, painting, and cleaning upon your moving out. The landlord should present you with a detailed list of charges and repay you the amount left from the deposit fund.

□ Will you be charged a fee for submitting the credit application (the form a landlord asks you to complete in order to check your credit history, which may include details of bounced checks, prior evictions, and credit card late payments)? If so, how much is it?

□   Do you have to pay a first and last month's rent up front? It's not uncommon for a landlord to require both—and a deposit on top of that amount. (Yikes! Moving can sure be costly!) Note that in the event you choose to move out, your last month is already paid for if you were required to front the last month's rent before moving in.

*Hip Tip*   *When in doubt about your rights, check with your local renter's association found on-line or in the phone book. They're there to help.*

□   What type of work (such as cleaning the carpets and painting the walls) will be done to the apartment or house prior to your moving in?

□   Do the refrigerator and other appliances come with the place? Does it have a washer and dryer? Are they all in working order?

□   Are pets allowed? If so, what other pets are in the building?

□   When will the apartment or house be available?

□   If the rental property is an apartment, does it have shared facilities (like a deck, backyard, or laundry room)? These are great places to meet the neighbors. Just remember to be respectful of their share of the space.

□   Is there parking, and do you have to pay a separate fee for it?

□   Has there ever been a bug, mouse, or—dare we say it—rat problem?

□   Ask around. If you run into one of the neighbors, ask about the building. Inquire what they enjoy and do not enjoy about living there. This should help give you a good feel for the neighborhood too (and you may make a new neighbor friend).

◆ Read the lease *before* signing it. Yes, the lease can be a form printed in very small (and deadly dull) type, but when you sign it, you are obligated to live up to its requirements. For instance, if the length (or term) of the lease is one year, you are obligated to pay the rent for a year whether you move out or not (with some exceptions). Make sure you understand what it says, and that its terms match your understanding based on the answers to the questions you previously asked. If there are repairs the landlord has agreed to, make sure they're included in the lease.

## Need a Roommate?

Let's face it. The idea of living by yourself may sound appealing (the reality of juggling bathroom schedules and tolerating different musical tastes can sometimes be strenuous). But living alone may not work within your financial budget. Having a roommate not only cuts the cost of living in half, but when you choose the right one, can add quality companionship to your life. Here are a few things you should keep in mind when looking for a roommate:

◆ **Best friends don't always equal best roommates.** Even though you and Keiko have been buddies since kindergarten, that doesn't exactly mean she'll be great to have living in the room next to yours. Asking your best buddy to take out the trash or clean up her dirty dishes may be difficult since you're so close. You may also find that your pet peeves about each other will intensify and may end up ruining your friendship.

◆ **Publicize.** Whether it's putting an ad in the newspaper or designing a flyer to hang in a coffee shop, at work, or in the dorms, get the news out. Word of mouth works well too. E-mail or talk with friends. Chances are they may know someone that needs a place to live. Another option may be to contact a service. Many cities have roommate finder agencies. All you need to do is fill out information about you and your wish list in qualities of a potential roommate, and they do all the work. (It's almost like a dating service. And hey, who knows? No, no, never mind. We definitely don't recommend snagging dates in roommate interviews. You don't know these people. Besides, we all know that kind of thing only works on *Friends*.) Look in the yellow pages of your local phone book, on the Internet, or ask around for roommate-finder services.

◆ **Start the hunt early.** Like a huge sale at your favorite department store, start looking for a roommate early on for the best selection. Out of sheer desperation, you don't want to get stuck with a roommate who reminds you of a certain movie involving a single, white female! Allow yourself at least a month to weed through all the weirdos.

◆ **The interview.** It's a good idea to have a few questions in mind to ask, but be ready to answer a few as well. Be honest with your answers. After all, if you end up living with this person, he or she is bound to see the fun-loving you and the cranky, selfish side as well. Here are a few sample questions:

**For both interviewer and interviewee:**

☐ Do you smoke? What are your feelings about alcohol?

☐ How clean are you in the common living areas (kitchen, living room, bathroom)? For instance, how often do you like to clean the bathroom?

☐ Do you have a boyfriend or girlfriend? If so, will he or she be staying over with you often? If not, do you see a lot of people and what's your dating style—sleepovers or after-hours get-togethers with strangers?

☐ What's your morning schedule? (You don't want to compete for the shower.)

☐ What types of things do you enjoy doing outside of school or work?

- ☐   Have you had roommates before? What was that experience like?
- ☐   Are you into the social scene? Do you like giving parties or having a lot of people around? Or do you like "alone" time?
- ☐   Are you an early bird or a night owl? (Early morning cooking or late-night partying might conflict with your sleeping plans.)

**If you are the interviewee:**

- ☐   How are household chores divided?
- ☐   How are space and storage divided?
- ☐   How expensive are utilities and how are they split? (You can ask for copies of recent monthly bills.)
- ☐   What types of amenities are there (such as laundry, storage, roof deck, or backyard)?
- ☐   Is there parking? If so, is there enough for both of you?
- ☐   What is the landlord like?
- ☐   What are the neighbors like? Make sure to get all the scoop, including whether they are single, married, or have kids or pets (and what kind); whether they are loud or quiet; whether they travel a lot or not; what kind of hours they keep. You'll want to know what to expect!
- ☐   Has there been any crime in the building or neighborhood?

◆ **Do a background check.** If you have found someone that seems like a good fit for you, you'll first need to find out if your prospective roommate can afford the rent, and second, whether she will pay it. Ask how that person will pay the rent. Is she employed (how long) and what is her salary? Call her employer and make sure the information is correct. Are her parents footing the bill? If so, how much will they be providing each month?

Next, find out your prospective roommate's credit history. Even if she is bringing in enough money each month, make sure she is responsible with her bills. Ask to see her credit report (make sure she really is who she says she is by asking for copies of her ID) and check out anything that looks suspicious or indicates this person doesn't take her obligations seriously. Also, ask to speak with her former landlords, making sure you find out how promptly she paid her rent and in what condition she left her last living space.

If you feel awkward asking these hard questions, talk to your landlord. Chances are he or she may need the same information and may help you in retrieving it. Keep in mind that this is first and foremost a business arrangement, and if you are saddled with a roommate who doesn't pay her share of the costs, you will be stuck with paying them! So make sure your basic financial requirements are covered. Then if your responsible roommate ends up being a bridesmaid in your wedding, all the better!

◆ **Go with your instincts!** We girls can be very intuitive, which is why some guys say they don't always get our logic. But in order to use your instincts as a tool for success, you must listen to them. When it comes down to it, you are the best judge of whether you and your lifestyle fits with a prospective roommate or not. Is she a wacko or someone you can see yourself spending a lazy day on the couch with watching 90210 reruns? If you are not at least 90 percent sure, continue looking around. You don't want to make a snap decision about your roommate choice!

## Self-Move vs. Hired Help

There's no doubt! We always recommend hired help! However, your bank account may not agree with us. Here are a few factors to consider:

◆ **How far you have to go.** If you're simply moving between dorms, a self-move is possible to carry off.

◆ **How much money you are willing to spend.** Need we say that doing it yourself is always cheaper?

◆ **What you are moving.** If you are moving between apartments or houses and have a lot of furniture and other stuff to move, matters may be more complicated and may require renting a truck or hiring pricey professional help.

Once you have decided whether hiring movers or managing your own move makes sense, read on for more details about each option.

## Hiring Movers

Hiring a mover is not as easy as opening up the phone book and letting your fingers do the walking. It's imperative that you do your homework before you decide on one. Why? If you don't, you may end up paying way too much and possibly hiring someone who isn't properly qualified. If possible, ask friends or family for recommendations. Check how long your mover candidates have been in business and call the Better Business Bureau to see if there have been any complaints about them. Start your research early (instead of procrastinating as if it were a dreaded describe-yourself-in-500-words essay for your psychology class). Most movers need to be hired as early as six to eight weeks in advance—especially if you want to move on a weekend, at the end of the month, or anytime except the winter months.

Professional movers mean professional pay. Hiring help can get expensive. Here are some tips for hiring dependable movers without dipping into your new car fund:

◆ **Call several moving companies, and ask some questions**. Ask what their specialty is: local moves or state-to-state moves. Generally, you don't need a state-to-state mover if you are moving across town (and local movers are usually cheaper). Ask each company if they will send an agent out to your home to give you a free estimate, but specify that you want that estimate to be a "binding" estimate (meaning that the price they quote you is the price you will actually pay) or a "not to exceed" estimate (meaning that the actual cost of the move cannot exceed that amount, although it can be less). Note that some companies will charge you for a binding estimate. You can usually get a rough estimate of what a move will cost over the phone if you describe what you are moving (generally, how many "rooms" of furniture), but that estimate won't be binding. A binding estimate, even if it is higher than other nonbinding quotes, may end up being cheaper in the long run. Get *all* estimates in writing.

Hip Tip *Go to imove.com for helpful tips on moving, packing, and hiring professional movers. You can get a moving estimate right on-line. This website also provides helpful checklists for moving out of your apartment.*

◆ **Apples and Oranges.** When comparing your estimates, pay attention to how they are estimating their fees. Long-distance movers may charge you by estimated weight, while local movers may charge you by the hour. (If comparing long-distance movers, make sure that their estimated weights on which their quotes are based are the same.)

◆ **Check out the moving companies you are going to deal with.** How long have they been in business? Does your agent seem experienced and pay attention to your concerns? Call your local Better Business Bureau and see if there are any complaints against them.

If you are checking out a national company that moves state-to-state, ask about that company *and* the local affiliated company that you will be dealing with. Also, state-to-state movers are licensed by the Federal Highway Administration, which you can call to check on the mover's registration and insurance at 202-358-7106.

Don't be afraid to ask the moving company if their employees are bonded and whether they are full-time or temporary—if they are full-time, it is more likely that they are experienced and trained.

◆ **Be very clear about what you want them to do.** When the agent comes, tell him or her exactly what is moving and what is staying—you don't want to include your roommate's couch in your estimate, do you? Also, tell the agent exactly the path that your things will take. Do you know, for instance, that the only way to get your dresser out of your room is to lower it from the window? Describe the mover's destination. Will they be able to park and unload in front of your building? Are they limited on the times they can do that? Some apartment buildings have restrictions on moving in and out times, and may also require that you go in and out of a certain door or elevator. Are there steps in front of your building? Is your new apartment five floors up? Is there an elevator? All of these factors may affect the price of your move.

◆ **How are you and your things protected?** Who pays if your things are broken or lost? If you already have renter's insurance (see more about that later in this chapter), you may have some coverage. Make sure of it by talking to your insurance agent. The moving company may also have to reimburse you, but it might not be a lot. Ask if they have additional coverage available and how much that costs. Is the coverage for replacement value (you are reimbursed for a new item) or current value? Get the former—your four-year-old stereo may not be worth much today, but you'd sure miss your music!

Doing your own packing can save you quite a bit of money. But if you are packing yourself, some moving companies may not cover you if the things you packed are broken or ruined. Check with them. After all, certain clothing items are so precious to your fashion statement that you practically consider them family heirlooms.

Speaking of insurance, make sure that the company has workers' compensation insurance for its employees. You don't want to be held responsible for somebody's bad back—or worse!

◆ **Protecting Unusual or Valuable Items.** If you have your grandma's antique dishes or the piano you've played on since you were six, you may need to make special arrangements. Many companies specialize in piano moving (and may even tune it when it gets to its destination). A moving company may also not want to take responsibility for moving antiques or other valuable items, but will probably be able to refer you to specialty movers for those items. Or check with a local antique store—they may be able to help. You are better off keeping small valuables, like your jewelry and personal papers, with you.

◆ **Read any contract carefully.** Ask to see your contract before moving day—in the all the hustle and bustle, you won't have time or the attention span to do it. Make sure it includes a delivery date and that you agree with all of its terms. If there are extra costs you did not approve or it does not reflect additional items you requested, then get it fixed before you sign it.

◆ **Power to the people!** The most essential element for a self-move is creating a social gathering of your best friends. It's a good idea to line up your helpers ahead of time, and make sure that they are reliable so you're not stuck on moving day. (Hint: A few helpers with muscles couldn't hurt either.) As a thank you, let them know drinks and pizza are on you, and that you can be counted on to return the favor.

◆ **Figure out how much you have to move.** Will all your belongings fit in your car and a borrowed SUV, or will they require you to rent a truck?

◆ **If you need to rent a truck,** get one that is large enough. You don't want to wind up on moving day with more stuff than you can get in the truck. A truck rental company can usually help you determine the size truck you will need based on the number of "rooms" you are moving.

◆ **Use your shopping know-how,** just like when you dig for brand-name bargains in a discount store, to compare deals between several rental companies. (U-Haul and Ryder are good ones, just to name two.) When comparing prices, you may also want to ask the companies the following questions:

- □ How far in advance do I need to rent the truck?
- □ Are there driver age restrictions?
- □ What is your cancellation policy?
- □ What are the daily charges? When do I pay for the truck?
- □ Are there any time restrictions? If you book the truck for five hours, what happens if you go over that time?
- □ Is a deposit required? If so, how much and when do I get it back?
- □ What size trucks do you carry and how do I know what size I will need?

- Where do I pick it up and drop it off?
- Must I refill the gas tank before I turn the truck in?
- Can more than one person drive the truck?
- Is the truck covered by my auto insurance? If not, what are my insurance options?
- Are blankets and a dolly (it's a moving apparatus, not a Barbie®) included or are they extra?

◆ **Driving a moving truck is not exactly easy.** Recognize that it is different from driving your car. Take into consideration the comfort factor—many of the trucks do not have a stereo or an air conditioner. More importantly, trucks are taller and heavier, so you may have to make sure you have overhead clearance, and stopping takes more time. And forget about having good visibility to maneuver when backing up, parking, or passing! If you're not comfortable driving it, don't risk it. Enlist a friend or family member who is.

## Packing Supplies

If you decide to pack your own stuff, get prepared by putting together some essential items for a low-stress packing experience (okay, that may be a tad optimistic).

◆ **Boxes, boxes, and more boxes.** It's wise to start collecting boxes early, as you will be amazed by how many you need. Grocery stores are a great place to get free boxes, and if you call ahead, most stores will put some aside for you. If not, friendly produce workers may take pity and scrounge some on the spot for you. Apple boxes are ideal. They are sturdy, a good size, and easy to lift when full. You can also buy boxes from the moving company or a discount store, but they can get pricey. What may be worth buying are specialty boxes, such as wardrobe boxes (you can just hang your clothes in them instead of taking them all off the hanger and wadding them up in a regular box) or dish boxes (with dividers for glasses or plates). That way you can protect even your designer (okay, knock-off) dresses and fine china (okay, your mismatched hand-me-downs from your mother). Some moving companies will let you "borrow" these boxes for a small fee.

◆ **Your school supplies from second grade.** That means scissors, string, marker pens with wide tips, and different-colored dot stickers. Who said packing is no fun!

◆ **Packing tape and dispensers.** By packing tape, we mean the wide, shiny brown or clear tape. Don't balk at buying the dispensers, which cost a few dollars each. Trust us, they are worth it.

◆ **All kinds of stuffing.** Unfortunately, we don't mean the turkey kind. Save your newspapers, and invest in some Styrofoam peanuts, paper towels, and bubble wrap. Stack up your dish and regular towels near your packing area. Newspaper, Styrofoam peanuts, and towels are good for cushioning boxes and filling up empty spaces. Paper towels are handy for wrapping those *itty-bitty* fragile things, like your sample perfume bottle collection. Bubble wrap is ideal for your more fragile and valuable items, such as fine china or framed works of art. You can also wrap fragile pieces of furniture in it.

◆ **Plastic bags of every description.** Get large plastic bags for throwing out junk you have let accumulate. Get rid of it now—you don't need to pay to have it moved! Keep a bag aside for clothes you no longer wear and can take to the Salvation Army. If you are just moving across town, large plastic bags are also handy for putting pillows and bedding in— you can just dump them back on the bed in your new place. Small plastic bags are ideal for putting kitchen utensils in—they are just going to get dirty rattling around in the boxes. Zip-loc® bags are handy for keeping small essentials in one place, such as wall-hangers, nails, or screws from furniture that you will re-assemble in your new place. And don't forget lots of garbage bag ties—they are useful for wrapping up extension cords or bundling eating utensils.

◆ **Essential tools.** If you're taking apart any furniture, keep a couple of screwdrivers handy—both Phillips and standard. A hammer and a box cutter (or two) will be key to setting up your new home. See the *Tool Time* chapter for descriptions.

◆ **Essential friends.** Don't do it all alone. No matter where you are moving, it is always disruptive and kind of depressing to pack up your house, especially by yourself. Recruit a girlfriend, mom or other friends to help you out for an evening or afternoon—you can catch up with each other, and make plans for your new home. If you are moving across country, you may be saying goodbye to these people soon, so take advantage of your time together.

◆ **Essential tunes.** No two ways about it, packing is exhausting. Get your girl band CDs out and turn up the volume to keep you motivated!

## Packing Tips

Now that you've got all your supplies ready, it's time to get packing. As tempting as it may be, don't just start throwing everything into the boxes. Here are some helpful tips:

◆ **Label every box.** It'll save you time and headaches if you know where a box goes. List a brief inventory and what room a box belongs in. Use your felt tip marker so it's easy to read. If you want to color code your boxes by room, use your colored dot stickers.

◆ **Start early.** Pack a couple of boxes each day. First pack items that you'll not be using before you move, like your winter clothes if it's summer and so on. Packing a little at a time will make it less over-whelming (and allows you to maintain your social life).

◆ **Pack like with like.** Don't put your heavy cookware in the same box with your drinking glasses.

◆ **Use smaller boxes for heavier items** like books, photo albums, or your collection of nail polishes.

◆ **Wad up newspaper** to completely fill the bottom of boxes in which you're putting breakable items. Use Styrofoam peanuts, more newspa-per, or towels between items so that boxes feel "solid"—nothing is shifting.

◆ **Protect dishes with bubble wrap** and pack sideways rather than stacked. Use potholders, dish towels, or more wadded-up newspaper to cushion the sides of the box or fill in empty spaces.

◆ **Pack heavier items on the bottom** of boxes first. Be sure to distrib-ute the weight. (Don't we wish we had this as an option with our body weight!) No box should be over fifty pounds (anything more than that and you might not be able to move it). If you're doing a lot of the mov-ing yourself, you may want to make it less heavy, depending on how much you are comfortable lifting. Try lifting each box after you have filled it halfway to make sure it isn't getting too heavy.

◆ **Packing a large mirror or picture?** Wrap it completely in bubble wrap, then cover it with heavy cardboard. Finish up by securing the cardboard with packing or masking tape.

◆ **Towels, sheets, and bedding** can be stuffed at the bottom of wardrobe boxes or into plastic garbage bags. (Have no guilt if you opt to load the bags in your car yourself, while your male friends build their muscles with the heavier boxes.)

◆ **Be sure to mark a box "Fragile"** if it contains any breakable items. Write it on the side as well as the top of the box.

◆ **Pack an "Open First/Pack Last"** box (or two). This way you'll have all immediately necessary items handy. Include items such as a utility knife, cleaning products, paper towels, toilet paper, soap, first-aid kit, flashlight, cellular phone and charger, and your essential tools. Having these items handy will ensure that your unpacking goes as smoothly as your packing did. Don't forget to include aspirin or ibuprofen and antacids. Moving is stressful!

◆ **General rule.** Remember the opening scene of the movie *Ace Ventura: Pet Detective*, when Jim Carrey impersonates a delivery man who kicks the package he's delivering all the way down the block? Assume that your boxes will get similar treatment, and pack accordingly. Of course, your boxes will be better treated, but you can rest easier knowing that you have planned for accidents.

## Before You Move In

Now that you've found the perfect place, signed your lease, and begun getting your belongings packed, there are a few more last-minute items to take care of before the big moving day.

◆ **Turn utilities on!** Just in case you may actually have to turn on a light, flush a toilet, or use a phone the day you move in, it's a good idea to get your utilities turned on a day prior to moving into your new place. To find out the names and numbers of the utility companies, simply check the phone book or give your landlord a call. Don't forget to turn off the utilities at your old place the day after you move out.

◆ **Get your address changed.** In order to make sure that everything from your subscription to *Glamour* magazine to your dreaded credit card bills follows you to your new home, you need to file a change of address. To do so, go to your local post office and ask for a change of address form.

All you need to know is your new and old address. It's as easy as that. Once settled, it's a good idea to contact your bank and credit card companies and others in order to give them your new info. The post office will only forward your mail up to six months, so don't let this slide for too long (or you could never get that letter from your ex admitting the breakup was all his fault and begging for you back!).

**Hip Tip** *Your post office has a handy list to remind you who you need to contact with your change of address. Get one!*

## Renter's Insurance: Is It For You?

When moving into a new apartment or house, you may want to look into getting renter's insurance for your new pad. But before you can decide whether spending the extra cash each month for insurance is worth it for you, it's important to understand what it involves.

◆ **The basics.** If you have a car, chances are you have insurance for it. (If not, better read the *Auto Insurance* chapter!) Having car insurance protects your automobile in case of theft or accidents. Renter's insurance is similar to car insurance except it's for your home.

◆ **What does it cover?** Most basic home insurance policies are referred to by a code. Most renter's insurance policies are generally known as HO-4 policies, but you can just ask for renter's insurance. This type of insurance plan can cover just about any sort of hazard you can imagine. From natural disasters like windstorms and fire to crimes such as vandalism or theft, you can rest well knowing even your prized CD collection is covered (as long as it's not in your car, where it's not covered). Sound too good to be true? It just may be. A renter's policy may protect you from some occurrences but not from other devastating tragedies such as earthquakes, floods, and hurricanes. Read the policy carefully.

◆ **How does it work?** Different companies have different coverage plans. When shopping around for one, pay attention to the type of coverage the company offers. Does the company offer "actual cash value" (ACV) or is it "replacement cost coverage" (RCC)? Translation: ACV coverage pays only for what your belongings are worth at the time they were damaged or stolen. That means that expensive TV that you splurged on a few years ago may have been worth $300 at the time, but would be worth much less today. Although you're going to need to purchase a new one, your insurance agency will only pay for what your old one is worth, minus your deductible. RCC, however, will pay you the actual cost of replacing it (although your deductible will apply). You may have to front the money first, but keep your receipts and you'll be completely reimbursed. (Not replacing the item within a certain period of time, however, usually means you have settled on ACV.) Bottom line, RCC is more bang for your buck.

◆ **What is the cost?** The amount of money you'll need to hand over for renter's insurance depends a lot on where you live, your deductible (which is the amount of damage or loss you are responsible for before your coverage kicks in), which company you go with, and if additional coverage is needed for items such as your beloved computer. For some companies, your credit history is a factor in determining the cost of your insurance.

Keep in mind that some high-ticket or easy-to-steal items require a "rider." Like your computer, sometimes expensive jewelry, silver, artwork, or work items won't be covered or have a limit on coverage, so you may want to investigate buying a rider to cover or extend your coverage in such valuables. Liability coverage (the portion of the agreement that protects you in case someone slips and hurts themselves at your house or even if you smash into a car or person on your bike, or your dog bites someone—on or off your premises) can also factor into the monthly cost of renter's insurance. All renter's insurance policies automatically cover some accident liability, but you can choose to buy a policy that offers a higher level of liability coverage for a slightly higher premium.

If you shop around and compare quotes, you could find coverage that costs from $150-300 a year (that can mean as little as $13 a month). You might have enough money invested in just your wardrobe to make that worth it!

◆ **Ask questions.** Since all insurance companies differ, it's important to get information about policies from several agencies. After all, if you're shelling out money, it's important to know exactly what's involved in your coverage plan.

◆ **How do I get it?** To find a company that offers rental insurance, search your local yellow pages for insurance providers. Surf the Internet, or check with your auto insurance provider to see if they carry renter's policies as well.

◆ **Discounts! Discounts!** It never hurts to see if your insurance company offers any discounts for renter's insurance. Most companies offer a discounted rate for having "protective devices," including fire and smoke detectors, burglar alarms, and fire extinguishers. Plus, if you carry more than one type of insurance with a company (such as your auto and renter's insurance), you might save money.

◆ **Break out the camera.** If you get renter's insurance, you should take photos of every room, once furnished (and your closets, when filled) so you can prove what was lost later. Give a set to your parents with a copy of the policy or put them in a safe deposit box so they won't be destroyed in a disaster.

◆ **Bottom line.** Deciding whether or not to have renter's insurance depends on how much personal stuff you've invested in, and if something horrible happened, if you would have enough resources to replace them. Given the relatively low cost, however, we recommend it.

—◄∭ᶚ▶—

Exhausted? Of course you are! All that unpacking and lifting was a great work-out substitution. Now feed your soul: Rally your girlfriends for a home spa party.

# Savvy Safeguarding:
## Keeping You and Your Space Safe

—◈◈◈—

*"The morning after a late night out on the town, I was awakened by a strange phone call. A lady at the other end was calling because she'd found my wallet in her backyard earlier that morning. I quickly assured her that she must have made a mistake. There was no way that wallet was mine. After all, I had not even taken it out with me the night before. To prove that I wasn't going crazy, I dashed into the kitchen, the last place I recalled seeing it. To my horror the wallet was no longer on the kitchen counter. That is when I noticed the screen on the front window was missing, and so were most of my things from the living room."*

—Kris, 27

## Keeping Thieves Out

LET'S FACE IT. IF BURGLARS REALLY WANT TO GET INTO YOUR HOUSE, there's no stopping them. There are, however, various things you can do to protect your home from a thief who's looking for an effortless target. So pay attention to these easy steps and rest assured that even what seem like simple safeguards can make a difference.

◆ **Do the obvious. Secure your doors and windows.** Whether you are leaving for the evening or just running across the street to borrow a cup of sugar, lock the doors and take the key with you. If you have a sliding glass door, secure it by wedging a broom handle or piece of wood in the track of the door, so that it cannot be pulled open. This will help put a stop to unwanted guests wandering into your home.

Window screens are great for keeping tiny pests like flies and mosquitoes out but when it comes to bigger pests like burglars, they are no match. If you don't have the luxury of air conditioning or you're trying to conserve energy, it might be a good idea to invest in adjustable window stops. These stops allow you to have the window open but will not allow the window to be opened wide enough for someone to climb through it. Also: Window locks are a *must*.

**Hip Tip** *According to the National Crime Prevention Council (NCPC), almost half of successful home burglaries occurred with burglars walking in through unlocked doors or crawling through unlocked windows. Keep 'em locked!*

◆ **Be clever.** Many thieves are experienced and smart, so they know all the good hiding places. Don't hide your spare key in the obvious places, such as under the doormat or flowerpot. Instead, leave an extra key with a trusted neighbor. Going for a walk and want your hands free and pockets empty? Put a spare key on a long rope chain worn around your neck or on a safety pin, which can be fastened to your shirt or pants.

◆ **Although you got it, don't flaunt it.** Don't place valuables where they can be seen from the window, especially if they can be easily whisked away. Burglars generally won't want what they can't see (maybe like your take on blind dating). Also, it isn't a good practice to leave large amounts of cash or jewelry around your house. (Refer to "Best Places To Stash Stuff" below.)

◆ **Speak up.** If you are in an apartment building, make sure the landlord is taking proper precautions, especially if he or she lives elsewhere and doesn't see the property on a daily basis. Are all entrances well-lit? Are all doors leading outside locked at all times? What about the door to the common areas, such as the laundry room and wherever recycling and garbage goes? Are the fire escapes easily accessible to someone from the street? Are there shrubs which are easy to hide behind or tree limbs that reach to your window? If you think there is a safety issue, or light bulbs simply need replacing, call your landlord. Insist that action be taken.

◆ **Outside activity.** Sometimes safety inside requires that you do more about the outside. Trashy neighborhoods simply attract more crime. Report abandoned cars and burnt-out street lights. Or go all out and organize a neighborhood cleanup. It will allow you to get to know your neighbors, make your neighborhood more attractive to its residents, and less attractive to criminals!

◆ **Get to know your neighbors.** Don't be afraid to chat it up with the people who live near you. Neighbors who know each other are more likely to be familiar with each other's routines and can learn to distinguish the people who belong in your home and those who don't. Feeling really motivated? Join a Neighborhood Watch group, or form an Apartment Watch if you live in a multiple unit building. See the NCPC website for details how: ncpc.org.

◆ **Ask a friend.** If you're planning on being away for a while, ask a buddy to drop by and pick up your mail and newspapers. Nothing else screams, *"NOBODY'S HOME!"* like piles of papers or a stuffed mailbox. You can also ask the postal service and your newspaper service to suspend delivery until you return. (See the *Stolen Identity* chapter to spare you even more misery.) What more can you do? Invest in a couple of light timers (available in most hardware stores) to approximate your schedule when you are away. Don't leave all the shades or drapes closed—it's another sign that you aren't home.

◆ **Change your message.** Modify your answering machine or voice mail message to tell callers that you'll "return shortly" or are "on the other line." This may help prevent prospective thieves from hearing an invitation to a vacant home. Live alone? Try not to indicate that you live by yourself in your message. Finally, if possible, check your messages while on vacation and delete them periodically. A long beep on your answering machine might alert a potential burglar that you're away. (Besides you might discover that guy from your chemistry class called for a little home-tutoring session.)

**Hip Tip** *More about doors: If you are renting, ask your landlord to install deadbolt locks on all your doors and a peephole (door chains are flimsy).*

◆ **Pay attention.** If you notice something wrong when approaching your house, such as a door standing open or a broken window, or the situation just doesn't "feel" right, don't go inside. Get help. There are worse things than getting your stereo stolen.

## Best Places to Stash Stuff

If you've ever hidden any of your valuables in your bedroom, then consider yourself lucky if they've never been stolen. Those hiding places are the first places a burglar looks. Instead, pay attention and get ready to change your unsneaky ways. Of course, the best place to hide your valuables is in a safety deposit box at your bank. But if there are things you wish to keep at home, here are some of the best hiding places to stash your stuff:

◆ **The bathroom.** Yes, you read correctly. As suggested by Kirsten M. Lagatree, author of *Checklists for Life,* the bathroom is commonly passed up by burglars and can be a sneaky place to hide your valuables. (If the thief is male, he'll probably be too afraid of discovering tampons. Okay, just kidding.) You can even purchase fake toiletry or cleaning supply cans in which to store valuables (see below). However, in case your burglar is a bit drug dependent, it's best not to stash items in the medicine cabinet. Put them in another strange place.

◆ **The kitchen.** We aren't referring to the cookie jar either. Hiding items in the kitchen can be a smart step—the trick is remembering where you stashed it. Before you hide your valuable items, place them in a sealable plastic baggie. If you have any bulk dry goods, such as jars of rice, popcorn, or sugar, you can hide small treasures inside and store the containers in the back of your cabinets. Kirsten Lagatree suggests putting your riches on ice by wrapping them in aluminum foil, then tossing them in the freezer—just don't mistake it for an icy ingredient to add to your morning smoothie! Want to be really tricky? Place your bagged valuables inside a frozen vegetable package (you can even defrost the vegetables, then refreeze them with the valuables in the middle). Unless your burglar is a healthy eater with a case of the munchies, you should be home free. Warning: Use caution when storing any delicate jewelry or valuables in freezer, however. Softer stones such as opals or paper items may be damaged.

◆ **Devious decoys.** Tennis anyone? Grab a tennis ball and make a small slit in it. Squeeze the ball to open it and stuff it with your valuables, then toss it in your closet. Just be careful not to let anyone borrow it for a tennis tournament or a game of fetch with Rover. You can also buy items such as hollow books, and fake soda cans or rocks that are specially made to store your valuables discreetly. We've even seen fake lettuce! New ones become available as burglars figure them out. Log on to safetybuddy.com, which offers a large selection of decoys. Or check with your local hardware store and see if they're hip to these clever items.

**Hip Tip**   *Check out CHECKLISTS FOR LIFE for more great hiding tips!*

---

All this safety talk got you wigged out? Don't be. Just proudly twist the term "safety girl" into a whole new statement of protection.

# Tool Time:

## Basic Gear and How to Use It

*"Freshman year in the dorms, my parents were just about to bid me farewell when my dad mentioned that my room was missing one important thing. As he mysteriously left my room, I thought, 'What more could I possibly need?' I already had a fridge, sandwich maker, TV, VCR, and, of course, new bedding. He proudly returned with a gray tackle box full of tools. Little did I appreciate then what a great gift that tool kit was. It saved me and my entire dorm wing from a ton of frustration time and time again!"*

*—Patricia, 27*

### Hip Girl Handtool Must-Haves

TAKE A SECOND AND THINK HOW MANY TOOLS YOU HAVE for your hair—curling iron, dryer, ponytail holders, clips, brushes, mousse, gel, hair spray, and so on. No doubt you agree each of these items is absolutely needed! These items, in a sense, are a tool kit for maintaining your hair. Having a tool kit for your home should be just as important.

Having a well-stocked tool kit will not only save you time and money, but will also help give you a greater sense of independence when you tackle small fix-it jobs. The trick to owning a tool kit is knowing what items to include and the purpose of each one. Here is a list of basic tools as well as some information about how to use them:

◆ **Hammer.** You know this tool is useful for pounding nails into the walls or elsewhere, but you'll be surprised at how many different weights there are. Check them out for yourself, but 12-ounce hammers are often preferred for the simpler household tasks (because their light weight is easier to handle than the heavier ones). You'll need it when hanging anything from your beloved framed posters to your precious sun-shaped mirror. (Pounding your TV with it when it's not working properly is not suggested.) One word of caution though: watch your fingers! A hammer can ruin a manicured nail in one simple slip. To hammer a nail in the wall, start by holding the nail in place with one hand while the other gives it a few gentle taps with the hammer. Once the nail is stabilized, remove your fingers from the nail (this is very important)! Using a more forceful stroke, begin pounding the nail in—being careful to come straight down on the nail head. Hammer the nail in until it is securely in the wall, but not all the way. If your hammer is a claw hammer (which we recommend), the other end of the hammer head (the side with the slit) is for removing nails. If you're going to hang heavier items, such as a mirror or a large framed piece, you might want to consider using a stud finder for more security in hanging (it helps you locate a solid base for the nail behind the wall). Stud finders can also be purchased at your local hardware store.

◆ **Screwdriver.** If you need to assemble furniture or install knobs, chances are you'll need a screwdriver to get the job done. To resolve any confusion, screwdrivers are used for twisting screws, and for our purposes, they come in two different styles and a variety of sizes. What type of screwdriver you use depends upon what type of screw you're dealing with. If the screw has one straight, indented line across the top, you will need a **flat-head** screwdriver. On the other hand, if the screw has two indented lines that form an "X" shape, grab what is referred to as a **Phillips** screwdriver. In order to be prepared for any scenario, it's best to have at least two of each type, one smaller blade and one larger blade.

◆ **Adjustable wrench.** In case you ever have a clogged sink, or want to upgrade your showerhead to a fancy massage nozzle, a wrench that can be adjusted to fit the job is the tool to help you.

◆ **Pliers.** Although there are many types, the standard pliers are the ones most commonly used. This tool has two hinged arms ending in jaws (think of a lobster claw) that are closed by hand pressure to grip something. These tools are great for tightening bolts (which are the octagon-shaped pieces which serve as the "head" on some screws) or plumbing work. You may need this tool when putting together your new fancy bed frame or a community garage sale kitchen table.

◆ **Swiss Army Knife.** This multi-tool device is so useful. You may want one with you wherever you go (just don't take it on a plane). Depending on which one you buy, it can contain a screwdriver, a knife, a file, a corkscrew, a bottle opener, and scissors. (Oh, how we love its multi-functional capability. Something to consider when selecting your dating partners!) You'll be surprised at how much you use this one.

◆ **Tape measure.** A tape measure, made of somewhat flexible steel, works like a ruler but is much longer. It's great when you need to figure out if that "antique" couch that your grandma gave you will actually fit along a certain wall or what size rug you'll need to cover up that spill from the party you hosted. If you need to measure something, this tool is perfect for the project.

◆ **Utility knife with razor blade.** If you've ever struggled with opening a large package, then struggle no more. This little tool is the answer to your problems. A utility knife is a hand-held tool with a retractable pointed razor. It will make opening even the most overly taped boxes a breeze. Or use it with a ruler and you have a great device for cutting everything from shelf paper to carpet. Word of advice: Cut away from yourself. This knife cuts skin just as easily (easier, in fact) as carpet or cardboard.

## Some Handy Extras

Now that you have the basic tools, here are a few extras you might want to consider throwing in. Think of these as accessories for your tool kit. Sure you can live without them, but just like that matching purse and belt you just bought, they help form a complete set.

◆ **Super Glue.** In case you ever accidentally break your roommate's favorite Hello Kitty mug, Super Glue will be there to help put it back together. This amazingly strong glue will help mend minor mishaps in a jiffy, but watch out for your fingers! This substance is capable of temporarily bonding them together.

◆ **Duct tape.** Duct tape is a very strong, wide, adhesive tape that is typically silver in color. This tape may just be the queen of all tapes. It's great at temporarily fixing things in an emergency. (Some women have even been known to use it as an emergency push-up bra.) If a window screen is torn or if you lose the battery cover for your remote control, place a strip of duct tape on it. It may not look that pretty, but it will do the job until you can get it replaced or fixed.

◆ **Scissors.** It's always a good idea to have a few pairs of these around the house. Keeping one pair in your tool kit will save you from searching all over for them. Use this tool for cutting duct tape or trimming down snapshots for your scrapbook.

◆ **Glue gun.** Like duct tape, the possibilities for this tool are endless. This is an electrical gun-shaped tool accompanied by glue sticks. The gun heats up the glue that shoots out when you pull the trigger. Read directions on the package before using this device. A glue gun is extremely handy when doing crafts or repairing various household items, such as broken pots or frames, but can be messy if not used correctly.

◆ **Assorted nails and hangers.** Want to share your artistic talent with your guests or have that snapshot of you and your girlfriends rollerblading at the beach blown up for your wall? It's always a good idea to have a few extra nails around. You can purchase nails that come with matching hooks, which are designed to hang pictures. Because what you hang will vary in weight and size, it's a good idea to purchase an assortment of nails and hooks in different sizes.

—◄▩ ▩►—

Got it? Not quite? No worries. Working with tools requires practice. Before you know it, you'll be scopin' out a how-to book on electrical drill usage.

# Computer Mumbo Jumbo:

## Figuring Out What Works for You

*"For Christmas, my parents kindly offered to purchase a computer for me. All I had to do was find the one I wanted, and it was mine. Simple, right? Wrong! Shortly after entering the computer store, I was bombarded by salespeople asking me how many megabytes I was looking for and if I was more of a Mac or Windows girl. I learned that day that, unlike shoe shopping, this was going to take some research."*

—Gloria, 25

### Choosing a Computer That Suits You

WHETHER IN SCHOOL OR JUST STARTING A NEW JOB, every Hip Girl is probably going to need to use a computer. Many new students are happy to get the computer that their big brother or aunt is getting ready to ditch for a new system, and aren't going to be faced with the choices offered in buying a new one. And any computer you use at your work will likely have been chosen for you. That's great! Using a computer is the best way to figure out what features you like, and what features you would like to change, so that when the time comes for you to purchase your own brand-spanking-new machine, you'll know exactly what you want.

Even if you're already computer-savvy, walking into a computer store to pick out a new machine can be daunting. Not to mention risky—making the wrong choice in buying your machine can be a very expensive mistake. So if you're a novice computer user faced with buying a new machine, and you walk into a store where you hear the phrases such as operating system, Mac, PC, RAM, CD-RW, and baud rate all used in a three-minute period, you may feel like ducking and running!

However, a Hip Girl is up to the task. Learning what a few features are and thinking about what you need will get you a long way in making a decision about buying a computer.

**What do you need?** It depends on how you will be using it. If you're out shopping for a dress, the salesperson might ask you where you'll be wearing it. Is it for work, a wedding, or a hot night out on the town? Shopping for a computer is no different. Have in mind what you'll be using your computer for. Will you mainly be doing word processing such as writing papers? Will you be downloading frequently off the Internet? Or will you be running an essay-writing business and be in need of some financial software to organize all your accounts? Will you run many programs at one time? Make a list of all your needs before you go to the computer store.

**What components should my computer have?** While there is a huge variety of computers you can buy, the good news is that their components, or parts, are all fairly similar in function—you just need to decide how fancy your parts need to be. This is a bit like deciding what car to buy—they will all get you somewhere, the only difference is how fast you'll get there, how many features you want, and how much you are willing to spend. If you are typical of most people, you'll probably start using the computer to write reports and papers, send and receive e-mail, play computer games, and perhaps keep track of your finances.

If you are just heading off to college or graduate school, some of your research may already be done. Your school probably has a new student orientation program to call, or you can go to the school's website to find out what computer specifications your school recommends. (If you are going to graduate school, make sure you check with your department, as your advanced curriculum may require an advanced computer.) If you're really lucky, your school has already negotiated with computer companies for some well-priced packages.

*Hip Tip*   *Some of the schools whose recommended computer specifications that we checked out are located at the following web addresses. Check it out or ask a friend to print out some of them for you:*

HARVARD UNIVERSITY—*fas.harvard.edu/computing/newcomers/#hardware*
PRINCETON UNIVERSITY—*princeton.edu/CIT/CITware/personal_standards.shtml*
STANFORD UNIVERSITY—*rescomp.stanford.edu/inrooms/config.html*
UNIVERSITY OF CALIFORNIA AT BERKELEY—*rescomp.berkeley.edu/gc/newcomp/*
UNIVERSITY OF CHICAGO—*o-fest.uchicago.edu/computerrecommend.html*
CHICO STATE UNIVERSITY—*csuchico.edu/stcp/about/ownership.shtml#comp*
UNIVERSITY OF NORTHERN IOWA—*uni.edu/its/us/purchase*
UNIVERSITY OF SOUTHERN CALIFORNIA—*usc.edu/isd/services*
UNIVERSITY OF CALIFORNIA AT LOS ANGELES—*icompass.ucla.edu/orgs.html*
UNIVERSITY OF TEXAS AT AUSTIN—*utexas.edu/computer*
NEW YORK UNIVERSITY—*nyu.edu/its*
COLUMBIA UNIVERSITY—*columbia.edu/acis/welcome/#buy*

Even if you're not starting school, you may log onto the Internet and check out what a college thinks is a good starting place for a new computer. Because specifications change so quickly and vary a lot depending on whether you are using a MAC or a PC or a laptop or desktop, we aren't going to list them here. Instead, we'll describe important computer components and list other factors to keep in mind when shopping for your computer.

◆ **CPU (central processing unit).** Also known as the microprocessor or simply referred to as "the processor" or "chip," the CPU runs your computer system. Don't let its tiny chip size fool you. The witty CPU takes your instructions and tells the rest of the computer how to process them. The higher the CPU's speed, which is measured in megahertz (MHz), or millions of cycles per second, the faster your system works.

◆ **CD-ROM (compact disc drive, read-only memory).** The CD-ROM drive is the tray or slot in your computer where you load a CD. A CD stores data, and these doughnut-shaped discs hold more data than those old-fashioned, square floppy discs do (don't be confused—floppy discs aren't actually "floppy"). And yes, the drive can also play your favorite Destiny's Child or Frank Sinatra CD. Unlike the sunroof on that new car you're longing for, CD-ROM drives are now standard on most computers. The higher the speed of a CD-ROM drive, the faster it can pull information from the CD. For example, a 32X disc drive will be faster than a 24X one. Also, once data is on a CD-ROM, you cannot erase it or write over it. For that, you need a CD-RW (see the next paragraph).

◆ **CD-RW (compact disc drive, rewritable).** Wow! That's a mouthful. Throw that one at a computer salesperson and he or she will think you're far too computer-savvy to try and sell you more than what you actually need. This CD drive does everything from reading and recording data to erasing it.

◆ **Ethernet card.** If you're a student and want to be able to log onto a university network, you may be required to get an Ethernet card.

◆ **Hard drive.** The hard drive is the closet of your computer, which holds all your software programs and data. Just like the beloved walk-in closet, the bigger the hard drive, the more software and data stored. The higher the number of gigabytes (GB) a hard drive has, the more you can store. Now if only we had a gigabyte of a closet to work with!

◆ **Modem.** You may not even know it, but every time you check your e-mail you're using a modem to retrieve it. This communication device allows you to connect with the Internet using your phone system. If you need to connect from home or your dorm room, you will likely use your phone line, and unless you have two lines in your house, you won't be able to receive calls while on-line.

HipTip *Worried you'll miss a call? Look into getting a voicemail system. Unlike an answering machine, it will still record messages when someone is on-line. Better yet, check out cable modems or DSL hook-ups. Although these devices may be a bit pricier, they won't disturb your phone line, or the Real World marathon you're watching on MTV, and they provide even faster connectivity.*

Just as you would expect, the faster your modem is, the quicker you can download from and surf the Net. Modem speed is measured in baud rate. The higher the baud rate, the faster the modem.

◆ **Monitor.** Much like the TV screen you veg out in front of, your monitor is the display area for all your computer activity. When you have a desktop computer, the monitor usually is a separate piece, but it is built into a laptop.

◆ **Printer.** Printers now come in a wide range of prices and functions—from a simple "dot-matrix" printer on the inexpensive end to a fancy, expensive "laser" color printer. For home or school use, a lower end printer should be sufficient. Even with just a couple hundred dollars, however, you can purchase a dot matrix printer with fax, copier, and scanner capabilities!

◆ **RAM (random access memory).** Sometimes we girls think our guys suffer from this syndrome. But seriously, consider this to be the place where memory is stored, but only for a short time. The RAM holds the information and the software programs the computer is processing at any one time. Much like the part of your brain that temporarily stores the knowledge for the final exam of the class you detest, this is only a temporary holding place. Once the data you're working on is saved or the program is closed, the information in your RAM disappears. Like the hard drive, the RAM's capability is measured in megabytes, and determines how many programs you can open and run at the same time.

◆ **Sound card and speakers.** You'll need the sound card for...well, sound. This allows your computer to play the recorded sounds you hear when you turn on your computer, play a game, run a program, or listen to a CD. You may want speakers, especially if you're using your computer as your stereo stand-in.

◆ **Software.** Your software needs depend on the tasks you need the computer to do. Often software is "bundled"—these are several programs sold together, and may already be loaded on your computer. Your software needs or "applications," will help determine what size hard drive and RAM you will need (the hardware requirements will be listed on the software box). Make sure your system can support the software you want to purchase.

◆ **Surge Suppressor.** To prevent unwanted excitement in your life, you may want to buy a surge protector for your computer. It will prevent electrical surges, such as those that happen when power goes off and then comes back on, from frying your computer.

◆ **Investigate! Investigate!** Ask other people what they like and don't like about their computers, and where they recommend you buy one. Here's your chance to strike up a conversation with that computer-clever hunk in your class or office. (Chances are his head will turn if you ask him how much RAM he has.) Stock up on a variety of computer magazines and learn a few new words. Look at many stores and systems. You wouldn't buy the first car you laid eyes on—the same goes for your computer. Check out *Consumer Reports* for quality and price comparisons. (The 2001 September issue is a recent one addressing home computers.)

◆ **Try them out.** Experiment at stores, friends' houses, or at work or computer labs with different models. It's the only way to know what you'll like.

◆ **So are you a Mac or PC girl?** Some people really do have strong opinions about this, and once you have tried each of them, you probably will too. Macintosh and Windows are types of computer operating systems. They act as the basis or "platform" for other software programs, such as word processing. The Macintosh operating system works with Apple computers as Windows does with IBM or IBM-compatible PCs. Although Macs have traditionally been associated with education-related software and Windows with the business world, they have many similar features and both are ever-changing. Take some time and explore each type of system. Only then will you be able to decide which type is more "you." And the next time someone asks if you're a Mac girl, you won't think they're asking about your makeup preferences. In fact, you can wow them with your computer knowledge. Note: Some schools have definite preferences about what you buy, so if you're a student, check it out.

◆ **Will it be a laptop or desktop?** The better questions here are, how much room do I have for my computer and how much money can I spend? Most everyone agrees that desktop machines provide more for the money, but laptops are handy little machines that are perfect for the on-the-go girl, or one who lacks space. Much like those powerfully packed mini-mints, these small-in-size, transportable treasures can be as powerful as desktops, and can go home with you on Christmas break or vacation, allowing you to check your e-mail wherever you are. However, laptops tend to be pricier. Laptops can also operate on a battery, so you don't have to be near an electrical outlet to use it. (Most batteries last for two hours max.) If you're leaning toward a laptop, remember that the screen will probably be smaller than that of a desktop computer and the keyboard and mouse (some laptops have a "touch-pad" instead of a mouse) may take some practice getting used to. Adding memory or storage capacity may be more limited than the desktop and laptops are also more easily stolen or lost.

◆ **Don't buy the "latest and greatest."** If your computer needs are typical of most users, you don't need the top of the line. If this is your first computer, buy the ol' family wagon instead of the sweet convertible.

◆ **Go where you know.** You could just as easily get a Kate Spade designer handbag from that expensive department store as you could get a fake one from the bargain street vendor outside. But let's be honest, you're not exactly expecting the same quality from the $20 purse as you would from the $200 one. And if the bargain beauty you just bought immediately falls apart, a refund is most likely not in your future. Point being, unless you're a savvy sister when it comes to computers, shop for brands and in stores that you recognize. Gateway is one such company. Get recommendations from friends who are owners.

◆ **Know their policy.** When shopping for clothes, we all pay attention to a store's return policy. After all, if your roommate laughs when you're modeling those too-tight new pants, chances are you may want to return them. Although a computer may seem a perfect fit, what happens if something goes wrong? Is there on-site repair or will you need to send it off to the manufacturer. What is the store's return policy? Is there a warranty for the computer? How long is it covered? To put your mind at rest, you may want to inquire about getting additional warranty coverage for your new pal. It may cost you more now, but it could save you more in the future. Whatever you do, keep all your receipts!

◆ **Ask about technical support.** Does your computer come with technical support? If so, ask if that support includes a round-the-clock-800-number. You will need to reach a tech repair person when your computer crashes at midnight while you're cramming to finish that report that's due the next day.

◆ **Don't be pressured.** A computer store can be an intense place. Take your time, make sure you understand what a machine has to offer, and only engage with a salesperson who doesn't talk down to you.

HipTip *Once you've purchased your computer, protect your investment (and your sanity) by investigating virus protection. A computer with a "software bundle" may already include some virus protection software. But it always needs updating—new viruses are out there all the time!*

—————

Got your RAMs from your ROMs and your monitor from your modem all figured out? Check your bad self out! Now nourish your soul and donate your old, hand-me-down computer to an underprivileged little girl or boy.

# Blackouts and Blowouts:

## When You Find Yourself in the Dark

*"One night I was in the middle of taking a shower when the lights went out in the bathroom. I panicked! All my roommates were out of town. How could this have happened? After lighting a candle that my roommate thankfully had put in the bathroom, I realized that the whole neighborhood was facing a blackout. Relieved that it wasn't some stalker who had shut off my electricity, I enjoyed the rest of my candlelit shower."*

*—Joy, 26*

### Preparing for a Blackout

ELECTRICAL-BOX BLACKOUTS LEAVE YOU IN THE DARK. Literally. Despite what you may think, however, there are ways that you can prepare yourself for a blackout.

Although usually occurring during stormy weather, blackouts can happen just about any time of the day or year. Preparing yourself for this event means that being in the dark won't be such a scary thing.

◆ **First things first:** get a flashlight (or two or three). It's a good idea to have a few working flashlights around your house. Store one next to your bed and in that junk drawer in the kitchen. If you live in a multi-story home, make sure there's at least one on each floor. It never hurts to be prepared. Do some homework: It's easiest to prepare for a blackout before you have one. Find your electric box in the light of day. A breaker box, which is sometimes referred to as an electrical or fuse box, is usually located in the garage, laundry room, or hall closet. It has a small metal-like door which, when opened, reveals switches (which look like oversized light switches) inside. Call your apartment manager in advance of an emergency to find out where your breaker box is located in your apartment. Hey, here's your chance to introduce yourself to a neighbor. Ask where his or her breaker box is located—chances are it will be in the same place in your apartment.

HipTip *A lot of older homes and buildings have "fuse" boxes instead of "breaker" boxes. If you look into the electrical box and see what look like knobs or plugs (they have a glass window) instead of big light switches, you're looking at a fuse box. If you have "blown a fuse," the fuse will have to be changed. Don't do this yourself. It's not that you can't do it, it is just that these are more dangerous to change—you have to make sure that you have the right kind of fuse. Call your landlord!*

◆ **Get romantic and buy some candles.** Candles not only improve your décor, but are functional too. Placing them around your house will not make you seem overly cautious, but instead may help put a little romance in the air. And let's face it, a girl can always use more of that! Don't forget to keep matches nearby.

*Remember to use candles with caution: Candles have an open flame, so don't get the flame close to drapes, bedding, or other things that will burn. Don't put lit candles too close to walls or ceilings either—at worst it is a fire danger, at best you will end up with soot marks there. Make sure the candleholder is sturdy. After all, there's no need to start a fire just to get you out of the dark!*

◆ **Go old-fashioned.** Cordless phones truly are one of the world's best inventions. (You can paint your toenails in the bathroom and dish the dirt with your long-distance best friend all at the same time!) But no matter how high tech your cordless is, it simply won't work if there's an electrical power failure. It's a good idea to have at least one old-fashioned, non-cordless phone—even if it's the first phone you ever got and has Hello Kitty stickers all over it—to keep you connected to the outer world.

## What to Do if You Get Caught in the Dark

We can think of lots of things you can do in the dark that are fun, so if you're caught in the right place with the right person, enjoy. But when you find yourself caught without lights when you'd really like some, don't panic. Despite what you see in the movies, the chance that a man with a golden claw is creeping down your hallway is really very slim. Most often you either tripped a circuit breaker or are caught in the middle of a blackout.

**SCENARIO ONE: The electrical power is not working in one area of your home but is in other areas.**

In this scenario, you may have just tripped a circuit breaker. How can you tell? If you were in the middle of blow-drying your hair or blending a smoothie and the blow dryer and/or blender stops working (get the picture?), it may be that you overloaded the electrical system in your home. Too many electrical devices on at the same time can cause that to happen. So, if you've got your dryer, curlers, iron, and stereo all plugged in while you get ready for a big night out, be prepared to show up late…you're bound to trip a circuit.

◆ **Turn off the appliances** you had on when the blackout occurred, such as the hair dryer, TV, and blender, and heat-producing appliances like space heaters, and stoves (you don't need to turn off the big stuff, like your refrigerator, which are always on). And turn off your computer! Turning on the electricity again could result in a power surge that fries your appliances. You could also just re-trip the circuit breaker again.

◆ **Find the breaker box** to fix this power blunder. Open it and take a look at the switches inside. Don't freak out. Most of the circuit-breaker switches should be going in one direction (usually the breaker box will indicate an "on" position). If you see any switches that have been flipped in the opposite direction to "off" or midway to the opposite direction, flip them off (if midway) then flip them all on (one at a time). Now all your switches should be going in the same direction.

◆ **Still no power?** Go back to the breaker box and give all the switches a flip—first one way to "off"; then all back to the other way, to "on." Do them one at a time. Although you may have to reset your alarm clock, it could fix your power outage.

*If the power keeps switching off, or if one of the switches feels hot,* Hip Tip *call your landlord or an electrician. The problem could be faulty wiring in your home or a problem with a particular appliance. Don't ignore it—the problem could eventually cause a fire!*

◆ **Power up and running?** Right on! Now you don't have to worry about your hair gettin' that frizz while you waited for the landlord (sometimes as long as a day) to get your power fixed. Next time, why not save yourself the hassle? Wait a few minutes for your roommate to finish blow-drying her hair before you start in on yours.

◆ **Power still not running?** You've done the basics, now give your landlord a call and fill him or her in on your situation. There are some types of electrical problems that an electrician should fix.

SCENARIO TWO: **The power is not working anywhere within your home.**

◆ **First, take a look outside at your neighborhood.** Are you the only home stranded in darkness, or are there others joining you in your misery? If you live in an apartment complex, peek your head out the door and check around you. Do you hear any TVs or stereos, or see any lights under the doors?

◆ **If your house or building is the only one in the dark,** turn off the appliances you had on (including your computer), grab a flashlight, and head to the breaker box. (Once again, a breaker box is usually located in the garage, laundry room, or hall closet. It has a small metal-like door, which, when opened, reveals many switches inside.) Give every switch a flip, one at a time (first "off," then "on").

◆ **Nothing happened?** It may just be this one is out of your hands. If you haven't already, give your landlord and/or your local electric company a call. Hopefully you'll be out of the dark in no time at all—and if not, it makes a good excuse for putting off your homework, or reorganizing your closet, for another night.

◆ **Is the whole neighborhood caught in a blackout?** At least you're not alone—misery, you know, loves company. Unfortunately there's not much you can do in this situation other than unplug most of your appliances (including your computer) and wait it out. Call your local electric company—it's a good idea to put that number and other emergency numbers by or on your phone (the one with the cord!)—and alert them to your situation. If it's daylight, now is a good time to take that jog you've been putting off. Just be careful—the traffic lights are probably out too. Is it late at night? Suggestion: Light some candles, grab your roommates, and enjoy an evening of girl talk.

—◅◊◆▻—

Who knew getting stuck in the dark could be so enlightening? With all your new blackout knowledge, you can spare the candles for a more romantic or social opportunity.

# Stopped-Up Drains:
## An Adventure under the Sink

—◄◊◊◊►—

*"My beloved college roommate was notorious for leaving globs of her hair on the shower wall. Aside from the fact that her routine nauseated me, it caused our drain to constantly stop up. I finally confronted my roommate about the problem, suggesting it was her hair that was clogging our shower. After we laughed about it, her hair globs not only disappeared, but so did our shower problems."*

—Andreea, 23

## Down Right Dirty Damage Control

HAVE YOU EVER GONE TO TAKE A SHOWER only to find a puddle of ankle-deep water already living in it? Ever tried brushing your teeth only to realize adding the tiniest drop of water made your sink back up? If so, you've been a victim of the dreaded stopped-up drain.

Before heading out to your local grocery store for drain cleaner, which usually contains lye or sulfuric acid and can be dangerous to handle, give these simple steps a try. However, if you or someone else has already poured drain cleaner into the drain, don't do any of these steps. This is because drain cleaner could splash back at you if you try any of these fixes, and can cause burns and blindness. Don't add any other cleaner either, which may cause a chemical reaction that creates a toxic gas or an explosion. (Oh boy. Would you just listen to us? Our greatest fear is happening: We're starting to sound just like our moms! Yikes! But we really don't mean to freak you out; we just want to make sure you're clear on all the unforeseeable consequences of using cleaners incorrectly. That's all. We won't nag you about it anymore. We swear!) Call your plumber and let him or her know the problem and that you have already poured in drain cleaner.

Hip Tip *If you have a septic tank (your landlord can tell you), drain cleaners can hurt it too.*

◆ **If your sink is slowly draining,** you may be able to dissolve the clog with hot water. First, grab a plastic cup (the one left over from last week's party will do just fine) and remove as much standing water as you can.

◆ **Next, turn up the heat** (or the stove, that is). Get a large pot, pour in some water, and boil it. Once the water is bubbling hot, slowly and carefully pour it down the clogged drain. This may help dissolve the blockage. (This may not work if you have a completely clogged drain.) If the hot water doesn't completely do the trick, go to the next step.

◆ **Now seize a plunger.** Hold it proudly! You're about to do battle with it. That's right, plungers aren't just for toilets; they can also be your best defense against pipe monsters. Warning: Do not use a plunger on a sink with a garbage disposal. It won't work. The garbage disposal mechanism blocks the pressure you will be exerting with the plunger.

◆ **Before you plunge,** any drain plugs or stoppers need to be removed. (Duh! Hey, it's okay. We're all allowed our ding-y moments.) They would block the pressure that you're going to create with the plunger. From the kitchen sink, you can usually just lift out any unattached "food trap" or basket type of plug. However, if you have a built-in stopper in the bathroom sink, you'll have to remove it. It's actually not too tough depending on the type of stopper you have. If you look under your sink and see a skinny or flat rod coming down from the sink that connects with another metal rod (forming a cross or an "L"), you can unscrew the bolt that connects the rods and just lift out the stopper. If there are no rods, you may be able to simply lift out the stopper or twist it slightly and pull up (but don't force it).

◆ **If your clog isn't terrible** and there's still some drainage from the sink, however slow, try fishing out the clog with an unbent wire hanger (the kind left over from one of your many trips to the dry cleaners) after you remove the drain stopper and before you plunge. That may be all you need to do. If that doesn't do it, read on.

◆ **Ready?** Princess Warrior is about to attack. Take the plunger and pump the drain at least four or five times, making sure that the plunger completely covers the drain, and the seal of the plunger is tightly around the drain. There must be enough water in the sink to cover the bell of the plunger. Repeat if necessary. If that doesn't budge the clog, see the next step.

**HipTip** *If, after you pump the drain once, there is water coming out of the overflow drain (located at the top of the sink or tub), plug up that drain before pumping again (with tape or a rag).*

◆ **Feel daring?** You go, girl, with your bravery! If your sink is the problem and you think you're up for it, find a bucket, a wrench, and a wire hanger (if you don't already have one). Some rubber gloves wouldn't hurt either.

◆ **Prepare for war.** Now that you've collected all your materials, go beneath the sink. Place the bucket under the U-shaped part of the drainpipe. If you're lucky, there is a plug at the bottom of the pipe, which you can twist out. If not, unscrew the U-portion of the pipe with a wrench. If you find yourself short on muscle power, enlist your room-mate and indoctrinate her into the Hip Girl world. Be kind enough to forewarn her that a scary surprise may lurk inside the drain.

◆ **Once the plug or pipe is unscrewed,** take the wire hanger and bend it so that it fits inside the pipe with ease. Poke the hanger up toward the drain to pry the gross goop loose.

◆ **Fished out the foreign substance (yuk!)?** Chances are you fixed the drain. Water may be pouring into your bucket. Screw the plug in or the pipe back together.

◆ **Now test your handy Hip Girl talent** by turning on the faucet.

◆ **Still clogged?** You've already valiantly gone above and beyond your call of duty. Call your landlord for help.

Hip Tip    *As a preventative measure, pouring boiling water or a handful of baking soda and a half a cup of vinegar down your drain every week can help keep your pipes clear.*

———❦———

Eww! We hear ya! Clogged drains are simply gross. 'Nuff said.

# Le Toilet:

## When You Have to Deal with the Unmentionable

*"I was at this guy's house. I'd been dating him for a month. My stomach started to not feel so hot, so I discreetly made a dash for the toilet. My tummy felt better, but my pride was shattered when to my horror I realized I'd clogged the toilet. I frantically found a plunger and prayed to the porcelain god as I profusely plunged. When that didn't work, I resorted to a one-woman bucket brigade to refill the toilet tank with water. It still wouldn't flush. I hurried out of the house without a word, leaving my embarrassment for my guy to discover on his own later."*

—Marisa, 25

## The Basics

WITH THE AMOUNT OF TIME WE GIRLS SPEND IN THE BATHROOM, you'd think we would know all there is to know about a toilet. However, if you are like most of us, you probably don't think twice about the wonders the toilet offers. Better get friendly (or at least acquainted) with your toilet just in case the two of you don't agree on what it should do. Now's the time to plan ahead to save you from your messiest nightmare!

If you've never taken the time to see how this marvelous invention works, take off the lid of the tank (which is the oval or rectangle-shaped container behind the toilet), give the toilet a flush, and watch in amazement. Heck, make a party of it! Invite your dorm room buddies or neighbors in for the thrill. Seriously though, knowing how your toilet works may help you figure out problems that arise in the future.

◆ **The tank holds most of the toilet's hardware** and is also the container which holds the clean water that will be used in the next flush.

◆ **Whenever you lift or push the arm,** or toilet handle, on the outside of a toilet, the flushing action begins. The handle, or outside arm, is connected to a chain located inside the tank. When you activate the arm, it lifts the chain and raises the black rubber plug at the bottom of the tank, sometimes referred to as the "stopper." As the stopper is lifted, the water located at the bottom of the tank pours out into the bowl, and then down the drain.

◆ **When all the water is out of the tank,** the stopper is lowered onto the "flush valve seat" (which, for us nonplumber princesses, is a brass or plastic seal, which surrounds the drain at the bottom of the tank), which closes the drain. As the water falls, so does the "float," or ball-like object in the tank. The float, when it reaches the bottom, tugs the refill mechanism so that more water comes into the tank, ready for the next flush.

## Some Toilet Dilemmas

*Dropped your jewelry?*

You're almost ready for work—all that's left is to put on your earrings. Oops, you've dropped one into the toilet! Don't freak out, just roll up your sleeves and plunge in to fish it out. Remember that it is clean water that has just come from the tank, which came straight from your water line (and therefore is just like the water coming out of your sink faucet). Don't let the stigma attached to toilets make you afraid to salvage your precious jewelry. Just wash your hands and earring and go on your merry way.

## Unclogging a Stopped Up Toilet

Okay, the toilet is clogged, now what?

◆ **Flush just once!** If you've flushed your toilet once already and it did nothing more than raise the water level in your bowl, chances are flushing it again will only result in a wet floor. Save yourself a headache and let the water drain down as much as possible.

◆ **Grab a plunger!** Stick the plunger in the toilet. Situate it over the hole while pushing up and down firmly, making sure the plunger cup fits tightly around the hole. Repeat a few times if necessary.

*Hip Tip* *Many plumbers recommend a ball-type plunger for use in the toilet. Regular plungers may "fold back" when you press them over the drain hole in the toilet.*

◆ **Pour a bucket of boiling water into the toilet bowl,** if room in the bowl allows. Then use the plunger. This may help dissolve the blockage.

◆ **Still clogged?** Put an "Out of Order" sign on your door and grab the phone. It's time to call a professional. If you're renting, call your landlord. You've done all you can and it's your landlord's responsibility to fix it.

*Running Toilets*

Like a co-worker or classmate who's always gossiping, having to listen to a toilet that constantly runs is annoying. Besides being noisy, a running toilet is not working properly, and can waste a lot of water. (And if you're the one paying the water bills, would you rather save money for the latest Banana Republic bag or shell it out for wasted water that literally goes "down the drain?")

◆ **First get jiggy with it.** Give the flush lever a little jiggle. This triggers the chain inside the tank to re-position the stopper so it completely covers the hole it was designed for. Whew! Does that seem like a whole lot of mechanical trivia you didn't need to know? Then just remember this: Simply jiggling the flush lever may be the only action required to stop that annoying sound!

◆ **Still running?** There are many reasons why your toilet may be acting up. Chances are there may be a problem with your chain or stopper. To help figure out the problem you're going to have to be tough and go in. Inside your toilet tank that is.

◆ **Lift the lid** to the tank and take a look at the chain. Make sure that the chain is not twisted, kinked, or caught under the stopper. If it is tangled, straighten out the chain or remove it from under the stopper. This should allow the stopper to rest back upon the flush valve, therefore stopping the unwanted flow of water. If it isn't the chain, it may be the stopper or seal, which sometimes wear out and have to be replaced. Replacing toilet parts is a matter for a pro, or for the extremely adventurous Hip Girl.

◆ **Still running?** It may be out of your control. It's time to give your landlord or a plumber a call to take care of the toilet troubles for you. At least you tried! And you'll sound more credible and probably get taken more seriously by the person you call if you tell him or her what you have already attempted.

*Hip Tip* *If the toilet's running is driving you crazy and you're waiting for the plumber to arrive, just shut off the water valve leading to the toilet. It usually is on the wall behind the toilet. Turn it all the way to the left. Just remember, you'll need to turn it back on if you want your toilet to refill.*

Didn't ever think you'd be so intimate with your toilet bowl, did ya? Probably not. But at least you now know what to do if you're ever a victim of toilet trouble.

# Unclogging Garbage Disposals:

## An Unsavory Task Made Easier

"When I was still in high school, my friend and I thought we'd try those at-home waxing kits for hair removal. That was our first mistake. Our second mistake was leaving the melted wax in a pan on the stove. My mom came home and thought it was water and tossed it down the disposal. By the time she realized it was wax, it was too late. The disposal and pipes were completely clogged. My dad came home and broke out a blowtorch to loosen it up. When that didn't work, we called a plumber, but ended up having to replace everything anyway."

—Jackie, 28

# Defeating Your Disposal's Troubles

Y OUR PARENTS HAVE SPRUNG A SURPRISE VISIT ON YOU. Like all surprise visits, the timing is rotten. Your sink is full of dirty dishes from the gourmet meal you attempted for last night's weekly girl get together. And as luck would have it, your disposal isn't working. But if your mom and dad just pulled into the drive, you just might have enough time to get your disposal (if not your apartment) in order, depending on the problem:

SCENARIO ONE: **Is there a horrible clattering sound? If so, there may be something in your disposal which doesn't belong there.**

◆ **First step:** TURN OFF THE DISPOSAL! Better yet, unplug it all together (the plug is probably under the sink). This is the most important step, otherwise you may have one less finger to manicure.

◆ **Roll up your sleeves,** because it's time to take the dreaded plunge. (We recommend wearing latex gloves. After all, who knows what gross fungi is growing down there?) Now, with one hand, carefully dive in and feel around. Remove any large or hard objects that you find, such as a pit from that peach you ate last week or pieces of your roommate's mismatched silverware.

◆ **Once you've discarded the evidence,** run cold water down the disposal and turn it back on.

SCENARIO TWO: **Does nothing happen when you turn on the disposal?**

◆ **Be prepared for drastic measures.** After turning off the disposal switch, get on your hands and knees and go where no girl should ever have to go: underneath the sink. Most disposals have a reset button, otherwise known as the "red button." Give that little baby a push and try the disposal switch again.

*Hip Tip*   *Does your disposal smell less than April-fresh? Put a cut-up lemon or lime—skin and all—through the disposal. To help keep your disposal clear, run some ice cubes and baking soda through your disposal every two weeks.*

**SCENARIO THREE: Does the disposal make a humming sound but doesn't move? It may be stuck.**

◆ **Again, turn the disposal off** or unplug it.

◆ **Prepare yourself.** This next tactic requires a tool. Don't be alarmed, it's only a broom. Standing firmly on the ground or on top of the kitchen counter, it's time for Princess Warrior to attack. With broom in hand, submerge the handle into the garbage disposal. Turn the broom handle counterclockwise so that you're moving the disposal blades opposite to their natural direction. Don't force the blades to turn. You don't want your landlord accusing you of breaking it. Take out the broom handle, cross your fingers and give your disposal a try once again.

◆ **Still clogged?** You've done your Hip Girl best. Time to call your landlord. Hey, that's why you pay rent!

◆ **Problem fixed?** Save yourself the hassle next time. Don't put metal, grease, wax, plastic, fruit pits, rice, or too much of anything all at once down the disposal. Oh, and always run cold water in the disposal while you have it on, unless you had such a good time playing Princess Warrior you want to do it again.

——◦∭∫∭◦——

Yeah, we know. This task ain't so pretty. But gettin' down and dirty with your disposal is sometimes simply unavoidable.

# Barbecuin' 101:

## The Fun and Fundamentals of Outdoor Grilling

*"On an all-girl camping excursion to Yosemite, my girlfriends and I decided to tackle our barbecuing fears. After all, how hard could it be? But we soon found out. After finally getting a spark, but no flame, smart me decided to douse lighter fluid all over the grill to speed up the process. Well, I succeeded. Only much to my terror, the flame burst just high enough to singe off my eyebrows. Luckily, the worst of the damage could be fixed with an eyebrow pencil, but nothing but time could mend my damaged ego."*

*—Gail, 26*

### Buying What You Need

ARE YOU HAVING A CRAVING FOR BARBECUED CHICKEN, but don't know where to start? Start with shopping, of course! Here's what you'll need to get started:

◆ **First things first, you need a grill.** When you shop for a new blow dryer, you look for not just any dryer, but also check out the features like temperature variations and speed levels, and finally choose one that will give you the best results. You should shop for a barbecue grill the same way. Knowing exactly what features you want and need is the key. Then you can decide if you want additional features that might make your barbecuing experience easier.

Despite what your guy friends say, you do not need a Cadillac-type grill. In fact, you can purchase a fun and very functional barbecue for $25-80. Check out the grills at your hardware store, or your local discount store. The Weber Kettle Grill is probably the best-selling charcoal grill. If you just have a tiny space in which to grill, or are only going to use it for yourself or a couple of friends, you could get away with a hibachi. *Note: In this chapter we are referring to charcoal grills, not gas grills, which require a propane tank or other fuel source instead of charcoal. Gas grills are preferred by many grillers, but they are more expensive. Don't commit to one until you know you enjoy this type of cooking.*

What do you really need? Think of your barbecue as a guy for a moment. You wouldn't date just anyone who crossed your path, rather, he must meet certain standards. According to the experts at Barbecuin' on the Internet (barbecuen.com), your barbecue should too—it must have sturdy legs, an adjustable grill (this will allow you to move food closer to and away from the fire if needed), and a lid with vent holes. (This lets you put out a fire with ease.) You should be able to control air flow to the fire (which allows you to control the heat of the fire) through adjustable vents in the base. Some other questions to consider: Is there an attached surface where you can set plates, sauces or marinades, and cooking utensils? Is there an easy way to clean out the ash from the bottom of the grill when you are done?

Once you've brought your perfect grill home, we recommend that you do a trial run with it—without actually cooking any food. "Cooking" the grill will burn off impurities left over from the manufacturing process. The instructions that come with your grill may tell you how to do this. Otherwise, the barbecuen.com experts say you should let a fire burn at 350 degrees for several hours. When finished barbecuing and the ashes have cooled, wipe down the grill and the inside of the lid, and empty the ashes.

*Check out the commercial sites such as bbq.about.com for information about different lines and dealtime.com for purchasing on the Internet.*

Hip Tip

◆ **Second, buy what you are going to burn.** Love won't fuel this fire. Charcoal will.

◆ **Third, get what you'll need to light the fire.** You can get your charcoal going in a couple of ways—either with lighter fluid or without, by using a chimney or electric starter. If you use lighter fluid, you can buy it separately or buy charcoal which already has lighter fluid in it. It's like buying your shampoo with or without conditioner. If your charcoal contains lighter fluid already, purchasing additional lighter fluid is not needed. (After all, you don't want to overcondition.) See below for using lighter fluid safely. *Note: Some states or local governments have put restrictions on the use of lighter fluid and charcoal with fluid because it has been found to impair air quality.*

Whether lighter fluid use is restricted or not in your area, you may wish to use a non-lighter fluid alternative to start your grill. An electric starter or charcoal "chimney" (or bucket) can be used instead.

Much like the rod that heats up an electric oven, an electric starter is loop-shaped and is very easy to use, not to mention an environmentally safer alternative. As you may expect, an electric starter needs electricity. If there's no outlet nearby, an extension cord may be needed. A chimney starter is a hollow cylinder (with no base) that you place on the bottom of the grill and fill with charcoal.

◆ **Gather your cooking tools.** You've made your big purchase, the grill, and have your fire building materials ready. What else do you need? Basic grilling utensils: Because you are cooking over fire and heat, we recommend getting some long-handled metal cooking utensils, such as a spatula and a set of tongs (both of which are useful for turning meat without spearing it and losing the good juices), a big fork (for spearing vegetables), and a basting brush. But if you don't want to splurge just yet for special barbecuing utensils, use the ones you already own from your kitchen collection—just be extra careful when using them. Regular kitchen tools lack extra-long handles. And no matter what, never use plastic utensils when cooking on the grill. Plastic melts . . . duh!

Also useful are hot mitts and a spray bottle for water, when putting out small flare-ups. Finally, invest in a bi-therm instant thermometer to use when cooking any type of meat. It really is the only way to tell if the meat is cooked enough, without drying it out too much. You'll have better food, without making you and your guests sick! To use it, insert the probe into the meat to determine the meat's internal temperature. Then take it out right away!

**Hip Tip** *For safety, keep a box of baking soda near the grill. While water will put out small flare-ups, baking soda will handle bigger ones. Forget about eating the food though, baking soda only improves baked goods, not chicken and vegetables! Even better, keep a fire extinguisher nearby and know how to use it. You have one in your home, right?*

# First Time?

Who said, "Barbecuing is for men?" Most likely a man. Well, you and your grill can prove that man wrong. Grilling is a lot easier than you might think. Much like putting on makeup, you'll get better with practice.

*Hip Tip* *While we, like most people, use the terms interchangeably, "grilling" and "barbecuing" are actually two different cooking methods. Cooking directly or indirectly over high heat is grilling, which is what we are talking about in this chapter. Barbecuing is generally cooking with indirect heat at low temperatures for longer time periods.*

◆ **Choose your guests.** Is it just you and your roomie? Or is it time to repay your neighbors for watching your house while you were sipping margaritas in Mexico? Whoever it is, don't invite so many people that you'll feel stressed. (Yes, volunteering to barbecue your family's traditional Thanksgiving turkey counts as stressful.)

◆ **Choose a nice day if you can.** You don't need to start playing with this fire when it's really windy or rainy. Besides, what fun is that? If you have guests coming you can always opt to cook on the stove. Never use your barbecue grill inside! The fumes are lethal.

◆ **Choose your menu.** You may want to prepare all the food yourself, or if you want to focus only on the grill, ask your guests to bring a dish. If you are going to marinate your meat or veggies, read the marinade recipe or bottle to see how long the food needs to sit in the marinade.

◆ **Fresh versus frozen meats.** Start with these food preparation tips: Fish and meat bought fresh (not frozen) at the market usually have the most flavor. However, if you buy your meat or fish frozen, remember that it has to thaw before you throw it on the grill. Thawing is best done in the refrigerator. If you are planning on barbecuing for dinner, take your meat or fish out of the freezer and put it into the refrigerator that morning. (Thicker pieces may need to begin thawing the night before.) Any additional thawing may be done in the microwave. Don't thaw meat or fish on the counter. It's a good way to attract bacteria and make you (and your guests) sick!

◆ **Fire up the grill!** Grab your charcoal and head for the grill. Lift the lid off the base and take out the grill (or grid). Which way you light your charcoal will depend on whether you wish to use lighter fluid or not. We prefer the non-lighter fluid way, as we find it more friendly to the environment, and not so dangerous. Also, some expert grillers insist that using lighter fluid leaves food with a petroleum taste, especially if the fluid doesn't completely burn off before putting food on the grill. How's that for motivation?

◆ **Using a chimney.** If you don't want to fool with lighter fluid, then a charcoal "chimney" or an electric fire starter are the tools for you. With a chimney starter, you will need a newspaper and your charcoal. At the bottom of the starter, place a few wadded-up pieces of newspaper, enough so that the bottom of the cylinder is packed solidly, then fill the rest of the cylinder with charcoal. Then light the newspaper with a long-handled match through a slot at the bottom of the cylinder and wait for the charcoal to start burning. Once it is lit and the coals become red-hot, simply lift (very carefully!) the cylinder up by the handle (with your oven mitts on), leaving the coals at the bottom of the grill.

◆ **Using an electric starter.** If you don't like the chimney approach, you can use an electric fire starter. To use an electric starter, spread a thin layer of charcoal briquettes on the bottom grate of your grill. Place the electric lighter on top of the briquettes. Next, spread another layer of charcoal on top of the lighter. Plug the starter into an outlet and let it work its magic for eight to ten minutes until the coals start to burn, then carefully remove it from the briquettes. *Remember: Electric starters* *may differ depending on manufacturers. Be sure to read the directions before using yours.*

◆ **Using lighter fluid.** Add enough coals to cover the base generously. Light the charcoal. You can do this two ways. If your coals contain lighter fluid already, you do not have to do anything further on this step. If the charcoal is without lighter fluid, however, take your lighter fluid and squirt it all over your coals. Check the directions on the charcoal bag to determine how much fluid to use. (Don't use too much. You're trying to start a fire, not put one out.) Let the lighter fluid soak into the coals for a few minutes. This will make it easier to light. *Remember: Never use gasoline to start a fire and never pour lighter fluid onto a flame or a glowing coal!!*

◆ **Lighting the coals when using lighter fluid.** This next step is probably the most dangerous of all so be cautious and read on. Once your charcoal is juiced carefully, light a match and toss it into the coals. (Make sure you've put the lighter fluid can far away from the grill.) Don't lean over the fire while you do this, otherwise you risk singeing your newly waxed eyebrows off (or worse). Better yet, use a long kitchen match to help with this task.

◆ **Got it going?** Great! Kick back while the coals heat up. Remember, you can always add more charcoal if needed. Check on the coals every fifteen minutes or so to check their color. If the coals are turning white, get ready to rock and roll.

◆ **Still no flames?** If you used lighter fluid or charcoal already containing it, try lighting another match. If there is still no fire in sight, try adding a few more coals and sprinkling more lighter fluid on them, but only if there's absolutely no fire or embers yet. Be careful! If the coals have begun to burn and you just can't see it, the lighter fluid will flame up and could seriously burn you. If you used a charcoal chimney, start the process over, making sure not to handle any hot coals. Use tongs instead. If you used an electric charcoal starter, reinsert it into the charcoal and give it another eight minutes to ignite. Don't forget to remove it once it has done its job, otherwise you'll be shopping for a new one.

◆ **Still no luck?** You gave it a good shot. This is the point where a Hip Girl should feel zero guilt about asking for some 411. Get on the phone. If your mom, dad, or friend is a master of the fire pit, call for some advanced barbecuing expertise.

# Let's Get Cooking

The tough part is over. Time to get cooking. Gather your food along with a spatula and/or tongs and head to the barbecue.

◆ **Carefully place the grill back on the fire.** You may want to use your tongs in this task to avoid the heat. Remember that the closer to the fire you place the grill, the higher the cooking temperature, so start by placing it somewhere near the middle height. You can always adjust it later.

◆ **Check the temperature of the coals** after the fire dies down. According to Steven Raichlen, author of *The Barbecue! Bible*, you can use the following method for checking your fire's temperature. Being extremely cautious, hold your hand palm down about six inches over the coals, without touching the grill. This will help you determine the approximate temperature depending upon how long you can keep your hand over the grill. *Note: When using this method it's best to count slowly. For example, "one one-thousand, two one-thousand, three one-thousand." You get the picture.*

| 3 seconds | = | 500 degrees F | HIGH |
| 5 seconds | = | 400 degrees F | MEDIUM-HIGH |
| 7 seconds | = | 350 degrees F | MEDIUM |
| 10 seconds | = | 325 degrees F | MEDIUM-LOW |
| 12 seconds | = | 300 degrees F | LOW |

◆ **Too hot to handle?** Does the idea of holding your hand over the coals scare you a bit? No problem, there is another way to check how hot your coals are. Diane Worthington, author of *The California Cook*, suggests that medium-high heat is evidenced by red-hot coals with just a thin layer of ash and an occasional flare-up. Medium-heat coals have a thicker layer of ash and no flare-ups. As you can see, these methods of figuring out the heat are not an exact science! All the more reason to use a thermometer to check whether food is done!

◆ **When you've gotten the approximate heat** you're looking for, toss your food on the grill. (Most grillers recommend leaving the lid off while grilling, unless you need to put the fire out. Having the lid on may cause the fire to go out or ruin the meat or vegetables with soot, a combination of smoke and ashes.)

## Food Preparation and Cooking Times

Just like you really never know how long it's going to take you to get ready (friends may call, your hair might not be cooperating, your roommate may hog the bathroom), the same is true about barbecuing. One can never tell how long it will take to cook something. It all depends on what you are cooking, how thick it is, the heat of the fire, and the weather outside.

The key is to get your food to the right temperature, and that all depends on what you are serving. (Barbecuing experts may suggest lower meat temperatures than listed here, but we recommend being safe, and are listing the USDA recommendations.)

**Hip Tip** *You can find recommended food temperatures at foodsafety.gov or by calling the USDA Meat and Poultry Hotline at 800-535-4555.*

**Fish**—If you can afford it. Use a medium-high fire. Coat the fish with a little butter or oil, place on the grill, and turn often. For delicate-textured fish, such as sea bass, you may want to enclose it in aluminum foil on top of the grill, so it doesn't fall apart into the fire. Let the fish rest a bit after taking it off the grill and before opening the foil. "Meatier" or thicker cuts of fish, such as swordfish or shark steaks, can usually withstand being cooked directly on the grill. Unsure if your fish needs the care of aluminum foil? Ask the person helping you at the meat and fish department if your fish is more on the delicate side. How can you tell when it's done? With a little help of a fork and your eyes you can figure that out. If the fish starts to flake when breaking it apart with a fork, it's done.

*Tip Tip* *Good butchers can be a great source of information. Don't be afraid to ask questions about grilling—they can make recommendations as to cut of meat and cooking tips. Don't shop where they can't or won't help you.*

**Chicken**—The college favorite. Use a medium-high fire. Lay the seasoned chicken on the grill. The chicken will first stick to the cooking grate. When it releases you should turn it over. How do you know when it's done? Simple, when chicken breasts reach 170 degrees F and chicken thighs and wings reach 180 degrees F, the pieces are ready to come off the grill. Here's where the bi-therm instant thermometer comes in handy.

*Tip Tip* *Thermometers should be inserted into the thickest part of the meat without touching bone, fat, or gristle. When using an instant thermometer, take it out of the meat once you've read the temperature.*

**Burgers**—Another college favorite (or necessity). Use a medium-high fire. Make your own patties with ground beef, pressing them into about half-inch patties. Cook until brown on one side, then flip. Don't press down on the meat or you can dry it out (and cause grease flare-ups). Cook all the way through!

**Steaks**—Usually saved for when you are trying to impress a date, or your parents are visiting—and paying. Use a hot fire. Ask your butcher what cuts he or she recommends for grilling. Flip when one side is brown. It will probably take about five to ten minutes on each side. You may use a knife to check the color inside, but most good cooks we know recommend using a bi-therm instant thermometer to avoid losing the meat's juices. (The various levels of "doneness" can be determined by the color or temperature of the steak's interior: red or 145 degrees F = medium rare, pink or 160 degrees F = medium, brown or 170 degrees F = well done.)

**Veggies**—You don't have to be a vegetarian to love them. Grilling veggies is a piece of cake. Cook at a high heat to seal in juices, then move to the edge of the grill to finish cooking. The rule of thumb is to cut the vegetable (whether it be a bell pepper, asparagus, eggplant, or zucchini) into pieces that will cook evenly and quickly. Make sure all pieces are cut to an equal thickness (no more than three-quarter to one inch thick). Before tossing your veggies on the grill, soak them in cold water for half an hour (this will help keep your veggies from drying out), then brush them with oil to prevent them sticking to the grill. Place small veggie pieces on skewers or use a grilling basket. Larger pieces can be placed right on the grill. Turn them frequently and brush with additional oil to prevent drying. When the skins begin to blister or the middles become soft, it's time to remove your veggies. Remember: different veggies will take different amounts of time to cook. Depending upon what you are grilling, and how thick it is, it may take anywhere from five to twenty minutes.

Congratulations! If you were still a Girl Scout, you would have just earned yourself a badge for your efforts. Give yourself a pat on the back! Better yet, give your parents a call and brag—they'll be so proud!

## Easy Cleanup for Your New Friend!

Be nice to your grill and it will be nice to you. Rubbing your grill surface with a paper towel drizzled with a little cooking oil, before you use it, will help keep food from sticking to it. After every use, clean your grill (once it is cool) to keep from building a residue that is difficult to remove (and not too appetizing to look at, either). Most grillers prefer a long handled wire brush with a scraper on the end to remove pieces of food. Scrape, brush, then wipe off with paper towels. If the grate gets too crusty, try soaking it in hot, soapy water. Make sure you remove the ashes from the grill periodically, as they'll eventually cause the grill to deteriorate. But not right away—we have a friend who started a fire she *didn't* want when she got eager and cleaned out the ashes before they were dead!

## Barbecuing Not for You?

Let's face it—barbecuing just may not be for you, or if you live in an apartment, you may not have an outdoor grilling space. Don't fret! Fortunately, today's technology allows us to bring the taste of the great outdoors…indoors. (It's much easier too.)

You can find an indoor grill just about anywhere from Target to Sears. Hamilton Beach and George Foreman are two popular brands.

These grills provide an excellent and easy way to barbecue inside without all the hassle of outdoor grilling. Depending on the size you want, they run anywhere from $25-100 in price. This grill can cook every type of meat and is great with vegetables too. Although it may lack the flavor of a true, smoky barbecue, indoor grilling (unlike outdoor grilling) can be done in your pajamas.

## Ins and Outs of Marinating

Flavor is everything. Sure we all love the basics, but tell the truth. If you had to choose between plain chocolate ice cream or super-chunky-fudge-and-peanut-butter ice cream, which would be more appealing? My money is on the chunky-fudge-and-peanut-butter. Well, much like ice cream, meat, fish, and vegetables need to be spiced up at times. Here are a few ideas for marinades:

◆ **There's a huge selection of marinades** out there in the grocery stores. Most marinades will specify whether they are made for fish or chicken, vegetables or beef. Trial and error and asking around are the only sure-fire ways to find your favorite. We've included some basic marinades below, but we also persuaded Papa DeGregori to share his favorite marinade recipes.

Hip Tip  *Salad dressing for meat? Don't underestimate the power of clear (not creamy) Italian dressing, which makes a tasty marinade for chicken or fish. See Papa DeGregori's recipe below.*

◆ **Lost on what marinade goes with what meat?** Here are some tips, for quick, "no fail" marinades:

**Beef**—Some popular marinades for hamburger and steak, which you're probably already familiar with, are A1 sauce or Worcestershire sauce. Or if you want a more Asian flair, try using teriyaki sauce to spice things up. After all, they say, variety is the spice of life.

*Hip Tip* *Check out The Barbecue Source at bbqsource.com for a selection of hard-to-find barbecue sauces and marinades. This website also offers a great "frequently asked questions" section where anyone can log on and get her barbecue questions answered.*

**Chicken**—An extremely versatile meat, everything from honey mustard, barbecue sauce to teriyaki sauce can be used on chicken.

*Hip Tip* *Stephen Raichlen and other grilling experts recommend that you not put sugar- or tomato-based sauces, which would include most bottled barbecue sauces, on the meat until it's almost done grilling. Otherwise, you run the risk of drying out the meat.*

**Fish**—"I love fish, but only if it doesn't taste fishy." Ever hear that one before? Fish is another type of meat where trial and error comes into play. Fish and Italian dressing mix well, but mainly on white fish only. A lemon and butter combination is a safe bet for all types of fish (although it's not a safe bet for your waistline).

**Vegetables**—For tempting veggies, try brushing them with olive oil and sprinkling garlic salt, parsley, Italian seasoning, or your favorite spice on top. We bet you never knew that something so good for you could taste so great.

Bottom line, marinating is purely a personal choice. If you don't have time to marinate before grilling, you can do it as you grill. Just brush the marinade on the meat, fish, or veggies as they cook. Otherwise, we recommend marinating your food for at least an hour or two before grilling, keeping in mind that the longer your meat, fish, or veggies soak in a marinade, the more intense the flavor.

*Chicken:*

## YUMMY ITALIAN RECIPE

◆ **Marinate boneless, skinless chicken breasts** in a light, clear Italian salad dressing. *Note: If breasts are frozen, pour dressing into a sealable plastic bag and add the chicken breasts. Allow the breasts to thaw, in the refrigerator, with the dressing around them in the bag.*

## 21-AND-OVER-RECIPE

◆ **Put your culinary skills to the test** and cut a chicken in half—or have your butcher do it for you.

◆ **Measure,** in a small bowl, one-third cup white vermouth and two-thirds cup vegetable cooking oil.

◆ **Sprinkle** a pinch of dried rosemary and thyme leaves on the vermouth and oil.

◆ **Stir** a few drops of Worcestershire sauce into the marinade.

◆ **Brush** the sauce on the chicken halves while barbecuing, making sure to not let the chicken get dry.

◆ **Hint:** If you like your food saucy (after all, you are a saucy kind of girl!), add some Tabasco or other hot sauce to the mixture.

*Beef:*

## MY-PARENTS-ARE-COMING-STEAK:

◆ **In a hurry** but want to impress your parents who are coming for their first visit to your apartment? Just season some steak with black pepper and garlic salt or powder to taste.

◆ **Put the steak on a hot grill.** Cook the first side until blood starts to seep out of the top, uncooked side.

◆ **Next, turn the meat over** and cook until the desired doneness: rare, medium, or well. *Note: Don't keep turning the steak over from one side to* the other. *Every time you flip a steak it loses more juices. Constantly flipping it will make your steak tough and chewy.*

### First-Date-Impressions-or-Anniversary-Steak

◆ **Got time to spare** and want to pretend like you're completely in control in the kitchen? Mix some red wine, finely-chopped onions, and garlic powder together.

◆ **Pour the marinade** over the steak and let it soak for about one hour.

◆ **Put the meat on the grill** to cook.

◆ **Sprinkle black pepper** on the steak while grilling.

◆ **Grill to the desired doneness,** only turning the steak over once. See the note above.

## Fish:

### One-Stop-Shopping Salmon Recipe:

◆ **Salmon** has enough of its own oils, so all you need to do is season it with a little black pepper and garlic powder. Mmmm…yum!

### You-Got-into-Grad-School Treat:

◆ **Swordfish** or any other "firm" fish merely requires a brush of olive oil and topping of crushed garlic before grilling. Or try teriyaki sauce.

Everybody step back! A Hip Girl's ready to roll with the big boys. Now fire up the grill and school the guys in your 'hood on your barbecuin' skills. (And watch 'em drool as you tame those wild flames!)

# Automotive Antics

Does car-buying get you frazzled? How about that car insurance—are you paying a bundle? Don't trip! Get a grip! Read up on this section for insight and Hip Tips for everything car-related, like shopping for a good mechanic (because you can't buy 'em at Target) and how to calmly handle a car accident (so not to cause more harm than good). And before you know it, you'll be changing tires quicker than the guys at the Indy 500.

# Car Shopping, Part I:
## The Homework

---

*"My car completely junked out on me two days before I started law school. I was freaking because I needed a car. But my funds were low and I could only afford to buy a stick shift, despite the fact that I'd never driven one before. I sure learned quickly as I half-drove, half-stalled my new car on the freeway going home."*

—Jen, 29

## What's Your Car Personality?

PICKING THE RIGHT CAR is just as important as choosing your friends wisely. Ask yourself a few simple questions when you are making a list of candidates:

◆ **What kind of car fits you?** This is the fun part: What type of car do you see yourself in? For every type of car, there is a wide range of prices and models to choose from. For instance, are you a nature lover whose passion for exploring the outdoors requires a truck or Jeep? Would a roomy SUV fit all of your girlfriends or your three dogs? Or would a hot red sports car be the perfect thing to match your free spirit?

◆ **What specific amenities does your lifestyle require?** Do you need air conditioning for driving around your heat-sensitive grandmother; a leather interior because it's easier to clean off the grease from late-night dashes for cheeseburgers and fries; good gas mileage to satisfy your environmental consciousness or live within your budget; or four-wheel drive for your hiking and snow-skiing getaways? Prioritize your wish list by thinking about what you simply cannot live without (an important rule to remember when choosing your dating partners too)! But also think about the things you don't *have* to have. Options that maybe aren't necessary, but seem important, can add a lot to the price, especially for a new car.

◆ **Where do you live?** Keep in mind that the kind of car you really want may not be appropriate for where you live. That hot little convertible with the cloth top may be really cold in the wintertime! Similarly, a new car may not be the best thing—if you're in school, college campuses are often prime locations for car thefts. Or perhaps your neighborhood is notorious for vandalism. Further, if you live in a city, your car is going to get a lot of nicks and dings. Weigh what's more important to you: A car that looks good and rides really well, or a car that you're not worried about being stolen (or damaged), but you know is reliable enough for toting you around town.

◆ **Narrow down your search.** Check out various autos by taking note of cars that catch your eye (not to mention the drivers) cruising by you on the road, logging onto individual car makers' websites, or by doing car-lot drive-bys. Does your eye candy share any similarities? How are your candidates different? By the way, consider yourself warned: Since you haven't completed your car shopping homework yet, don't get out of your car to have a closer look at a car on a dealership lot. If you can't resist stopping, just leave your money at home. A car salesman's job is to persuade you to buy right on the spot. Sometimes even the smartest and most strong-minded people can fall for a sales job done well. But without the proper research, you could end up losing more than you gain!

## Money Can Buy You Love!

So after scoping it out, you think you've found your true love at last! It's everything you've ever dreamed of! Okay, at least you've found a few cars that meet your basic "true love" standards. Now that you've chosen a few candidates, make sure you find out which of them has all the amenities you want, at a price that won't force you to eat rice cakes every day for lunch. Remember that you need to look at the up-front price of buying the car, as well as figure out how much it's going to cost you every year in maintenance, insurance, and registration. Here are some key pricing factors to consider for all your car candidates:

◆ **What is a fair price for the car?** If you're looking at new cars, get on the Internet to look at manufacturers' sites, where you can check out different models, the options available, and usually, the manufacturers' suggested retail prices. Also, keep your eye on newspaper advertisements for the prices of new and used cars. Watch to see if there are price cuts for certain models. For a comprehensive list of cars and prices (both for new and used), go to the library or bookstore and get a copy of the Kelly Blue Book, which is an independent guide to tell you what you can expect to pay for a car. If you're borrowing cash to buy your car from a bank or a loan provider or if Mom and Dad are sportin' you the dollars, ask them what they think is a fair price for the car you want to purchase.

*Hip Tip* *You can save yourself a trip to the library by logging on to the Kelly Blue Book website at kbb.com. You can also find great price information at the National Auto Dealer Association website, nadaguides. com. There is an amazing amount of car information available on the Internet if you want to check it out—just punch in key words like "car" and "prices"—but we know these particular sites are sponsored by companies that have been around for a long time and have good reputations.*

◆ **How will you pay for it?** This question will probably weed out some of your candidates. Not many people can afford to buy a car, especially a new one, with cash, so they have to borrow some money. You'll need to figure out what you can afford for a down payment, as well as for monthly loan payments. Check with your bank—a loan officer will help you figure out what works within your (virtually nonexistent) college or first-job budget! (See later in this chapter for some tips on your auto loan.)

*Hip Tip* *There are a ton of car loan calculators for your use on the Internet. Type in "car loan" to get to them. Go to bankrate.com for calculators on how much to put down for your car, as well as how much your monthly loan payment will be. You can experiment with different car prices and interest rates to see what you can afford. Or go to CarsDirect.com to determine how much you can afford by starting with the monthly payment you'd like to make.*

◆ **How much is insurance?** Generally, the more expensive the car, the higher the loan, and the younger the driver, the pricier the insurance will be. Better check into auto insurance rates for the models you're considering. No need to drool over a cherry-red convertible Porsche (yeah, right!) if you can't afford to insure it! (See the *Auto Insurance* chapter, too.)

◆ **How much is the registration fee?** At the time of purchase, all cars must be registered with your state's department of motor vehicles (some states have different names for that agency, but we'll refer to it as the DMV for shorthand). This agency keeps track of the car and the owner (yep, that's how the DMV knows exactly where to send all those parking ticket reminders). Sometimes the cost of registration can tack on a whole lot of extra dough (upwards of $200-500 or more), depending on your state's registration fees. If several hundred dollars is enough to completely drain your account, you might want to consider another vehicle for this reason alone. Additionally, registration must be renewed annually, and the amount you pay may or may not decrease after you buy your car, depending on how your state calculates its registration fees. So if this amount will bust your account every year, consider another car that better suits your spending (and earning) habits.

◆ **How much is sales and other taxes?** As if the registration fee isn't enough to bear, there's also sales tax added to the cost of the car. You know how much money that adds to your clothing purchases, so you can just imagine how it feels to add it to the cost of your car! If you live in an area with a high sales tax, this can make a significant difference in the real price of your car. And wait, some states charge a personal property tax on your car too! Make sure you know what applies to you.

## New or Used?

Consignment shops can sometimes be a Hip Girl's best friend for the latest fashion trend of vintage clothing made hip again. The same is true with cars. Decide whether you want (and can afford) a shiny, new car, or if there's a more classic, used style that toots your horn. (Sorry, we couldn't resist the pun.) Below are the pros and cons of buying used and new cars:

## Pros of Buying a Used Car

◆ **Costs less.** The car is used, so clearly it won't cost what the same, brand-new model does. Cars are lasting a lot longer than they used to, so if you're careful about what you're buying, you can buy a quality car that will last you a while for less cash. Plus, depending on the state in which you live, insurance, sales tax, and possibly registration fees may run a little less.

◆ **Less depreciation.** Have you ever heard someone say you lose money as soon as you drive a new car off the lot? They're talking about depreciation, which is essentially the loss in a car's value after you buy it. The sad truth about buying a car is that, unless you are buying a very valuable collector's car, it's going to decrease in value the longer you own it. And they decrease in value very quickly. Cars depreciate most in the first few years of their lives. If you buy a car that is three to four years old, a big chunk of the depreciation has already been incurred and you won't be paying for value that will immediately be lost after the purchase (like you would with a new car).

◆ **Get more bang for your buck.** By buying a used car, you might be able to get the fully-loaded model complete with a CD player and a leather interior. In contrast, a new version of the same model with all the extra features will likely cost a lot more money than you've saved up from all your tutoring jobs.

◆ **Lots of good inventory.** There are a lot of quality used cars out there. Leasing programs are being pushed by many car manufacturers, and many people choose to lease a car instead of buying. (We'll talk a little more about leasing later.) Anyway, all those leases are up at some point or another (usually in three to four years), the people who leased the cars turn them back in to the car dealership, and the dealer sells them as used cars. Since leasing programs require that the cars be kept in excellent condition, and not driven over a certain number of miles every year (usually 15,000), there are a lot of good quality used cars available on the market.

◆ **But I have to have that model.** For the same reason you can't throw out that old, raggedy pair of jeans you've had since your freshman year, sometimes newer versions of the model you want just don't have that same appeal. Only the old model has the features you want or the style that fits your Hip Girl image.

## Cons of Buying a Used Car

◆ **No or poor warranties.** Boyfriends don't come with guarantees or warning labels for problems that might arise, and some used cars don't either. You do need to pay close attention to see what, if any, warranty comes with a used car. To make things easier, all dealers (or at least those who sell six or more cars a year) are now required to post a "Buyers Guide" in every used car they have for sale. The Buyer's Guide will tell you a lot of useful information, including whether or not there is any warranty with the car. If there is a warranty, the Buyer's Guide will spell out what it is—which systems of the car it covers, how much the dealer will pay, and for how long the warranty lasts.

Hip Tip *If there is a box checked on the Buyer's Guide that says "as-is," that means there is no warranty, and any problems you have are all your problem.*

There are a couple of important rules to remember about the Buyer's Guide: First, if you negotiate any change in the warranty with the seller from what is listed on the Buyer's Guide, that change *must* be shown on the Buyer's Guide. If you have a disagreement with the seller after you buy a car, what is shown on the Buyer's Guide controls the outcome of the argument, *even if you have a contract with the seller that says something else.*

**Hip Tip** *There is a bit of homework in understanding what different warranties there are out there. Check out the Federal Trade Commission website for a good explanation of what to look for at ftc.gov/bcp/conline/pubs/autos/usedcar.htm.*

Second, people who sell less than six cars per year (which means most private sellers, such as those you would find through the classified ads), are not required to post a Buyer's Guide in their used cars. Most likely, private sellers will only sell a car to you "as-is."

**Hip Tip** *Some car manufacturers sponsor a certification program whereby their dealers make sure that used versions of that maker's car are up to par with certain standards before reselling the car. These certified used cars often come with some warranty, although usually with less coverage than if you buy a brand-spanking new car.*

◆ **Repair nightmares.** The older the car, the more worn certain parts may be (kind of like our joints from playing too much rugby in college). Repair costs for a used car can become your biggest nightmare if you don't have the car inspected really well before you purchase it. You can guard against this risk, however—we'll talk a little bit more about inspections later.

◆ **No interest in your pride and joy.** For convenience sake, many people will trade in their old car when buying another one, whether new or used. If you don't trade in your old car, you'll have to sell it on your own, usually through the classified ads or by word of mouth. That includes the inconvenience of setting up appointments and talking to several people about your car. And how can you sell your trusty old friend to a buyer you don't like? The agony! We understand. However, if you purchase a used car from a private seller, they probably won't consider a trade-in at all and you'll be forced to do it. The upside is that you're almost sure to make more money if you sell your old car on your own (a dealer can only pay so much, because they'll have to prepare the car and probably do some minor repairs to sell it again).

*Pros of Buying a New Car*
◆ **Overall fewer headaches.** A new-car warranty buys an owner more peace of mind, which means you can instead focus on writing your thesis, taking your GREs, or prepping for your promotion-request meeting with your boss. New-car warranties are more comprehensive, are backed by solid companies, and extend for longer periods of time or greater mileage than used cars. Because cars tend to be better built and last longer, however, that warranty may not last long enough to cover big problems that will come along some day. Talk about good news/bad news!

◆ **A new best friend.** Like your best friend, if you treat your car right, usually she'll be good to you too. If you buy a new car, you'll have the benefit of knowing it has been well taken care of from the first day off the lot, and probably won't face the problems that a badly-cared for used car may have. Plus, unlike your best friend, your new car doesn't mind your singing, you can always count on her to go road tripping, and her feelings won't get hurt if you start spending more time with your new boyfriend! You can rest easy knowing all the TLC you've given your new car from the very beginning is the foundation for a decade of good performance and fond memories.

◆ **Because you deserve exactly what you want.** New-car buyers can get dealers to order straight from the manufacturer a variety of features—right down to the CD player, mags, engine, and color that you've been drooling over since you saw your favorite actress driving it in the movies. If you gotta have it, you gotta have it.

◆ **State-of-the-art safety.** Manufacturers are continually coming up with new safety features. If you want them, you'll need to buy new.

## Cons of Buying a New Car

◆ **Cha-ching!** New cars are by far more expensive than used ones, unless you go for the cheaper or stripped down model! Bye-bye, sunroof!

◆ **No appreciation.** Buying a new car is like spending a pretty penny on trendy clothes, instead of investing in timeless, classic pieces. Remember that old demon called depreciation? The moment you drive a new car off the lot, it loses value—some say as much as twenty percent of the purchase value in the first year alone.

◆ **Total disaster strikes.** If you total your car in an accident, you run more risk of the insurance proceeds not being enough to replace it. This means you are left to cover the remaining balance all by yourself. Better insure that baby completely—and that's going to be expensive. If you take out a loan for the car, it's likely you'll have no choice about it. And full coverage insurance costs more than just liability insurance (see *Auto Insurance* chapter for details).

# Lease or Buy?

The next step in getting a new car is to decide whether to lease or buy. Leasing is basically a long-term rental. Think of it like renting an apartment—except at the end of a car lease, you have the option of buying the car or giving it back to the dealership to sell to someone else.

**Hip Tip** *Keep in mind that you can even lease a used car, backed either by the manufacturer or the dealership. If you are considering a pre-owned car lease, we recommend leasing a manufacturer-certified used car, which may be refurbished to like-new condition. Dealer's standards may vary.*

Many auto industry experts recommend that you buy instead of lease, especially if you plan on holding on to your car for more than two to three years. But you can make up your own mind. Below are the basic pros and cons of leasing versus buying a car:

## Pros of Leasing a Car

◆ **Lower monthly payments.** How much can you pay per month? If not a whole lot, leasing might be an option to consider.

◆ **You'll look hotter in a convertible.** Generally speaking, because monthly payments are lower in a lease (determined by the length of the lease term, any down payment, and your ability to wheel and deal), you may be able to lease a car you couldn't otherwise afford to purchase.

◆ **Less money spent on maintenance.** A manufacturer's warranty usually expires after two or three years. As long as you don't sign a lease longer than that, you'll spend less money out of your own Coach purse for repairs and maintenance on the car. You got it—that means more money for that laptop computer fund!

◆ **Little or no down payment.** You shouldn't have to put a lot of money down for a leased car. *Warning: A car salesperson may try to convince you otherwise, but don't do it. Leasing is not like a layaway plan for that new leather coat. You're not necessarily going to buy the car at the end of the lease, so paying a hefty down payment isn't "getting you ahead" of the game.*

◆ **No worries about selling it.** Plain and simple: You don't own the car in a lease, so it's not yours to worry about getting rid of. If school's done or you're in-between jobs and your auto lease is up, you have the freedom to go backpacking in the south of France.

◆ **Less money on taxes.** Depending on your state law, you may only pay taxes on the monthly payments under a lease, not the entire cost of the car.

## Cons of Leasing a Car

◆ **No investment.** Because you are only paying to lease the car, you don't have anything to show for it at the end of a lease—just like when you're renting an apartment. That means starting from scratch all over again when you turn in your car. And unless you've saved up some money for a down payment (or won the lottery), you'll likely have to lease again.

◆ **It costs you more if you keep the car too long.** You'll make monthly payments all the way to the end of a lease, whereas if you buy, there are no more payments once you've paid off your loan. So if you opt to buy and you keep your car for a while, it's almost like free money in your pocket (but not quite).

◆ **Regular grooming required.** Basically, unless you can personally detail your car (or can have it done inexpensively for you) as well as you groom your nails and hair, be prepared to be overcharged from your leasing company for little nicks and dings when you return the car.

◆ **Expensive road trips.** Most leases stipulate a limit on the number of miles you can drive—usually twelve to fifteen thousand miles a year. If you go over your allotment, you'll really rack up some extra charges. So unless you buy extra mileage up front (which is much cheaper than buying it in the end), you're better off to chip in for gas and rely on your friends to drive on weekend road trips. Speaking of road trips, better make sure your lease allows you to take your car into other countries, just in case you go wild after your final exams or need a vacation and want to try authentic Mexican margaritas.

◆ **Higher insurance rates.** Leasing companies require full property coverage and higher liability coverage on the car, which raises the cost of your monthly insurance payments substantially. And if you're at an age where insurance rates are already high (or your driving record reflects your need to put the pedal to the metal), paying more on insurance could mean less money available for going out. You may also have to pay for "gap" insurance, which covers the difference between the amounts you've paid on the lease and the value of the car if it's totaled or stolen (less the amount the insurance company pays you in these events).

◆ **Leases can be very complicated,** consumer unfriendly, and filled with fine print. If you're seriously considering a lease, do some more homework about the various terms to watch out for, and get some help with calculating what a lease really costs you. Check out bankrate.com for tips and a lease calculator. You can also read more about leases in the resources we've listed in the back of this book.

―⊸⧅⊷―

Make the car-buying process more enjoyable by asking your friends about their own tactics and nightmares. (Their stories just might save you from the same hassles.)

# Car Shopping, Part II:
## Getting Down to Business

—◦◦◦—

*My Dad took me shopping for my very first car one day. One of the dealerships we visited didn't have anything I liked, except for a cute salesboy. So when my girlfriend asked me to tag along to find her a new car, I quickly stepped up to the plate. I took her right back to that same dealership where I'd met Mr. Right (for right now). Let's just say, my friend got a great deal on a car, and I walked away with a date.*

*—Erin, 20*

## Ready to Go?

YOU'VE DONE YOUR HOMEWORK. You know exactly what you want, how much it's worth new or used, and whether you want to lease or buy. Just like you'd make a game plan before an important basketball game, it's now important to develop a car-hunting strategy. Try these places to find your true love:

◆ **Friends and family.** Sometimes a friend or family member is ready to part with her current ride, or may know someone else who is. Word of mouth and referrals are often the best way to get about anything done. Just make sure you trust the person you're buying the car from, and just to be safe, take it to a mechanic anyway before buying it. Even with the most honest seller, take the car for a look-over, because sometimes a car might have a problem that the seller isn't aware of. If the seller balks at your request or gets offended by your wish to have the car checked out, walk away from the deal. You're too smart to be messed with!

◆ **New and used car dealerships**. Grab your most business savvy of girlfriends to tag along for a day of car shopping fun. Now is the time for all the support you can get. You may also want to throw a guy in the mix (whether that be Dad, big brother, or just a good friend), because, while many dealerships are trying to create a more woman-friendly environment, many car salespeople still see a woman as an easy target. You know (and we know) that you know your stuff, but we urge you to bring a guy along even if just for show. Let him sit and listen to the salesperson ramble on about all the mirrors in the car while you check out the horsepower under the hood. Plus, the extra people tagging along will get you more opinions and ups your chances of fewer hassles. And your goal should be to get your car as quickly, inexpensively, and painlessly as possible.

◆ **Private sellers.** Like finding a great bracelet at a local art-in-the-park exhibit or flea market, you can find the perfect ride through a private seller. There are many ways these days to find just the right used car and seller—we've listed a few below. But don't forget to bring your best male friend along! He's especially important as a safety factor when dealing with a stranger.

- ☐ Try flipping through the classified ads of your local and college newspapers.
- ☐ Scan campus and apartment bulletin boards.
- ☐ Get on the Internet and shop ebay.com or other websites that are a forum for direct sales between individuals.

◆ **Web cruiser.** Maximize your techie skills by looking for your hot new wheels on the Internet. Try searching key words "women" and "car." Pairing the two key words will usually locate websites on this topic specifically designed to make used car buying more girl-friendly. Check out a few different websites by punching in key words like "auto" or "car" and "prices" or "dealerships," as well.

◆ **Superstores for used cars.** These are basically the largest used car lots you can imagine. They're set up as chains across the country, and promote themselves as no-hassle auto centers (prices are already set) with a friendly environment. Two superstore chains are Auto Nation USA and CarMax.

◆ **Auto brokers.** Hip Girls are go-getters who work for what they want. But we're also intelligent enough to take whatever feels like the simplest route. Using an auto headhunter, who does all the work for you, may be your ticket. If you belong to an auto club service, like AAA (American Automobile Association), or are a member of a discount club like Costco, you can participate in their no-hassle auto programs, in which the club has prenegotiated a range of prices with certain dealerships in your area, all at no or minimal charge to you. Or you can pay a fee (which can be more costly) to an independent auto broker. Look for one in the local telephone listings, on the Internet, in newspaper advertisements, or through family and friend referrals.

◆ **Dealer auctions.** This is an option only if you know someone in the automobile industry like a dealer or a fleet manager. (Try to befriend one. Hey, it doesn't hurt to make a new friend whenever possible!) A dealer auction is where dealers and manufacturers dispose of slow-moving inventories, fleet cars are sold, and used cars are wholesaled. Have your buddy scope out a car for you based on your preferences, but be prepared to be able to front the money for the purchase. And talk to your friend first about all the specifics involved in purchasing a car this way, including the availability and quality of warranties and whether or not your mechanic can come along to inspect the car.

◆ **Fleet sales.** Fleet sales take place when corporations (like car rental companies, sales firms, utility companies, etc.) sell their used cars to the public at what are supposed to be lower prices. Much like a dealer auction, fleet sales are a great option, but they require putting on your super-snooper to find one. Check classified ads in newspapers or log onto your favorite Internet browser and punch in the key words "fleet sales" or "fleet leasing" along with your state. If you really want to be thorough in your search, call various car rental corporate headquarters and ask who you should talk to about upcoming used car sales. (This, however, could be time-consuming and wouldn't you rather spend your time planning your Friday night out on the town? Oh, what were we thinking? We mean Friday night at the library studying. Yeah, that's it.) Again, be ready to pay up front, expect limited or no warranties, and bring your favorite mechanic with you to check out a car before making any purchases.

◆ **Public/municipal auctions.** Most of us love outlet malls for killer deals on brand-name items. A public auction for cars can be just as exciting. To find one, keep a lookout for auction announcements in your community paper's advertising/classified section. But beware: just as some items at an outlet mall are sold "as is," this too can be the case at a car auction. All deals are cash on the spot and usually don't come with any kind of warranty. Don't go alone! Our suggestion is to make friends with a car mechanic and persuade her to trek along to inspect the car before you do any bidding!

◆ **Go-get-it girl.** Empower yourself by going after the car you want, rather than waiting for it to find you. Use the same initiative and ingenuity you use for job hunting and advertise for exactly the car you're searching for. Include the features you want and the price you want to pay. No need to spend a lot of dough; in fact, you can advertise for free on various Internet websites. Check out marketplaces by punching in key words "woman" or "girl" and "motorist" or "auto" and "prices" for websites that make shopping for car prices more woman-friendly. Your local newspapers might offer good classified ad deals as well. Don't give out your name and home number, however, for safety reasons. Use a voicemail, anonymous e-mail address, or a P.O. box for replies.

## When the Love Bug Bites

Your heart's all aflutter. You can't eat. You can't sleep and you have no interest in working. Know the feeling? You've been stung by the love bug. Only instead of a lucky guy, you've finally found the car that has almost everything you ever wanted! Start this relationship off right. Don't just follow your heart, be smart and protect yourself. Once you've narrowed down what you want, check out these things:

◆ **What kind of safety features does the car offer?** Some features to ask about are driver and passenger airbags, side-impact bars, antilock or front and rear brakes, seat belts, central locking systems, alarms, delayed light extinguishing, and home security links for tracking your

car if it's stolen. Overwhelmed? Don't
bother memorizing all these. Just
ask the seller to list all the car's safety features for you and memorize all
the latest fashion trends instead.

◆ **If the car is used, ask where the car has been driven, under what
conditions, and how it's been maintained.** Was it driven in snow, in
the desert, or over rough terrain (like through a cornfield to get to a
keg)? Was it kept in a garage or parked outside? Was it parked seaside
and exposed daily to salt water? Who all has driven it, to the best of the
seller's knowledge? What kind of maintenance did it receive and does
the seller have proof of it, such as a maintenance report or history from
the original owner? Are there any recurring mechanical problems? Has
the car been in any accidents?

**Hip Tip** *Now you can investigate your prospective car's history on the
Internet, if you have its vehicle identification number (you can see
it on the driver's side dash through the front window). For just a few bucks,
carfax.com can tell you whether a car's been in an accident, and the mileage
when it was last transferred. Although not all states are included, this could
turn up some great info.*

◆ **Test-drive it.** You wouldn't just marry the first guy you ever dated.
You date different guys, and for a long time, to determine which man
is Mr. Right. Test-driving several cars is along the same line. Each test-
drive determines not only how smoothly a car runs, but how comfortable you feel in it. Take it on the highway and in town. Adjust seats and
mirrors, and check for blind spots. Are there any strange sounds? Do
you feel safe in it? Is it too large for you to maneuver? Go with your
gut. Your instincts are your most reliable gauge.

◆ **Is it reliable and cost effective to maintain?** If you opt to purchase a previously owned car, make sure to have it fully looked over by a mechanic and body shop before signing your life away.

HipTip *Before you have the car checked out, you should do some of your own snooping as well. Several websites on used cars offer a used car checklist, which can help you pinpoint specific problems you'll want a professional to check. Resources on buying a car listed at the end of this book also include helpful checklists.*

Make sure you know how much they're going to charge you to check the following:

☐ Overall condition. A mechanic can diagnose any weird noises and check whether there are mechanical parts that will need replacing now or in the near future, while a body shop can tell if the car had previous body damage. Get a written estimate for any necessary repairs. You'll want it if you decide to move to the negotiating process.

☐ Accidents and mileage. Specifically ask if they saw any signs that indicated it had been in an accident or if someone had tampered with the odometer (the gauge that tells you the car's mileage).

Even if a car is brand new, it may not be without imperfection. While it may not be necessary to have a mechanic check it over, we do recommend you test every option like the heater, air conditioner, CD player, sunroof, etc. The last thing you want is to be stuck in the desert with your girlfriends without—music (OK, no air conditioning would be a drag too)!

However, even with a new car, do investigate with a mechanic what your post-warranty maintenance costs will be, including how much various car parts cost (like a transmission, clutch, fan belt, etc.).

You can also log onto the Internet and search for key words "car," or "auto," and "parts," or the car manufacturer's website. If your warranty runs out or doesn't cover a specific part, you're left to fix it with the money you make from your part-time bookstore gig. Good luck!

Finally, whether the car is new or used, check for all incidentals. Make sure you get your owner's manual, a good spare tire, jack, and other tire-changing tools.

## Tracking Down the Cash

If you're paying for your car entirely with your hard-earned cash, you go girl! That fact may help you negotiate a better deal. However, if you're searching for a loan for your dream car, keep in mind some of the following tips:

◆ **Check several loan sources.** Financing for your car may be available through your bank or other banks, credit union, or through the dealer. And yes, check the Internet for going rates in your geographical area. Just enter "car loan" into your search engine. Make sure you check several sources before you agree to the terms of the loan (even better, before you start negotiating for your car).

◆ **New vs. used.** Loans for used cars have traditionally been for shorter terms and higher interest rates than loans for new cars, although that may be changing a bit. If you're set on a new car, however, remember that it loses value quickly in the early years of its life. If you decide to sell your car in the first few years of owning it (before the loan is paid off), the value of the car may not be enough to pay off the loan you have on it!

◆ **Do the math.** Add up how much you'll actually be spending on a car after adding the down payment and all the monthly payments. Compare that to the price of the car. Is it worth it?

# Time to Wheel and Deal

With her hard-earned savings (and pride) at stake, here's where a Hip Girl proves she's the queen of getting her way. Sure, a little compromising is important. But bending and being a pushover are two very different things. While girls may be made of sugar and spice and everything nice, Hip Girls exercise their strong-minded, business-savvy sides too. Just remember the basics of bargaining:

◆ **Show no emotion and stay cool.** Put on your best poker face before beginning the negotiating process. Focus on the task at hand. Don't let your opponent get a rise out of you or distract you.

◆ **Say as little as possible.** If you take a friend, he or she can do all the talking with the salesperson—giving you a chance to look at cars without being distracted or revealing your thoughts. And if your friend is male, his presence may help in hassle prevention and create the impression that he plays a role in the decision-making process—even if he doesn't. Your "team" spirit will also create more negotiating power. You can even rehearse your lines ahead of time. "Eh, I kind of liked the car we saw at the last dealership." "True, maybe we should check it out again," and so forth.

◆ **Know your limit.** Since you studied up on a fair price before going to look at the car you desire, you can already estimate what you'd like to pay. If it's a used car, take into consideration the cost of any necessary work the mechanic and body shop representative noted. And, as if you were lifting weights, know your limit and don't go over it.

◆ **Be willing to walk away at any moment.** Be strong. Remain in control of your negotiating power. If you can see you're going nowhere in your negotiations, smile at the seller, say thank you, and offer your number before you leave—in case he or she decides to come down in price later.

◆ **Know who you are dealing with.** Can he or she make the final decision? A dealership may try to wear you down through a tactic often known as "turnover." Turnover is where a car dealership will have you meet and work with many representatives during the negotiating process—claiming each person is responsible for a different aspect of the process. Before you know it, you feel like you have a hangover. Nicely but firmly insist that you will only negotiate the price with the person who can call the shots. Otherwise, you won't negotiate.

◆ **Keep notes.** Now is not the time to slack off on your note-taking skills. Be prepared to write everything down, including anything they promise or numbers they discuss with you. Your notes help make a seller accountable for anything offered, and pressures the seller to stick with his or her agreed-upon bargain.

Now that you have the principles down, you're ready for the actual negotiation:

◆ **Let the dealership or seller offer the price first.** Most likely, they will offer the list price or close to it.

◆ **Counteroffer.** Oh, the friendly bargaining begins. Bargaining at a garage sale is similar, only the cost and risk during car shopping are much higher. Reciprocate with a price that is close to the wholesale price you had previously determined, but less than you are actually willing to pay. Maintain a very professional tone.

◆ **Be prepared for an objection.** The seller's objection often comes in a tone that is meant to make you feel guilty or stupid. (Whatever! They don't know they're dealing with a Hip Girl.) Again, keep a straight face. Play the game.

◆ **Ask what they consider to be a reasonable offer.** The seller will likely respond with what was originally quoted to you.

◆ **Quote your research material.** Offer the seller substantial and justifiable reasons why you're standing your ground by quoting whole-sale prices straight from the *Kelley Blue Book,* or if you're at a dealership, by asking them to see a copy of the dealer invoice. Show the seller you've done your homework.

◆ **Wait for them to lower their price.** If they don't, smile, say thank you, and get your walking boots ready. If they drop their price first, now you know you're in business.

◆ **What if it's still more than you feel it's worth?** Stick to your guns and work your charm. Don't be afraid to repeat yourself several times by asking the same questions or making the same statement three or four times more. (This is good practice for future salary negotiations. Rely on your experience of negotiating for your childhood allowance. Stay tough. You can do this!)

◆ **Make small concessions.** Repeat that you'd like to stay as close to the amount you originally suggested, and then raise your offer by a little. Wait for their response.

◆ **Be persistent.** Restate your position and explain the reasons why you deserve to pay less than what they are now requesting. If it's a used car, show repair estimates or other documentation to support your reasons. (You go girl with that "I won't be messed with" attitude!)

◆ **Handling concession reversals.** If you get to a point where you think you've agreed on a mutually fair price and out of the blue, the seller tries reneging on the deal, pull out your best "I don't have to take this" attitude. Thank the seller, hand over your phone number on a piece of paper, and tell the seller to call if he or she reconsiders. Then walk out. The seller may run after you, dropping the price again significantly as you are walking out the door. If you feel the figure they've come back with is workable, then hang around until you close the deal with a number that satisfies you. (It's a strategy that sometimes works in love affairs too. You want a commitment so you make your demands. Then you get up and walk away. Hopefully he'll run after you realizing he's already got the deal of a lifetime. But in love, just like in car-buying, you have to be prepared to really walk away—and possibly for good.)

◆ **Check-out counter.** You've got the deal you want? Don't let your guard down yet. Beware of last minute additions to your bill when buying from a dealer. The dealership may try adding dealer prep, extended warranty, or undercoating costs at the last moment. Skip the extras (although some people say you may want to look at extended warranties if you have no warranty on the car you're buying). Firmly remind the seller the price already had been agreed upon and resist further changes. If they are insistent, walk away, and feel no guilt! You were ready to live up to your word, and so should they.

◆ **Look at the car one final time.** Don't take ownership until all of the work that is promised you on the car is done. Be picky—once you've taken possession, it will be harder to get earlier promises fulfilled.

## Signing on the Dotted Line

◆ **Read the Contract.** Sweet! That baby is almost yours. But don't let your enthusiasm cause you to overlook final details. When buying from a dealer, carefully read the contract before signing, making sure everything reads as it was promised to you verbally. If it doesn't, question it and ask to have it reprinted. If you're buying a used car, remember to make sure the Buyer's Guide shows any changes you and the seller agreed on. If you have any doubts, listen to your brain and intuition and walk out.

◈ **Feeling too overwhelmed to buy just yet?** Is your studying best done in the library, not in the student center or lunchroom where there are lots of distractions? If you want the car and the deal, but want to study the paperwork where there's less noise and commotion (and more time to get a trusted friend's opinion), see if the dealership will let you leave a small deposit in exchange for taking the paperwork home to read. Put the agreement for the deposit in writing, clearly stating you get the deposit back if the terms of the deal are not what was negotiated. (Note that most dealerships aren't going to give back a deposit without a fight. So expect to lose your deposit if the terms appear the same as what you negotiated, but you back out.) And despite the myth, most dealerships do not offer a three day "cooling off" option. Once you make the final decision to buy, it's all yours.

◈ **Private seller contract.** Whether you're buying from a neighbor or a stranger in a private transaction, present the seller with your own contract to sign. Give a basic description of the car (including make, model, year, and VIN—Vehicle Identification Number), stating that this is the vehicle which is being sold to you. The contract should also simply spell out the agreed-upon price, subject to the review of an independent mechanic. Incorporate a grace period for such an inspection (usually a few days) and book an appointment with your mechanic that works within that time frame. You'll probably need to pay some "earnest" money, or down payment, before the seller lets you take the car. Specify that you can get the money back if the car doesn't check out. Leave space for additional language where you can address any other concerns you have with the seller's claims (like they'll pay to have the car detailed or to fix an existing mechanical problem within a specified time). Get it signed by the seller, then sign it yourself. Compare your homemade contract with one you've scoped out on the

Internet before exchanging your hard-earned cash. Womanmotorist. com has one already written up, but check for others on sites dealing with used car sales. Or even easier yet, just model yours after samples you find (making sure to tweak any language you need to first). Awesome!

◆ **Get your insurance.** You'll need your policy (at least a temporary one) before you drive off in your car. Call your agent, and she will be able to fax proof of insurance to you or the dealer.

◆ **Making payment.** This is more exhilarating (and exhausting) than finding a swimsuit that fits! Don't pay with cash. Paying with a money order, cashier's check, bank check, or even traveler's check is the safest. If you're buying from a private person who insists on cash, ask for him or her to follow you to your bank (but not an ATM) and exchange the money there or in another public place. Always get a signed receipt.

◆ **Get proof of ownership.** Make sure to get the title to the car signed by the seller, then take it with you. This step is of the utmost importance—the title gives you the right to call the car yours. If you're getting a loan for the car, most states require that the loan provider retain the title until you've paid off your loan. However, there are several states that give you the title to hold onto even with a loan. This is known as a "title holding" state. Check with your local DMV office (or ask a dealership) to find out what the law is in your 'hood.

Hip Tip    *If the seller still owes money on the car, you may have to meet at his bank to get the title released to you. If you don't live in a title holding state and you bought your precious car from an auto dealer, then the dealership will most likely handle getting the title to your loan institution for you. Otherwise, it's up to you to send it to them yourself.*

◆ **Register the car.** Congratulations. You did it. Take pride in your feat! Now go straight to your local DMV and register that baby as yours. Some dealerships will do it all for you. Or, if you belong to an automobile club (like AAA), you may be able to take care of your vehicle registration at one of their local offices—and very possibly enjoy the convenience of a shorter line. There will be costs to register the vehicle in your name, and the costs vary state by state. Make sure you follow your state's requirements for keeping your car legal to drive, including putting your license plates on your car, taking your car in for smog checks, and keeping your tags current.

Huh? What the heck are tags? They're stickers issued annually by the DMV reflecting the last month and year through which your car is legally registered. If you buy a car from a dealership, the seller will handle sending for plates and tags from the state for you. If your car is from a private sale, registering your car for the first time is up to you (whereas the license plates usually just transfer with the vehicle). Grab your driver's license, title, and the car and head down to your local DMV (or AAA, if you're a member). Oh, and don't forget your checkbook or cash. Remember, registering your car can cost a good chunk of change (but not nearly as much as the  fine for not registering). Once you have your tags in hand, follow the directions and apply directly to your license plate.

And don't forget to renew your tags annually. Like yearly pap exams, it's annoying but important. Some states will even allow you to renew your auto registration (and driver's license) on-line. Yippee! No waiting in long lines! Log onto your state's DMV website to find out if you're one of the lucky residents. If not, your AAA membership generally provides the tag renewal luxury as well. (Ahh. If only our pap exams were this painless.) Otherwise, enjoy your afternoon at the DMV.

Shopping is the one thing we Hip Girls do almost innately, and car shopping isn't much different. Learning what accentuates your figure took years of research (with a few tragedies). Use your Hip Girl's car-shopping know-how to keep from making the same fashion faux pas when choosing your new ride. And don't forget to give back to your sisterhood: Put the car salesman in his place with your phat negotiating style.

# Auto Insurance:

## Protecting Yourself and Your Car

---

*"I was sixteen and had just gotten my driver's license. I stopped to fill my car up with gas on my way to see my boyfriend. I was in such a hurry that after I paid, I pulled away quickly, forgetting to remove the gas nozzle from my car. It didn't dent my car, but it practically ripped the nozzle off the station's tank. Thank goodness my dad made me get insurance which covered the gas station's expenses to fix the damage, or my momentary "ding-y-ness" could have put me hundreds of dollars in debt."*

—Kristy, 28

## Even the Safest Drivers Need Insurance

AUTO INSURANCE PROTECTS ONE OF THE MOST VALUABLE TOOLS for your independence—your car. After all, walking to the neighborhood coffee shop in your heels can be torturous! Depending on the type of insurance plan and the circumstances, it also covers medical expenses for you and other accident victims and provides protection from other liability. Most states require you to carry a certain amount of liability insurance that covers bodily injury to others and damage to other people's property.

*Hip Tip We're giving you a general overview of auto insurance in this chapter, but the terms and details of insurance coverage vary from state to state and from company to company. Make sure you understand what your coverage is!*

But what if you're newly on your own, and you've accidentally let your car insurance lapse—or never got it in the first place? Better start practicing the skill you were practically born with—talking on the phone. Not having continuous coverage can end up costing you thousands of dollars. (That means: There goes that spring break trip to Florida you were saving up for!)

Wondering where to begin looking? Ask your friends who covers them, open up the yellow pages to auto insurance or auto insurance agencies, or log on to the Internet. Insurance companies and agents want your business and most will give you a free quote over the phone. We suggest that you try working with an agent first. (Why waste your precious time hunting for auto insurance when you could be shopping for new shoes!) Keep in mind that some agents represent one insurance company and some represent several companies. Make sure you get quotes from several companies.

*Hip Tip Check out the Insurance Information Institute website at iii.org for helpful information about various types of insurance and what is required in your state.*

# Getting Ready to Ask for a Quote

Ever answered a roommate-wanted ad? Calling up unknown agents for auto insurance is similar. Only instead of swapping bathroom habits with a perfect stranger, you're exchanging car insurance needs and options. Before "cold" calling insurance representatives and asking for an auto quote, do some homework.

◆ **Collect your personal information.** Prepare yourself with information about your driving history, your car, and your current auto insurance, and specifically, answers to these questions:

□   Do you want liability coverage only (which would only cover other people and their property) or full coverage (covering you, your car, and others and their cars)? What other specifications are you interested in? Do you want insurance for someone *without* insurance hitting you? Read "Terminology and Policies" below for a description of some of your options.

□   What kind of safety measures does your car have—an alarm system, driver and passenger airbags, or automatic seat belts?

□   What's your car's Vehicle Identification Number (VIN) number? (See the "Terminology and Policies" section later in this chapter.)

□   How far do you drive in a year?

□   Do you own or lease your car? Does someone else (say your parents or the bank that holds your car loan) own the car? Regardless of your situation, you're going to need to know the name and address of the lending or leasing company that holds the title to your car, and its insurance requirements. If you're leasing a car or have a car loan, you'll likely be required to take out full coverage.

*If you're leasing, you may also need "gap" coverage, which covers*
**HipTip** *the difference between what you've paid under a lease, and the cost*

*of replacing the leased car if stolen or totaled (minus what other insurance coverage there is).*

☐ What's your driving record? Have you been in any accidents, whether they were your fault or not? How many speeding or driving-through-a-red-light tickets have you not been able to talk your way out of? Lay it all out on the table for the representative because the truth will come out in your driving record. Hiding anything will cause them to give you the wrong quote, as well as not trust you. And just because a police report was not made, don't assume the accident won't be discovered. Insurance companies by law have to report accidents to the state's department of motor vehicles (DMV). They also share information with other companies.

☐ When is your current policy up for renewal?

☐ What is your current coverage and deductible? (See "Terminology and Policies" later in this chapter for definitions.)

☐ Do you want to raise or lower the amount of your coverage, or keep it the same?

◆ **Get the skinny on your roommates.** Insurance companies will want to know if you think anyone else will be driving your car. If you plan to share, ask your roommates or friends for their birth dates and who covers them for their auto insurance. (Better hope they have good driving records, as their records affect your rate. If not, you may want to think twice about sharing with them.) Some insurance companies just might cover your roommate borrowing your car (usually to do incognito drive-bys of her ex's house). And if you don't divulge all the drivers of your car, the insurance company may deny coverage when she crashes into the tree in her ex's front yard.

# What Questions Should You Ask to Get the Best Quote and the Right Coverage?

◆ **No-fault insurance.** Remember when you were a child and you and your sisters blamed each other for breaking the lamp? If you get into an accident, the "other guy" might have a different opinion than yours of who to blame. In a "no-fault" state, blame may not matter. That's why you better ask if no-fault insurance (see the "Terminology and Policies" section later in this chapter) is what you need.

◆ **Discount shopping.** You work every angle to get the best deal on your clothes. Beef up on your bargaining style by knowing what kinds of premium discounts to ask about:

  □ Accident-free—You've not been found responsible for causing any accidents.

  □ Antitheft devices—Your car has built-in security instruments such as alarms, digital door locks, or electronic tracking systems.

  □ Good student—Your report card reflects your responsible behavior in the classroom. So if you're enrolled as a full-time student and carry a grade point average of typically 3.0 or higher, auto insurance companies may offer you a discount on the assumption that your responsible behavior will be reflected on the road also. Check for each insurance company's specific requirements—they vary.

  □ Good driver—A Hip Girl knows when and where it's appropriate to go wild. On the road isn't the time or the place. If your driving record reflects no or minimal moving violations (like speeding or running a red light) or accidents, you may be eligible for a good driver discount.

❑   Driver training—You passed a DMV-authorized driver work-shop and test. Now auto insurance companies may be willing to offer you a discount for your efforts to become a safer driver.

❑   Multiple auto or multiple policy coverage—If you're covered under your parents' insurance or have more than one vehicle of your own insured with one particular company, then you just may be eligible for this discount. You may also get a discount if you carry renter's or homeowner's insurance with the same company that's offering the auto insurance.

◆ **Coverage.** What are all the available coverages and specifically what does each cover? For instance, what if your windshield breaks? Do you have to pay a deductible (which is usually about $100 or higher, if you choose) or does your policy include windshield coverage with no deductible? Keep in mind that the types of coverage available and requirements for eligibility vary from company to company and from state to state.

◆ **What is required by your state?** Most states require that you carry bodily injury liability and property damage liability insurance. An agent should be able to confirm this, but log onto iii.org to make sure. It can tell you how much coverage you're required to have. Required liability coverage is typically stated in ratio form, such as 30/60/10. In translation, that means up to $30,000 of coverage for one person injured, up to $60,000 of coverage for all persons injured, and up to $10,000 of coverage for property damage.

◆ **Payment plans.** Premiums can cost even more than your makeup collection. Many companies offer a monthly billing plan and attach a minimal fee for using it. If this is the method that's affordable to you, inquire about paying your bill electronically so that the money is automatically deducted from your bank account (see the *On-Line (Not In-*

*Line) Banking* chapter for more information). Some insurance companies require you to pay half your premium up front and the rest midway through your policy. And of course, you can always pay the whopping bill all at once.

◆ **Car swapping**. It's your roomie's little brother's turn to have the family wagon. Is *your* gem now her only way around town? Better ask if she and anyone else in your house would be covered to borrow your car.

◆ **Wedding bells.** Found Prince Charming? It doesn't hurt to see if your rates go down when you get hitched.

◆ **Parental guidance.** As long as you are living under your parents' roof (ever heard that line once or twice in your life?) you can get your auto insurance coverage under your parents' policy—as long as they agree to it, that is. And let's hope they do, because auto insurance is usually cheaper for you in that case. This is one of those little dependent measures you may want to learn to live with. What if you're a college student away from home? Don't worry. As long as you're a college student, typically until you are 25 years old, you may be considered a resident of your parents' home and qualify for this perk. But, to have your car on your parents' policy, the car may have to be at least co-registered with your parents. If it's only in your name, you may have to get your own policy.

◆ **International warrior.** Taking a quick trip to Toronto or South of the Border? Better ask if your auto insurance covers your road trips into international territories.

◆ **Rental car coverage.** Does your policy pay for rental of a car in case your car is in the shop after an accident? If so, how much do they reimburse you for and for how long?

◆ **Towing.** Ask if towing is covered in your policy, or if you can pay a little extra to include it. Weigh the extra cost against becoming a member of a towing service. For a yearly fee, AAA offers roadside assistance nationwide 24/7, along with other member benefits. Their national number is 800-222-4357, or look up their local office number in the yellow pages or on the Internet at AAA.com. Compare their prices and services with your insurance company's roadside coverage to see which is more cost effective.

## Ways to Spend More Money on Clothing and Less on Car Insurance

◆ **Where you keep and drive your car** plays a big part in how much you pay. Do you have a garage, underground parking, or a carport to help protect from theft, vandalism, or weather-related damage? Plus, living in or near a city rather than the suburbs will likely cost you the extra dollars you were hoping to save for your next vacation.

◆ **Keep a good driving record.** Is it really worth jeopardizing your perfect driving record just to catch up with that cute guy in the next lane? You decide. Just one speeding ticket can raise your auto insurance rates dramatically. And if you incur too many speeding violations in a short time, many companies will even drop you as a client. If you're busted for a ticket, see if you can get it removed from your record by going to traffic school. Some states offer that as an option—although the number of times or frequency that you can use it may be limited.

◆ **Couldn't wait to turn twenty-one?** It's good for more reasons than one. Depending on which state you're insured in, your auto rates can get lower as you get older—either measured by your birth date or the year your driver's license was first issued. Check with your insurance company to learn their policy.

◆ **Do you go home every weekend?** Here's a reason to become just a little more independent: The number of miles you put on your car is a determining factor in the cost of your insurance coverage.

◆ **Hoping to get a BMW** convertible for a graduation present? Better hope your parents are also willing to pay for your auto insurance. A car that is expensive also costs more to insure, so cheaper may be better for several reasons.

◆ **Opt for a higher deductible** (see definition in "Terminology and Policies" below). It will lower your insurance costs, sometimes by a surprising amount.

◆ **Comparison shop**—when getting your first policy and every year or so thereafter. And we can't emphasize enough: Don't forget to periodically check on what discounts you might be eligible for, as insurance companies may add or change discount opportunities on their policies.

## Terminology and Policies

◆ **Bodily injury liability coverage.** This coverage pays for damages to others in an accident which is found to be your fault, such as medical bills, lost wages, and pain and suffering. Expenses are paid up to the amount of coverage you have selected. Most states require that you carry a minimum amount of bodily injury liability insurance. *Note: If you're relying on your parents as a main source of support, ask your agent if a victim's insurance company could try to collect the victim's costs that exceed your coverage from your parents. If so, make sure your policy limits are the highest you can afford.*

◆ **Collision.** This coverage reimburses you for the cost of auto repairs your car needs as a result of an automobile accident, up to the amount of coverage you previously selected or for replacing your car at its current value if it's totaled (as determined by your auto insurance company). If your car is totaled, this coverage will pay to replace your car at its current value. In other words, if you're sporting around in the 1985 family station wagon, you'll be reimbursed the amount of its worth today (which could be significantly less than when it was bought). You must pay a deductible. Collision insurance is optional in all states.

◆ **Comprehensive (other than collision) coverage.** This coverage is for theft or the cost to repair your car when damaged in other ways than in an accident, including fire, glass breakage, vandalism, wind, hail, and hitting an animal, such as a deer. Comprehensive insurance is optional in all states.

◆ **Deductible.** This is the amount of money you pay out of your pocket before your insurance coverage kicks in. Typically a deductible for collision coverage ranges from $250-1,000, and for comprehensive insurance, about $100-300. The higher your deductible, the lower the cost of your insurance.

◆ **Full coverage insurance.** Generally, this type of auto insurance covers, up to the amount of your coverage, the cost of medical and legal bills as well as auto and other property damaged in an accident, which are incurred by other parties who were not at fault, and property damage incurred by you. Full coverage includes liability, comprehensive, and collision coverage. (See additional definitions in this section.)

◆ **Medical insurance.** This is coverage for medical costs for you and other occupants of your car, whether or not an accident is your fault.

◆ **Liability insurance.** This type of auto insurance coverage is required by law in most states. Liability insurance includes bodily injury and property damage coverage for everyone but you and your car. If an accident is your fault, it covers the medical costs, pain and suffering, lost wages, and property damage costs of the other people involved in an accident—up to the amount of coverage you selected—and associated legal costs.

◆ **Odometer.** It's the mileage keeper on your car and is located on the dashboard, usually near the speedometer (you know, the thing that measures how fast you're going).

◆ **Property damage liability.** Property damage liability coverage pays for the repair or replacement of the other person's car and/or other property affected by an accident that is your fault (such as when you accidentally back into your ex-boyfriend's motorcycle). It'll also pay for the rental of a temporary vehicle until the, uh-hum, motorcycle is fixed. Check your state law's requirements and choose an amount that meets your financial ability.

◆ **Quote.** The price the auto insurance company says they will charge to insure you for the coverage. Obtaining a quote is generally free.

◆ **Rental reimbursement coverage.** This coverage covers the costs of renting other transportation while your car is being fixed. (Here's your opportunity to try out that new (well, almost new) SUV for a while—as long as it's within your rental car coverage guidelines.)

◆ **Towing and labor.** Usually you can get towing and labor costs covered only if you choose to pay for collision coverage. Towing and labor coverage reimburses you for the cost of hauling your car to a mechanic if it can't be driven—but not the cost of fixing it.

◆ **Underinsured motorist coverage.** This coverage under your policy pays for you and your passengers' medical, loss of income, and pain and suffering costs in an accident caused by someone else whose auto insurance policy doesn't completely cover your expenses. Typically, you must request separate coverage to protect your property against an underinsured motorist. This coverage is called underinsured/uninsured motorist property damage.

◆ **Uninsured motorist coverage.** This coverage protects you and your passengers who become injured in an accident caused by someone without auto insurance at all. It covers medical, loss of income, and pain and suffering costs at no more than the liability amounts you previously selected as your coverage. Check your state law's requirements and choose an amount that is within your financial ability. This coverage does not extend to property damage. However, you can request it as a separate coverage just like in the underinsured motorist coverage option.

◆ **Vehicle identification number (VIN).** A VIN is like a social security card for your car. It's the combination of letters and numbers usually imprinted on the inside of your car on the driver's side of your dashboard, or you can find it on your registration or last auto insurance form. The VIN tells your insurance agent the year, make, and model specifications of your car and is increasingly becoming a means of tracing its history.

—⊸⊸⊸—

Ugh! Is your head spinning from all the terms and coverage info? Just refer to it when taking on the insurance industry to get exactly what you want. Then loan your copy of *The Hip Girl's Handbook for Home, Car, & Money Stuff* to your girlfriends and help them learn the ropes.

# The Great Mechanic Quest:

## Finding a Repair Shop You Trust

*"I'd just gotten into a car accident and was flustered. I didn't have a particular mechanic, so I had my car towed to the mechanic my auto insurance company recommended. In my state of frustration, I signed a waiver without reading it over well. It apparently said I agreed to let the mechanic fix it. But the car had been totaled and fixing it would have cost me more than buying a brand new one. Ugh! I refused to let the mechanic bully me with his coercing tactics. So after much persistence, I demanded he release my totaled car to me without an exchange of any money. What a nightmare!"*

—Eva, 22

## Starting the Search

L ET'S FACE IT, FINDING A GOOD AUTO MECHANIC can be just as hard as locating your Prince Charming in a bar. Just as you have a checklist of standards for your potential prince, start conjuring up an additional list for the other potentially very important man in your life—

your mechanic! And if you're lucky enough to find a female mechanic, treat her like a sister. Instead of borrowing her clothes, borrow her car knowledge.

We should point out that you probably will not be able to find one mechanic to do all the work you may need over the life of your car. A good "solo" mechanic is hard to find. Why? Good mechanics soon have more customers than they can handle, so they hire other mechanics that they can train to their high standards. Soon there is a shop of good mechanics. In this chapter "auto mechanic" realistically means the owner or manager of an auto repair and service shop.

One thing to ask yourself before you start your mechanic search: Is my car under warranty? If you have a new car or a used one that has some type of warranty, make sure you will not void your warranty by going to a repair shop that is not approved by the manufacturer or dealer. Read the warranty and ask the dealer that you bought the car from if there are limitations and if there is a list of approved repair shops. That being said, knowing what questions to ask and what criteria to look for will help guide you on this puzzling quest for a repair shop you can trust. Here are some tips:

◆ **Start early.** It's a good idea to shop around for a trustworthy auto mechanic before trouble strikes. After all, you don't want to have to make a snap decision that will hurt your car (and likely your social life).

◆ **Start small.** Don't wait for a major problem to test out your mechanic. Start with oil changes and other simple jobs. That way you can see how you like their work without putting your car and your money at risk.

◆ **Ask around.** Your hairdresser quit and left you stylist-less on the day of a big date. You wouldn't dream of walking into just any salon to get your hair done. Can you say Disaster? Instead, you'd get recommendations from your friend or sister. The same should go for the person who will be maintaining your car. Talk with your friends, family, professors, co-workers, or any other person you trust to see where they have had satisfactory work done. Try to get an opinion from someone who has lived in the area for a while. If any of these people have the same make car as yours, they may go to a repair shop that specializes in your type of car. Who knows? They may have an old family friend who gives first-visit discounts to referrals. No leads? Call your local AAA to see if they have any recommendations.

◆ **Is the mechanic trained?** Take a look around the shop for evidence that indicates the mechanic or mechanics are competent in the automotive field. Certificates may be on the wall or they may show up as a logo on the window. Your auto shop mechanic may be certified by the manufacturer of your car, and if they are employed by the dealer of a particular make of car, probably has had some training in that make of car.

In other shops, mechanics may be "ASE certified." What does that mean? An ASE certification means the mechanic has a certain level of experience and has passed a difficult exam (which is purely voluntary—they don't have to do this) on one of eight car systems (such as the electrical or brake system). Also, ASE certification has to be renewed every five years, so you'll know that at least some of their training is up to date. But just as certification in CPR doesn't make someone skilled at giving mouth-to-mouth, simply having passed the ASE requirements doesn't make the mechanic an expert, nor trustworthy for that matter. Only one-third to one-half of all mechanics are ASE certified.

HipTip   *If someone has passed ASE exams for all eight systems of a car, they can call themselves ASE "master technicians."*

◆ **Can you get an estimate without a hassle?** Will the shop give you a written estimate before charging you anything? You should be able to see a list of repairs and their costs—and approve it—before you are charged a penny.

◆ **Check their honesty.** The shop's philosophy should be: If it ain't broke, don't fix it. To avoid money-hungry villains, get a diagnosis and estimate for any necessary work from at least two places, or take your car to an independent diagnostic shop for annual checkups. Members of automobile clubs like AAA are able to take their cars to auto diagnostic clinics in some areas. Getting two estimates, or taking your car to an auto clinic will help prepare you for any upcoming repairs your car might need, as well as tell you what repairs your car doesn't need.

◆ **Do they stand behind their work?** What kind of guarantee does the shop give for their work? If they don't believe in their work, neither should you.

◆ **Never trust a bargain price.** We all know that outlet shopping doesn't always mean we're selecting from perfect pieces of clothing. Sometimes things are cheap for a reason. Be cautious of a mechanic that quotes you a really low price. It may mean that the parts and labor used may be far from reliable.

◆ **What's their record?** Check up with the Better Business Bureau or AAA Approved Auto Repair Status for a repair shop's customer service record.

◆ **How clean is the workspace?** Would you date a slob, or someone who didn't groom himself well? Chances are if they don't take good care of themselves, they aren't going to treat you to manicures or pedicures either. A mechanic plays a very important role in caring for your precious car, so take into account his or her standards of cleanliness. Even though he or she is dabbling in grease and oil, how well a mechanic cleans up or keeps the garage organized says a lot about how he or she will treat your car.

◆ **It's smart to ask.** Ask the mechanic what brand of auto is his or her specialization. If your brand of auto isn't mentioned, watch out. Cars are much more complicated than they were in the past. It's best to work with someone who is familiar with the nuances of your car.

◆ **How are you treated?** Make sure you and your mechanic can communicate. Fixing cars is not your profession. Expect your mechanic to be courteous, and talk to you in plain terms, so that you are comfortable. If the shop personnel are not respectful and helpful, go elsewhere.

So get going and find your mechanic! Owning a car can be pricey, but not being prepared for car problems can make it even pricier. And don't ignore problems. The thought of forking over a lot of money to fix your car may not sound as appealing as a trip to the day spa, but not paying attention to problems will only make it worse. With proper maintenance and a good mechanic, your future with your car can be a smooth ride.

Yippee! When you snag yourself a reliable mechanic, consider yourself lucky (they're not so easy to find). Show your appreciation for his or her attentiveness to you and your car's needs by occasionally swingin' by a coffee or cookie shop and picking up a little somethin' for your mechanic. Drop the goodies by when you drop off your car. Your little act of kindness will put a smile on your mechanic's face (a little appreciation can go a long way in getting you great service at a good price).

# Road Trippin':
## Cruisin' Happily into the Sunset

—◦∽◦—

*"One spring break my girlfriends and I loaded ourselves into the car and took off. Destination: Florida! We were cruising along when a carload of guys pulled up beside us. They were totally obnoxious, making faces at us, even yelling obscene comments. We finally escaped them by pulling over to a rest area. Later, back on the road, we noticed an overheated car at the side of the highway. Yup, it was the carload of guys. We slowed down like we were going to help them and they looked up hopefully. I stuck my head out the window and yelled, 'Next time, change your oil every three months!' and we peeled away, leaving them in the dust.*

—Julia, 30

### Stockin' Up Before Hittin' the Road

YOU'VE GOT YOUR CAR, YOU'RE INSURED and you've found the mechanic of your dreams. What else do you need to do before you hit the open road? Make sure you're equipped! Just like you need a tool kit for your home, you need an emergency kit for your car. A Hip Girl can enjoy her independence much more when she knows she's prepared for emergencies.

## What Do You Need First?

First, check your car kit. We know a Hip Girl has got her car kit stashed in her trunk at all times. (Uh-oh, you don't? Busted! Now is the perfect time to start.) Read on for more detail about your car's essential needs before hittin' the open road:

◆ **Owner's manual.** The owner's manual is a font of useful repair, safety, and emergency information about your specific car, and will also tell you what kind of gas and oil your car requires, the optimal tire pressure, and other important information, such as a recommended service schedule. If you haven't laid eyes on it yet, look in your glove compartment. If you don't have one, order another one from the manufacturer.

◆ **Car jack and lug nut remover (and any other tools you need to change your tire).** Look at your owner's manual if you're not sure what tools you'll need to change your particular car's tire. For instance, if your car has wheel locks on the tires (to prevent them from being stolen), make sure you have the key with you. It may be located with the tire-changing tools.

◆ **Spare tire.** Make sure it is still where it should be and has an adequate amount of air in it, should you need it. (Air may have seeped out simply by sitting in your car for so long.) If you have a "limited use" tire, make sure it hasn't been used already. (A limited use tire is much smaller than a regular tire, and will only go so far in distance.)

# Your Own Emergency Car Kit

Now think about what you might need if you were stranded on the side of the road (and we mean the necessities, not just the latest copy of *Vogue* magazine) and throw it all into an old laundry or duffel bag inside your trunk. We suggest the following things for your emergency kit (you may want to include other items as well):

◆ **Medical materials**—bandaids, icepack, bandages, scissors, aspirin (need we say why?), hydrogen peroxide, prescription medicine, and your favorite tummy relievers (to get you through all that rest area, fast-food-eating turmoil).

◆ **Flashlight**—fully loaded with one set of brand-new batteries and a spare set too.

◆ **Jumper cables and tools**—especially screwdrivers, pliers, duct tape, and a pocketknife.

◆ **Weather-specific items**—like a window scraper, shovel, chains and rock salt for snow, extra blankets for the cold, and sunscreen for the convertible ride, etc.

◆ **Can and bottle openers**—no way to get to the food and beverages could be a major nightmare!

◆ **Travel sewing kit**—with all the anticipated eating and drinking, plan on zippers bursting and buttons popping.

◆ **Extra "5 Fluids"**—because you may need a refill in climates that are more demanding on your car. (See the *Give Me Five for Fluids* chapter.)

◆ **Garbage bags**—not just for tossing your empty pop cans and Doritos bags into, garbage bags can double as rain and snow attire while changing a flat tire roadside.

◆ **Old rug, towel, or curtain**—to sit on if you're changing a tire.

◆ **Work gloves that fit well**—to protect your hands from the heat and grime. No sense in ruining that new manicure!

◆ **Flares and matches or reflectors**—to help alert approaching motorists if you're by the side of the road. We'd recommend using reflectors in an accident at night—there may be gasoline or other flammable material on the road, and lighting a flare may cause a fire.

◆ **Funnel and a couple of rags**—if you need to add some fluids.

◆ **Two blocks of wood or rocks**—large enough to wedge under a wheel so the car won't roll when you're working on it. (You can also buy "wheel chocks" at an automotive store.)

◆ **Food that will keep**—energy bars, dried fruit, or nuts—and a big jug of water.

◆ **A blanket**—even if you're planning to drive in the desert, it can get very cold at night.

◆ **Paper and pencil**—just in case you need to take some notes after an accident (not to mention they come in handy for taking all those magazine quizzes).

*HipTip* *A new handy tool that should be kept inside the car and not in the trunk is a window-breaking tool. If you're traveling over or near water at all, have one of these handy in the event that your car ends up submerged. You may need it to escape from the car, as your windows may jam.*

## Need a Break?

Pack your bags, put the top down in your convertible, and gather all your Bare Naked Ladies tunes. A weekend road trip is overdue! But before you and your best friend hit the highway and venture across state lines for sightseeing, or across international borders for authentic salsa dance lessons, read on. Sound advice for making your excursion memorable, but safe, lies ahead.

# Planning

◆ **First, if your car is due or almost due for a tune-up, have it done.** (You can check your owner's manual for recommendations on when your car needs this servicing.) Make an appointment with your friendly mechanic. (By now, the two of you should have become fast friends, and taking care of you is like making sure his or her own daughter is safe.) If you still haven't found just the right one, it's time to start the hunt.

Hip Tip *Don't make your car appointment for the day before your trip— you'll want to drive around a bit to make sure that everything in your car is back in proper working order before you hit the road.*

◆ Tune-up or not, ask your mechanic to specifically do the following:

☐ **Fluids and coolant system parts**—Ask your trusty mechanic to change your oil, unless you've just had it done. It doesn't hurt to change it before it's due, and it will give you peace of mind knowing you have many miles to drive before you have to change it again. It's also time to check the other four fluids covered in the *Give Me Five for Fluids* chapter. (No pop quizzes here! We'll cover them for you.) Those are power-steering, brake, transmission, and radiator (coolant) fluids. And speaking of coolant, ask your mechanic to also check the rest of your coolant system; especially the hoses, and belts. When parts have names like "belts," how could you forget? (Think of it as the perfect accessory to your most important asset—your independence.)

☐ **Windshield wiper blades and fluid**—Have him or her check your windshield wiper blades and washer fluid. (Having streaks and a windshield full of bugs is kind of like wearing beer goggles. It's hard to decipher if the guys in the car that just passed you are worth a smile!)

□ **Tires**—Check the pressure and the wear on your tires. Balance and rotate tires if necessary. Don't forget to have your mechanic check your spare. (You never know what might happen on the open road.)

□ **Battery**—Plain and simple: You need energy. Make sure your car has its energy too by asking your mechanic to examine your battery and the battery fluid level.

□ **Lights**—Test all of your car lights: Turn signals, headlights (high and low beams), interior (for last-minute hair checks, of course), and taillights.

◆ **Map out your route** and keep that map with you. In case you get lost, or just need reassurance, having the route mapped out will mean one less stress for your road trip in your overstuffed car. If you belong to a road service club, they might be able to route your map for you. Hey, the less work for you the better!

**Hip Tip** *You can go to a website for maps as well. Some include mapquest.com, maps.yahoo.com, and randmcnally.com—just enter where you're leaving from and your destination, and you can get driving directions too.*

◆ **Leave at a good time.** If possible, avoid leaving during rush hour. Tell your notoriously tardy girlfriends you're leaving a half-hour earlier than your actual estimated departure time. You know how stressful it is for them to get ready just for a night of fun—imagine their dilemma when packing for a whole weekend!

◆ **If you're leaving at night, take a nap beforehand,** so you won't fall asleep at the wheel.

◆ **If you drive a stick shift** (also known as a standard or manual transmission), make sure that there's always at least one other road tripper that can too. The last thing you'll want is to get stuck doing all the driving. You'll want a break to join in the car dancing too!

◆ **Fill up the gas tank!** It'd be a major pain to run out of juice before all the madness even begins, not to mention losing two hours of good driving time as you wait for a service truck.

## Packing

◆ **Boys, sun, and fun—here you come!** A road trip is in your future and it's time to party! Since you already have your car emergency kit ready, the first step in smart packing for your girls-only road trip is compiling all your favorite CDs for hours' worth of gettin' your groove on.

◆ **Pack a cooler of ice and fill it with plenty of bottled water.** (While you're at it, throw in some of your other favorite non-alcoholic liquids too. Yes, we did just say "non-alcoholic." If your plans include exotic Piña Colada taste-testing, wait until you get to your destination before indulging. Drinking while driving, or even having an open alcoholic container as a passenger, isn't just illegal, it's plain stupid!)

**Hip Tip** *For maximum use of cooler space, and minimum waste of water, freeze some water bottles beforehand to use as the cooler ice. Then drink the water as it melts.*

◆ **Don't forget all the junk food.** Hey, it's vacation! Bring along all the chips, candy and doughnuts your little heart desires.

◆ **Bring a sleeping bag and pillow**—because when you get to the hotel, sleeping six to a bed after a crammed car ride suddenly may not sound so appealing!

◆ **Destination sun and swimming?** Better pack plenty of suntan lotion, sunglasses, a cute hat for shade, and of course, several bikinis for looking oh so hot while you get a great tan. You might also want to include a suit with more support for waterskiing with hot lifeguards.

◆ **Destination snow skiing?** Grab extra clothing, blankets, gloves, a scarf, and a space heater. (That quaint cabin in the brochure could turn out to be more like an igloo in the middle of a forest.)

◆ **A valid driver's license, current auto registration, and current proof of insurance.** Check to make sure you have all of these with you. Also, check to see if you have current tags or license plates on your car.

*HipTip*  *If someone else will be driving too, you might want to call your insurance agent to check if your insurance covers other drivers. Make sure those drivers bring their drivers' licenses—they may need their IDs for more than one reason!*

◆ **Take your cell phone, charger and auto service membership card.** Possibly the most important items, in case you have any problems with your vehicle!

*HipTip*  *Your cell phone may not work in more remote areas of the United States, or outside of the U.S. Call your cell phone company to learn your coverage. As a backup, keep a phone card or a pile of quarters or other local currency in your car so you can use payphones—you remember what those are, don't you?*

◆ **Last, grab your house key.** You certainly don't want to come home exhausted and ready to rest only to have to break into your home instead!

# What to Look Out for When Living Large on the Open Road

◆ **Exercise caution.** You and your soul sisters are jammin' to the tunes when a carload of hotties passes you by. Everyone's down for a little car flirting, so you catch up with them (without speeding, of course) and start the game playing. Try exchanging cell numbers via drive-by messages to one another first, before determining if you feel comfortable enough to meet up later. But just as you wouldn't wander off with a stranger at home, don't pull off the road to meet them unless it's at a highly popu-lated, well-lit, public place like a gas station or restaurant. And need we say it? Don't split up with your friends or leave with any strangers!

◆ **If your car breaks down** and you're unable to fix the problem your-self, stay in your car, turn your hazard lights on, and keep your doors locked while you wait for the highway patrol to come. If a stranger pulls over and offers to help, stay in your locked car, roll your window down slightly and if you don't have a cell phone, ask him or her to call for help. Do not get in a stranger's vehicle! If the stranger wants to try to fix your problem, just say thanks and politely but firmly ask him or her to just phone for help.

◆ **Lock your car doors** while you and your girlfriends cruise along. (If for no other reason, you don't want your car door flying open because, exhausted from your Hip Girl weekend, you fell asleep and leaned against it.)

◆ **Play it safe at the gas pump.** Filling up the tank on a road trip can be a peak flirting scene, believe it or not. But be sure to lock your doors whether you're in or out of the car. And watch your car mates' backs by always knowing where they are.

◆ **Take the same precautions at rest stops.** Don't stop unless they are well-lit (if at night) and there are lots of people around.

◆ **Ready? Now sing and car dance your little heart out!** The girls are on their way to weekend freedom!

━∿∿━

Woo-hoo! Road-smart Hip Girls rule! Just be sure to empower your girlfriends on road trippin' etiquette, too (after all, their actions can directly affect you)!

# Give Me Five For Fluids:

## Easy Ways to Keep Your Car Happy

*"I was on a date when I noticed my car was leaking green stuff. My date tried impressing me with his car know-how and took me to buy some transmission fluid. When the problem didn't stop, I took the car to a mechanic who discovered it wasn't the transmission fluid, but rather the coolant. As it turns out, not all men are automotive geniuses after all."*

—Regina, 30

### Prepare for a Drought

CAN YOU IMAGINE LIFE WITHOUT LIQUIDS? Sure, you could lay off the soda or coffee, but could you stop drinking water? Of course not! Cars, just like us, need fluids to survive, but instead of just one essential fluid, they need five. They are: automatic transmission, brake and power steering fluids, oil, and coolant. You can ask a gas attendant to check your fluids. Don't be afraid to flaunt your car maintenance knowledge. Being able to specifically identify what you want is a smart money-saving tactic (and one that will also save you lots of headaches in the world of dating).

All of these fluids can be purchased at an auto supply or hardware store (or even many drug and grocery stores), if you want to add the fluids yourself. Just check your car manual for the correct type of each fluid for your particular car. And if you don't have your owner's manual with you, most automotive stores will be able to look up the right type of fluid for you as long as you know your car's make, model, and year.

Hip Tip *For more details on how your car works and keeping it well-maintained, we recommend these two books:* THE LADY MECHANIC'S TOTAL CAR CARE FOR THE CLUELESS, *by Ren Volpe, and* CAR SMARTS: AN EASY GUIDE TO UNDERSTANDING YOUR CAR & COMMUNICATING WITH YOUR MECHANIC, *by Mary Jackson. Both written by women who know you may not have learned this stuff growing up, they use easy-to-understand language and explain clearly how a car's systems work.*

## Automatic Transmission Fluid

*What Is It?*

◆ **Automatic transmission fluid** lubricates gears that undergo constant friction. (Think of it like lotion.) It allows you to have a smooth ride whether you are in stop-and-go traffic or cruising around the countryside.

*How Do I Check It?*

◆ **First, if you drive a manual or standard transmission** (or "stick shift"), checking your transmission fluid is more complicated than you need to deal with. It is best to take it to a mechanic to have it checked and filled.

◆ **Drive an automatic?** All right! Find some level ground and place your car in "park" or "neutral." Don't forget to put your emergency brake on.

◆ **Is your car supposed to be on or off** when checking the transmission fluid? Most often, transmission fluid should be checked when the engine is running and warm, but some cars should be off. Some allow you to test when the engine is either warm or cold. Check your owner's manual to find out about your car.

◆ **To check your transmission fluid,** pop open your hood. Properly secure the hood in an upright position. Most cars have a prop stick on either side under the hood. If there's no prop stick, the hood should stay up by itself. Latch it tightly (there's usually a slot in the hood for the prop stick to latch onto or into).

◆ **Now find the transmission fluid cap** (it's often labeled), which usually is located near the back of the engine. Consult your owner's manual to make sure.

**HipTip** *We recommend you wear gloves when checking your fluids. While these products are good for your car, they aren't good for you.*

◆ **Once the engine is warm** (if your manual recommends a warm fluid test), unscrew the lid and pull out the attached dipstick. Wipe off the dipstick with a clean rag. This will help give a more accurate reading.

◆ **Put the dipstick back into its slot** and hold it there for ten seconds or so.

◆ **Pull it out again and check its level.** There should be a line on the dipstick that reads "Full" or "F," or there may only be marks whose meanings are explained by your manual. Don't be surprised if you find "Hot" and "Cold" levels, either. These are the "Full" marks for manufacturers that allow either hot or cold testing of the transmission fluid. If the transmission fluid is at the "Full" line then no additional amount is needed, but if it reads below the line you may need to add more.

## How Do I Add More?

◆ **Now that you've checked your transmission fluid** and found that you need to add more, don't stress. The hard part is over.

◆ **If you already have some spare transmission fluid,** then awesome—you're a prepared princess. If not, go buy some.

◆ **Ready to add?** Set that dipstick down and pick up a funnel. (A funnel is a cone-like tool used to pour liquid into a small opening. Gas stations usually have paper funnels for your use, or you can make one out of paper. Simply roll into an ice-cream-cone shape, with a large hole at the top and small one at the bottom. You can also get a plastic one from the automotive or hardware store just for this task.)

◆ **Slowly pour in the appropriate transmission fluid** and recheck the level. Continue until you have reached the "Full" line. It's important that you not overfill.

◆ **Finally, it is also good to check the color and smell of your transmission fluid.** Transmission fluid should be very clean, and a transparent pinkish-red color. If the fluid on your dipstick looks dark or feels gritty, or if it smells burnt, have a mechanic check it out. After all, checking the fluid regularly will help keep you from needing to replace your transmission, leaving you more money in the long run (for buying that bracelet you've been drooling over in the Tiffany's catalog.)

**HipTip** *Be good to your transmission and it will be good to you. A couple of basic tips to help your transmission live a long life:*

• *Let your car warm up for a minute after starting your engine before putting it in gear.*

• *Don't shift from "drive" to "park" or "reverse" (or vice versa) until the car has completely stopped moving.*

# Brake Fluid

## What Is It?

◆ **Brakes are a bit more complicated than they look.** In case you did not know, brakes work hydraulically. (That basically just means they operate using fluids. But don't worry. Just knowing that word will make you sound like a pro.) A master cylinder pumps out brake fluid by steel tubes or rubber hoses into smaller brake cylinders at each wheel. If there's no fluid to pump, then your brakes will not work. It's kind of like dry heaving when you had that nasty stomach flu, but worse, because without brakes, you can't stop your car. And speaking of heaving, brake fluid (like other auto fluids) is poisonous, so if you do ingest some, you will be very sick! Or worse!

## How Do I Check It?

◆ **Make sure your car is off with the emergency brake on.** Open the hood and take a look for your master brake cylinder. It's most likely located toward the back of your engine, on the driver's side. The reservoir (where you put the brake fluid) of the brake cylinder is usually a rectangular metal or plastic container. Consult your owner's manual.

◆ **If your reservoir is plastic,** just look at the fluid level from the outside of the reservoir. The cylinder should be at least halfway filled with brake fluid, which is a clear yellow-beige color. If it has enough fluid, you're done! If not, read on.

◆ **If you need to add fluid** or if your reservoir is metal and you'll have to open it to test the level, wipe the top of the master cylinder reservoir before opening it.

◆ **If your reservoir is metal,** and is attached by a metal clip, a flat-head screwdriver may be needed to pry off the clip, in order to open the lid.

◆ **Unlike checking your oil,** there's no dipstick to gauge how much brake fluid your master cylinder reservoir contains. Most newer cars will automatically alert you to a low brake fluid level with a light on your dashboard. Don't fill to the very top. Overfilling is to be avoided here too. Remember to check your owner's manual for the type of brake fluid to use and how full your reservoir should be.

Hip Tip *If your brake light keeps coming on, have your car checked. Also, have your brakes looked at if they feel "squishy" or are making any strange sounds, such as screeching, clicking, or grinding.*

# Power-Steering Fluid

## What Is It?
◆ **Big wheel keep on turning.** Have you ever driven with a friend that seemed to use all his or her strength to crank the steering wheel? Have you ever wondered how your car can maneuver with the slightest touch? Well, that's the beauty of power steering. Once again the power of hydraulics makes it easier to steer even the biggest of SUVs, but you need to have an adequate amount of power steering fluid to do so. If you are low on, or run out of, power steering fluid, you will definitely be in for an arm workout. In fact, you may not be able to turn the wheel at all.

## How Do I Check It?
◆ **Like all fluids in your car, this one has its own reservoir.** All you need to do is locate your power steering reservoir, which is usually near your power steering pump. But if you don't know where the pump is, that won't help, will it? The easiest way to find it is to look at your owner's manual, as power steering fluid reservoirs can be located in different places under the hood depending on your car. You can

also check out the caps of the different reservoirs—if you are lucky, it may say "Power Steering" on it.

◆ **Put your emergency brake on,** and your car in park or neutral, pop the hood and give it a look. Your car can be on or off, but to be on the safe side, turn it off. You don't need to get caught in any moving parts! Locate the power steering reservoir. If your reservoir is plastic, you may not need to remove the cap to check the level if there are lines on the outside of the reservoir. If the reservoir is metal, twist off the cap. Whether metal or plastic, the cap should have a dipstick attached to its underside.

◆ **Survey the dipstick.** Some may have two lines that read "Full Hot" or "Full Cold." Because the yellowish power steering fluid expands when hot, the two-line dipstick allows you to check the level with accuracy whether the car is hot or cold. If your dipstick only has a single "Full" line, it is then best to check your power steering level when the engine is cool.

◆ **If your level is low,** add only what is needed to bring it to "Full" or the "Full Hot" or the "Full Cold" line (whichever applies). Don't overfill. Once again, consult your owner's manual for the appropriate type of power steering fluid for your car.

# Oil

*What Is It?*

◆ **Oil is the fluid that helps keep your engine parts from rubbing against each other.** Imagine going down a water slide without any water. Sure you can do it, but chances are you'd get a bit of a burn from it. But, if you run water on it, you would zip down with the greatest of ease. Oil helps your engine zip through its routine when you're driving. Without it, your car would not last long.

*How Do I Check It?*

◆ **If there is one fluid that is most important to check, it's the oil.** Because your oil is considered the most important of the five fluids for your engine, it has a bit more in-depth directions for checking and changing. Consult the *Checking Your Oil* chapter for explicit directions.

# Radiator Coolant

*What Is It?*

◆ **Radiator coolant acts like antiperspirant for your car.** In other words, it's the fluid that helps keep your car's engine cool while your cylinders are working out. Coolant is a mixture of water and other chemicals like alcohol or glucose. (Don't confuse the glucose used in coolant with the glucose you eat. It's poisonous, and hard on the environment—make sure kids or pets don't get to it either.) Coolant has the remarkable ability to help keep your car's engine at an even temperature whether you are in the blazing heat of summer or the dead of winter.

*How Do I Check It?*

◆ **If your car runs low on coolant, it will do more than just sweat.** It will overheat. Because overheating of cars is a common problem, we've got a section devoted just to it. Consult the *Hot Under the Hood* chapter for more specific directions on how to check and maintain your radiator coolant.

# A Couple of Things to Watch for with Any Fluid

◆ **If you are frequently adding any of these fluids,** you may have a more serious problem with your car. Get it checked out by a professional.

◆ **If you see that fluids are leaking onto the ground** where you usually park your car, you may want to take it in for repair.

◆ **All of these fluids are toxic,** so keep them away from children and pets and wipe up any leaks. You'll want to protect yourself, too, by using gloves, and washing your hands after handling any of them.

◆ **After you've added any fluids to your car,** make sure you wipe off any spills or drips on the engine and car paint, too!

## Fluid Maintenance That's Hassle-Free

◆ **How can you have maintenance that is hassle-free?** Simple, have someone else do the work! Whenever you take your car in for an oil change, which should be about every three thousand miles (or every three months, whichever comes first), request that all your fluids be checked. (Most places usually do it for virtually no charge.) Many automotive experts recommend you also check these fluids every month (some say every week). Hey, it doesn't hurt to check them more often rather than less often—once you do this a couple of times, checking all your fluids will take less time than a manicure. And for maximizing your road trippin' freedom, check your fluids (or have them checked) before heading out for a long trip. If you don't want to do it yourself, ask a gas attendant to help check under your hood while fueling up.

—⊸◈⊷—

Wow! Who knew cars required so many different fluids? Remember, just like we require a little pampering, so do our cars. Maintaining your car will keep your busy social life up to par.

# Checking Your Oil:
## Your Number One Car Duty

—◦∞◦—

*"When I graduated from high school, my parents bought me a brand-new car to take to college. I was so excited! I cruised around campus all year as proud as can be. Then one day, my new car started getting really hot and emitted an awful smell. I remember thinking, 'What could it be? I just filled the gas tank.' But I hadn't changed my oil—ever! The engine had blown up. So now I didn't even have an engine. Now I get why my father was relentless about asking me: 'Did you check your oil?'"*

—Diane, 30

## Building a Lasting Relationship with Your Car

WITH ALL THE SOY MOCHAS, CHIPS, AND PIZZA you've shoved down, your body is fueled for the overnight shift or your all-night-long study session. But you'll eventually need to catch up on your sleep to keep from crashing and burning. This is also true for your car. It's important to remember to not only "feed" it with fuel for short-term results, but to check and change its oil on a regular basis for the long haul.

*Hip Tip* *If your "oil light" comes on in your car (it will be on your dash-board and may say "oil" or just be a figure of an oil can), do not ignore it. This is a serious cry for help from your car, and continuing to drive your car may ruin your engine.*

Checking, adding to, and changing your car's oil is crucial to the survival of your automobile, no matter how new it is. After all, oil lubricates your car's engine so that it operates smoothly. Keep in mind that oil, like all car fluids, is not good for *you* to ingest, however—even through your skin. Take good care of yourself by wearing protective gloves. Now, here is what you should do to check your car's oil level:

◆ **Park your car on level ground.** (If your water bottle rolls under the seat, that's a sure sign the ground isn't level.)

◆ **Put your car in gear or in park** and apply the emergency brake.

◆ **Turn off your car!** Leaving it running leaves room for potential disaster.

◆ **Reach below your steering wheel** for the lever that pops open your hood.

◆ **Now make your way to the hood.** (Don't be scared! You'll be a better person for it!) Properly secure the hood in an upright position, using a propstick if there is one.

◆ **Next, find the oil dipstick.** (That's dipstick, not lipstick.) Each car is different, but most oil dipsticks are near the front of the car and may have a handle that's bright-colored like green or orange. Some handles may simply have a metal ring at the end. Pull the dipstick out of the engine. Wipe it off with a tissue or a rag.

*If you're a "vintage" type of girl and have an old Volkswagen, take special care when checking your oil. The oil in your cute VW air-cooled engine can run over 300 degrees F. A metal dipstick in that oil will burn you good unless you use a rag or thick gloves.*

◆ **Once clean, reinsert the dipstick where you found it.** Make sure you place it all the way back in and give it a bit of a jiggle.

◆ **Take the dipstick out again and examine it closely** (as if you were studying a fine diamond). You are checking to see the level of oil that your engine contains. Normally it should be at the "Full" mark or between the "Add" and "Full" as indicated by the engravings on the stick. If your dipstick lacks a marking, you can judge the oil level by how much is on the stick. It should be coated with two inches of oil— or the width of two perfectly manicured thumbnails—from the bottom. If it's lower than "Add" or the width of your two nails, you need to add more oil until it's full. (See "Adding Oil" below). Hold up though, you're not done just yet.

◆ **OK, so you know your oil-level status,** but what you don't know is how clean your oil is. (Adding oil without ever changing it is like applying loads of perfume and deodorant without taking a shower. And you'd only do that if you were in a desperate hurry!) So, before putting the dipstick back in its place, check its color and condition. Here's where your herbal tea and nonfat-decaf-vanilla-latte-with-whipped cream expertise comes in handy. If your oil is extremely black, like a thick espresso, get your oil changed! If it is slightly brown like an iced tea, you're good to go. Not a Starbucks girl? Just remember this:

*If your oil is brown, don't frown.*
*But if your oil is black, it's time to take it back.*

# Adding Oil

◆ **Oil for cars is what shampoo and conditioner is for hair.** And we all know that changing our brands of shampoo every so often increases our hair's performance and volume. But that's not true for cars. Professionals recommend using the *same* type and brand of oil every time. For example, if you use Mobil SAE 15W-40, try to use the exact same oil next time for good performance.

◆ **No clue what type of oil your car takes?** Again, check out your owner's manual. Or do something that a guy would never do. Ask someone! Next time you're filling up your tank at the gas station, nicely ask the resident mechanic, if there is one, for his or her recommendation. You're likely to find out way more about oil than you ever wanted to know, but if you play your cards right, he or she just might add the oil for you. After all, getting under the hood could get a little messy.

◆ **On your own?** Don't sweat it. The tough work is already over. Before you add any oil, check the level once again, just to be sure you need it.

◆ **Next, unscrew the oil cap.** Check your manual for the location of your oil cap—if you open the radiator by mistake, you could be severely burned. The oil cap is located near the dipstick. It may have a drawing of an oil can on it.

◆ **Carefully pour the oil into the opening.** (For a cleaner pour, most gas stations offer free paper funnels.) Be careful not to overpour. Too much oil is bad for your engine too. We suggest stopping midpour just to check the oil level again.

◆ **Once done, screw the cap back on** and make sure the dipstick is back in place. Wipe up any oil drips. Close the hood and hit the open road.

# Changing Your Oil

◆ **Take it to a professional!** Please! Did you really think we would suggest you take on such a feat? This is above and beyond the Hip Girl call of duty. You have too much work to tackle between studying and starting that jewelry-making business to attempt this one on your own.

◆ **Find a professional.** In just about every city or town you can find a quick and inexpensive place to change your oil. You can go to a chain like Jiffy Lube (call 800-343-6933 for the Jiffy Lube nearest you), or ask your friends, employers, or professors for independently owned stations they trust. If you have a mechanic or repair shop you already trust, take it there. If not, you can start checking one out with a simple job like changing your oil. As we talked about in *The Great Mechanic Quest* chapter, trusting your mechanic is important, because as a woman especially (although men get ripped off too), some shady mechanics will underestimate your automobile knowledge and charge you for services not needed.

◆ **Wow your mechanic with your know-how.** We like a mechanic who's not afraid to get his or her hands dirty, especially so that we don't have to! But knowledge is power. Here's the 411 on having your oil changed professionally:

　□　Change your oil every three thousand miles or three months, whichever comes first. Most oil change shops will even put a small sticker on your windshield as a reminder when your next change is due.

　□　Change your oil filter every time you change your oil. You can request to see your old filter, which should appear dirty and black in color. This is just to make sure the mechanic didn't charge you for something he or she didn't do. Have the mechanic check all the other car fluids, too. This includes coolant, brake, power steering, and transmission fluids. Ask to have your windshield wiper fluid checked, too. Most places will charge you an additional amount to add or flush out old fluids. (See the *Give Me Five for Fluids* chapter for more detailed information.) You should not need fluids added every time you change your oil. If you have been charged for that each time, either you have a real problem with the car, or a real problem with the mechanic.

□   Check your air filter. You should only need this changed once a year.

□   And here's where you can really strut your stuff. Ask the mechanic to rotate your tires. You only need this done once every six to eight thousand miles to maintain your tires for their maximum life.

□   Sound pricey? Thinking, oil change or new halter top? Well, you might be able to have both. Most oil changes run from $20-30. Make sure to get quotes before turning over your keys. Certain services are extra. (We know that Jiffy Lube's $29.99 oil change also includes replacing fluids, checking tire pressure, minimal interior vacuuming, and exterior window cleaning, but anything else is an additional cost. After all, if you can hold off on getting that air filter changed until the next oil change, that halter top has your name written all over it!)

---

Wear any oil stains with pride. You earned 'em; they're all yours. Don't forget to humbly strut your stuff; enlighten your girlfriends by showing them how to check the oil in their cars.

# Hot Under the Hood:

## Time to Cool Off Your Car

*"I was on my way to my first day of college when I suddenly noticed smoke coming out of my car's hood. I began to panic. I thought, 'Fire! Explosion!' So I quickly pulled over to the side of the road and stupidly began knocking on the doors of random houses, in hopes of calling the fire department. An elderly man answered his door and as I desperately explained my problem, he choked back his laughter and assured me everything would be OK—that my car was simply overheating."*

—Michelle, 25

### First Things First

PICTURE YOURSELF DRIVING DOWN THE OPEN ROAD in the middle of summer, singing along to your favorite Madonna tune, when suddenly you notice a little problem with your car. The smoke billowing from under your hood suggests you're not the only one feeling a little hot—your car is too.

◆ **Don't panic!** Check your car's temperature gauge. It's located near your fuel gauge and ranges from red (hot) to blue (cold). If it isn't in the red yet, you're in luck. If your temperature gauge is not color-coded, check your owner's manual right away to learn how your car measures its temperature.

◆ **Lose your cool.** Not your composure, your air conditioning. If your air is on, turn it off.

◆ **Turn up the heat.** Although it may sound strange, give your heater a crank to full blast. But don't forget to roll your windows down unless you're in the mood for a sauna. Using the heater will draw heat from your engine, thereby cooling it down.

◆ **If your gauge is in its hot (red) zone** and/or if some unknown light that says "engine" or "temp" suddenly pops up on your dashboard, take the previous steps, turn on your hazard lights and pull off the road as soon as safely possible.

◆ **Turn your car off.** Once your car's temperature is in the hot zone, you only have a few minutes before serious damage to your engine results (plus serious damage to your bank account). Hopefully you're close to a mall or have a good book because your automobile needs at least a fifteen- to twenty-minute nap to cool down.

◆ **Don't junk your car just yet.** Remember, an overheating car doesn't mean it's time to purchase a new one. Think of your car as having a minor case of heatstroke. It simply means your car needs a little TLC. Most likely your car is thirsty for some coolant. No, not Kool-Aid, coolant. (Coolant keeps your car from overheating, like air conditioning does for you.) If you're already traveling with some spare coolant, which you can purchase at just about any gas station or drugstore, then purchase yourself a little somethin' (like chocolate or a new nail polish) for being so on top of things.

◆ **Help is nearby.** If you're hearing the word "coolant" for the first time, don't stress. Call AAA, or if a gas station is close by, thank the Lord! Let the gas attendant know that your car is feeling a little hot under the hood.

**Hip Tip** *Coolant is a toxic green fluid, and has a sweet flavor that animals especially love. Keep the coolant locked away, and clean up any leaks or spills right away.*

## No Help in Sight?

◆ **No gas station in sight and you don't belong to AAA?** Don't sweat it! If you have coolant, then great. More times than not your car is just thirsty for some.

◆ **To check your own coolant** (and add some if you need to), park your car on a flat, level surface and turn off the engine. If your car is really hot, wait till it cools off before you even open the hood, and especially before you open the radiator or check the coolant reservoir. If you don't, not only are you liable to get an incorrect reading, but you also risk severely burning yourself. And we aren't talking about the type of burn you get from too much sun either.

◆ **While you're waiting for your car to cool down,** it's a good idea to turn to your car manual to see where your radiator or coolant reservoir (you'll put the coolant in one of them) is located, and any special instructions for these circumstances. Generally, the radiator is at the front of the engine. If your car has a coolant reservoir (not all do), it is usually a plastic container that's connected to the radiator by a small hose that emerges from the top of the radiator.

◆ **Ready with your coolant?** Your engine has cooled down and the temperature gauge is out of the hot "danger" zone? Then it's time to pop the hood.

◆ **Lost your manual?** All cars are different, but all have a place where coolant is stored. You can still locate it. Look for the coolant reservoir cap that is marked with either the word "coolant" or a picture of a water drop. It's usually located toward the front of your car. If you have an older "classic" type of car, then you may not have a coolant reservoir. Instead look for the radiator cap, but don't touch it until your car has cooled down.

◆ **If your car has a non-pressurized coolant reservoir,** you can add coolant to it even when your car is hot. However, according to Ren Volpe, author of *The Lady Mechanic's Total Car Care for the Clueless*, a number of Volvos and German cars have coolant reservoirs that are pressurized. With these cars, therefore, and any others with pressurized reservoirs, your engine should be completely cooled before you open and add any coolant. Check your owner's manual for specifics about your car. If you're not sure whether it's safe to open your coolant reservoir when the car is hot, then *don't*. Waiting fifteen to twenty minutes isn't going to hurt you. Being sprayed by steam and boiling liquid will! Skip down two steps for directions on adding the coolant.

◆ **Don't have a coolant reservoir?** Then you'll have to wait until the radiator is cool. Otherwise you may severely burn your hand on the cap, as well as be burned by the overheated contents of the radiator that will blast out when the cap is released. Once cooled, use a rag to slowly turn the radiator cap counterclockwise, stopping after each quarter turn to allow any built-up pressure to release (and not harm you). Once a few seconds have gone by, carefully unscrew the cap the rest of the way.

◆ **Now it's time to pour the reservoir or radiator a drink.** (Come to think of it, hasn't all this manual labor got you thirsty, too?) There are usually markings on the side of the coolant reservoir that indicate how much to pour. Add until you get to the appropriate level. If you have a radiator only (with no reservoir), check your manual for the correct amount of coolant (it will probably be filled almost to the top).

*HipTip  Some coolants require you to add water to them before you put them into your car, so be sure to check the label on the coolant container before pouring any into your car. In an emergency, you can add water only to the reservoir to get you to a station or repair shop. However, your coolant/water ratio should be restored as soon as possible.*

◆ **If your gauge is still in the red (hot) zone,** or quickly returns to it after you've added coolant and started it up again, have your car towed and serviced. There may be something else wrong with your coolant system and remember, driving your car while it's too hot can seriously damage your engine in a matter of minutes. You've covered your bases. Now get some help.

*HipTip  To prevent your car from overheating, get in the habit of check- ing, or having someone else check, your coolant level whenever you get your oil changed (every three thousand miles, or every three months, whichever comes first). If it's summertime or you live in a hot climate, you might want to check it every week.*

≡》〇《≡

As you can see, you aren't the only one capable of getting a little hot and bothered at times. What's the rule of thumb? Play it cool. Rash reactions can cause bigger problems.

# Jump-Starting Your Car:
## When Your Ride Needs a Jolt

—◦∞◦—

*"I was notorious for leaving my car's headlights on. But really! Was it my fault? I mean, no alarm sounded to remind me to turn them off! Of course, my failure to turn off my headlights always led to a dead battery in the morning. So I turned to AAA to save me. Finally, when I'd called AAA enough times in one month that the agent knew me by the sound of my voice, I knew it was time to invest in some jumper cables."*

—Kim, 26

## Transcending the No-Turn-Over Trauma

HAVE YOU EVER HAD TO TURN ON THE INTERIOR LIGHT IN YOUR CAR to check your makeup or read directions and then, unknowingly, left that light on? Have you ever left one of the doors just a tiny bit open? If so, you most likely know what it's like to have a dead battery.

How do you know for sure if your battery is dead? The answer isn't as simple as you might think. If your car doesn't start, your battery may be dead. However, it may also be a few other things. If your car won't start, check your owner's manual for troubleshooting tips. As crazy as it may sound, cars with automatic transmissions may not start because they are in "neutral" instead of "park," or a car simply may be out of gas. It's best to check these basic items before taking unnecessary (and time-consuming) measures.

Car still won't start? Chances are you need a jump. No, it isn't time to show off your Double-Dutch talents. Your *car* needs a jump, the kind that requires cables, not a rope. Think of your car in need of a little jolt—just like some of us need our lattes fully loaded with caffeine to start our day.

◆ **In order to jump-start your car,** you'll need the following items: jumper cables (which is a device consisting of four clamps that look like lobster claws and a pair of connecting electrical cables), a friend and his or her car, and a bit of patience. If you don't have jumper cables and/or another car to use as a charging source, call AAA or another automotive service to take care of the problem for you.

Hip Tip　*If you follow our advice and buy your own set of cables, make sure they are good quality: 100 percent copper heavy gauge (at least four gauge) jumper cables long enough to reach between two cars (ten feet at least).*

◆ **Ready to do it your own Hip Girl self?** Situate your friend's car as close to yours as possible, but *not* touching. Hood to hood is best for making an easy connection.

◆ **To prevent a potential disaster,** make sure both cars are off before connecting the cables. Put both cars in "park" (or in gear if you have a stick shift) with emergency brakes on. Pop open both of the hoods.

◆ **Locate your battery.** Batteries are usually located near the front of the car. Consult your owner's manual for help.

◆ **Take a look at your battery.** If it looks damaged or cracked, jump-starting is not an option.

*⋮◯⋮* *You may also have a "charge indicator" on your battery. Check*
**HipTip** *your manual to find out. If you do, and the indicator is clear, don't jump start your car as it may cause an explosion.*

◆ **If the battery looks fine, grab the jumper cables.** These cables will connect the two cars' batteries allowing the "live" battery to charge the "dead" one. Make sure that both batteries are the same voltage (that will either be on the battery or in the owner's manual).

*⋮◯⋮* *Be safe! Remember how you tested the battery for your Walkman*
**HipTip** *as a little kid by putting your tongue on the positive end to see if you felt a "zap"? Yeah, well, that wasn't so smart. (Neither was the time your high school boyfriend got a mullet hairdo!) Playing it safe with your car's battery is a life-saving necessity. Car batteries contain sulfuric acid, which is highly corrosive to skin and clothing. Avoid contact with the acid, and wear gloves if you can. Sulfuric acid also emits explosive gases, so don't smoke or light a flame while you're doing this.*

◆ **Connect the cables in the following order:**

  ☐ First, attach one of the red clips from the jumper cable to the positive terminal (the one with the "+" symbol or "POS" written on it) of your dead battery.

  ☐ Next, attach the other red clip to the positive terminal of your friend's live battery.

□   Then, attach the black clip to the negative terminal (the one with the "–" symbol or "NEG" written on it) of your friend's live battery.

□   Finally, attach the remaining black clip to an unpainted metal surface on your car, away from your battery (*not* to the negative terminal of your car battery, which may cause sparks and an explosion, *or* to your car frame). It may sound odd, but it's a must!

◆ **Now that all the hard and technical work is done,** take a deep breath—you're almost there. Make sure everyone has moved away from the battery and cables. Have your friend start his or her car, letting it run for a few minutes.

◆ **Get into your car, cross your fingers, and give it a start.** Yeah! You should now have power.

◆ **Don't turn off your car quite yet.** Disconnect the cables, removing them in the exact *reverse* order that they were applied, starting with the black clips, then red.

◆ **Give your friend a big thanks and hop in your car.** To help recharge the battery, take it out for a little spin on the open highway for fifteen minutes or so.

◆ **You haven't gotten far and suddenly—oh no! Dead again?** If your battery gives out again shortly after the jump, there's most likely something wrong with it. Your car may require a mechanic's attention, and you may need a new battery. So you don't have to miss another kickboxing class because your car won't get you there, go get it checked out as soon as you can.

—◄◄∭∫∭►►—

Way to take charge of a situation! Next time a friend's car needs a jump, electrify him or her with your battery jolting know-how.

# Tire Trivia:

## Because Flat Tires Are No Fun

"While heading home for Thanksgiving break, I decided to beat the traffic and take the less bustling back roads. About thirty minutes into my ride, I noticed my car was acting a bit odd. When I pulled over to the side of the road, I was shocked to find a rear tire nearly flat. After calling my auto club and learning it would be almost two hours before they could come to my rescue, I decided to take matters into my own hands. Although I got a bit dirty, it was only a matter of time before my tire-changing talent had me rockin' and rollin' again . . . destination, Mom's famous stuffing!"

—Sam, 26

### Is Your Tire Feeling a Little Flat?

BESIDES BAD HAIR, nothing can put a damper on your day like a dreaded flat tire. If you're ever unlucky enough to find yourself in this situation, you have two choices: Change it yourself or have someone do it for you. Sometimes there's no one to help. Why not avoid much of the dread by learning tire changing from a friend before you're stuck for hours?

# First Things First

◆ **Do you have a spare tire?** Yes? Well, is it in top-notch condition? It may be a surprise to you that your car might be carrying around an object you've never seen, a spare tire. If your spare is not already visible, it may be hiding in your trunk. Take a second to locate it and check its pressure. (See the "Checking Your Tire Pressure" section below.) Keep in mind that your spare tire may look smaller or thinner than a regular tire. Make sure there is also a jack (the portable device which lifts the car off the ground) and a lug wrench (a hand tool used to turn or twist the lug nuts off your tire). These tools should come with your car and are usually located with your spare tire.

◆ **No spare or tools?** This one is out of your hands. Call a tow truck or your automotive club.

◆ **Spare and tools ready?** If you have a spare tire in good condition then remind yourself how wonderful you are for being so prepared. More women should take lessons from you.

◆ **Now: Decisions. Decisions.** What is the verdict? Are you going to call a professional to come help, despite the fact that it may take hours before your hero arrives? Or, are you willing to get down and dirty and brave it on your own?

## Preparing to Change Your Tire

Going for it? Great! Despite what you might be imagining, this is far from a truly troublesome task. It can be a messy one though. Unless you were about to go to the gym, changing clothes (if you can) will be in your wardrobe's best interest. A few safety tips:

◆ **Make sure your car is on level ground.** A muddy slope (or any slope, for that matter) is no place to change a tire.

◆ **If you're by the side of the road, get out your flares** or reflective triangle and place them seven or eight car lengths behind your car, alongside (not on) the road. (Of course, you can change your tire anyway if you don't have them—just try to move your car as far from the road as is safely possible.)

◆ **Make sure your car is in park** (if automatic) or in gear, *not* neutral (if you have a stick shift).

◆ **Put your emergency brake on.** It's important that your car isn't going anywhere.

◆ **Turn your hazard lights on** (you know, the blinking light you put on whenever you're double parking in your rush to pick up your dry cleaning).

◆ **Put a rock or piece of wood behind and in front of the tire** that is diagonal from your flat tire. That means if your right front tire is flat, put a block behind and in front of the left back wheel. This is to keep your car from moving while you have it up on only two of its wheels.

**HipTip** *Two four-inch by four-inch pieces of lumber, each cut the width of your tires, are perfect for this job and do not take up much space in your trunk. You can easily have these cut for you at a home improvement store or lumber yard.*

◆ **Now that you're dressed for the part** and have taken your safety precautions, it's time to gather all your necessary tools. You'll need:

The spare tire, the jack, and the lug wrench (and any other goodies in the tire-changing tool kit). If you have an old towel or apron and gloves, even better, because your time for getting dirty has come!

## Changing Your Tires

◆ **Check your kit to see if there's a special tool for taking off your hubcap.** If not, grab your lug wrench. Although a lug wrench is used mainly when working on lug nuts, it may help you pry off the hubcap (which is the circular shaped disc on your wheel), and also functions as the lever for the jack. If you have a newer car, you may have wheel locks, which will have to be "unlocked" to take the wheel off. That tool should be in your kit. (It's smart and safe to take out your owner's manual to get more specific details on how to change a tire for your car.)

◆ **With the flat tire still flat and on the car, pry off the hubcap.** Once off, you'll have a clear view of the lug nuts—the large nuts that screw onto a heavy bolt and are used to attach your wheel to your car. (Yep, that's what they're for, holding your tire to the car!)

◆ **Using your lug wrench and some muscle power, loosen the lug nuts** by turning them counterclockwise, but check your manual, because a few cars go the opposite way. Keep in mind, "righty-tighty, lefty-loosy." If the lug nuts are tightly fastened, try using some leg power. Position the wrench on a lug nut, then stand up and step firmly on the wrench with your foot (using your body weight to help out). Loosen all of the lug nuts, but don't completely remove them!

◆ **Now it's time to jack the car up.** Consult your owner's manual for the best place to position the jack for your car. Most cars have a place along the bottom edge of the car frame near each tire. Using your jack, raise your car to a level high enough to remove the flat and put the spare on. About six inches of space between the tire and the road surface is enough. Make sure none of your body parts are underneath the car. Remember all things that go up also come down, and the last thing you need is a crushed foot.

◆ *Now* **remove the lug nuts all** the way. Be sure to place them in a spot where they cannot roll away or into the road. You'll need them again soon enough.

◆ **Pull the tire towards you,** holding it at the "9 and 3 o'clock position." Be prepared, the tire is very heavy! Make sure that there's still plenty of room under the wheel well to put on your spare.

◆ **Hang in there, you're almost done.** Put on the spare. Make sure the tire is on the right way—the air valve should be facing out.

**Hip Tip** *Putting on the spare can be a bit tricky, because you have to hold it up while lining up the holes on the wheel with the bolts that hold the tire in place. If you can find a big rock or if you have an extra wood block, you can shove it under the tire while you are trying to line it up.*

◆ **Once the tire is on, take the lug nuts and fasten them on the bolts.** It's best to tighten the lug nuts by hand using a crisscross pattern (tighten one, then tighten the one opposite it). Make sure that the wheel is pressed flat. Do not use the lug wrench to tighten them yet. If you apply too much pressure now, you could push your car off the jack—didn't know you were so strong, did you?—and find yourself in a not-so-fashionable neck brace or a cast for your foot!

◆ **With caution, slowly lower the jack.** When the tire is fully on the ground, remove the jack. Now, take the lug wrench and finish the task by tightly securing all the lug nuts. Test all of the lug nuts again just to be sure.

*After the Tire Change*

Clear away all tools, as well as any blocks you may have used to stabilize your car. Put the flat tire, jack, and lug wrench back where they belong in the car. Brush yourself off. Remember: Your car now has a spare tire on it. That means you're capable of driving to a service station or to your favorite mechanic to get your tire fixed. Don't rely on your spare tire to get you around. Even if you have a full-sized spare in good shape, you still need to have a professional check to make sure it's on correctly and that the lug nuts are tightened properly.

Hip Tip    *If you have a temporary spare—it will be smaller than a regular tire—you must get to a shop right away for a new tire or to have the old one fixed. Temporary tires only go so far and they have to be driven at slower speeds.*

## Checking Your Tire Pressure

Whether you're heading out for a road trip or have neglected your wheels lately, it's a good idea to check your tire pressure.

Hip Tip    *Most auto experts recommend you check your tire pressure (including your spare) once a month and before going on a trip.*

*How Do I Do It?*

◆ **You can either check your pressure yourself, or have someone at the gas station do it for you.** This chore is nearly effortless so if you're looking for an easier Hip Girl car task, this is a good one to try. All you need is a tire gauge. This inexpensive tool can be bought at any auto parts store or borrowed at many gas stations. It's a good idea to invest in your own, well-made tire gauge. Often the free-to-use gauges on air pumps themselves do not give very accurate readings. Once you have a tire gauge, it's time to rock and roll. *Note: Just like cooling down before reciprocating during a heated discussion with your friend, colleague or employer, it's best to check your tire pressure when your tires are cool. If you've been driving around and your tires are hot, your reading will be off.*

◆ **Start at any one of your tires.** First, check the outside condition. Do you see any cracks or signs of foreign objects, like nails or stones? If so, your tire may be flat soon and need replacement.

◆ **Everything A-OK?** Next, unscrew the small black cap that covers the air nipple, which is a small valve on the tire that's the inlet and out-let for its air. (If you're missing the black cap, it's a good idea to replace it.) Remember doing this with your bike?

◆ **Press the tire gauge straight down** and firmly against the nipple. (This book is starting to read like a Danielle Steel novel!) Don't worry if you hear some air escape for a couple of seconds. It's normal—but if it continues to escape, you don't have the gauge on right. Try again. Depending upon the type of gauge you have, you'll either notice a plastic rod pop out or an indicator that measures the pounds per square inch—otherwise referred to as "PSI."

◆ **To find the correct PSI level for your car,** look for a label on the door jamb of the driver's door. It should tell you the proper level for the front and rear tires. If you cannot locate it, then check your tire. The maximum tire pressure level is typically printed on the side of the tire, although you usually *don't* want the maximum pressure in your tires, unless you are carrying a heavy load. (A better option, of course: Check your owner's manual.)

◆ **Screw the cap back on** if the gauge indicates that your tire is prop-erly inflated already. You're ready to proceed on to the next "patient."

◆ **Feeling a little deflated?** All you need is a little air. Make sure to head to the closest gas station, if you aren't already there. Don't forget the little black cap!

◆ **Although free air is all around us,** some gas stations may charge you for filling up. Apply the air hose to the tire nipple and let it pump away. Stop and recheck the pressure.

◆ **Don't overdo it!** (We know conquering this feat is empowering, but like eating too much at a good meal, stuffing yourself isn't healthy.) If you find that you got a little pump happy and put too much air in your tires, let it loose. To do so, locate the tiny pin inside the nipple and gently press it in. You should hear the unwanted air escape. (Too bad you can't release the pressure on your ex's over-inflated ego!)

◆ **Continue on to your remaining tires,** following the steps above.

**HipTip** *If one of your tires is regularly in need of more air, then you need to take it to be checked and repaired at a tire shop.*

◆ **Don't forget to maintain your spare!** If you ever find your car with a flat tire, you will be grateful your spare is in tiptop shape. (It's like maintaining standby duty with a good guy friend for those college dances or mandatory office parties at which you'd find yourself otherwise dateless.)

———

You rock! Whether you changed or inflated your tires on your own or with help, you made it happen for yourself. That's the ultimate sign you're made of Hip Girl stuff!

# Auto Emergencies:
## Controlling the Uncontrollable

—◦◦◦—

*"I was sporting around in my 1973 Omega. That beast was the ultimate party car! I was all dolled up for the big party; who cared that it was practically a blizzard outside. Nothing was going to keep me from seeing the guy I had the biggest crush on. Nothing, that is, except the icy road that sent me flying into a ditch in the middle of nowhere. Luckily I wasn't hurt, but that walk to the nearest farmhouse was freezing cold!"*

—Jennifer, 28

## OK, You Had a Car Accident

WE HOPE YOU'RE READING THIS SECTION as a proactive measure and not after the fact. But if you're consulting this section as the result of an accident, take a deep breath. What you do next is what matters now.

◆ **First things first: Stop!** If you don't, you become a fugitive of the law and your fifteen-minutes-of-fame dream may come true with a horrible picture of you splashed across all the local news as a hit-and-run perpetrator.

◆ **Turn off your vehicle.** It will help prevent a possible fire.

◆ **Next, check to see if everyone involved is OK, including yourself.** In an accident situation, it's easy to ignore some of your own injuries if someone else is hurt. If everyone is fine, move on to the item below. If not, identify their wounds: Are they bleeding? If so, where? Are they breathing? Are they unable to speak to you? *Note: Do not move an injured person unless necessary to save his or her life. You could end up doing more harm than good and you could be held responsible for it.*

◆ **Call the police, whether the accident is severe or seemingly minor.** Be prepared to answer the following questions:

☐ What's the location? What are the cross streets? Are freeway on-and-off ramps nearby? Which ones are they? Highways and free-ways are tagged by mile markers to give you a better idea of exact-ly where you are. Being able to relay this information to authorities can help get them to the scene more quickly.

☐ What's the number you're calling from?

☐ What kind of injuries are there and what, if any, help is being administered to the victims?

While on the phone, tell them what you need by giving any other information about the situation that they may need to know to send out the proper authorities and equipment—for example, if someone is sub-merged in water or a car is completely overturned. Finally, ask if you should move your car off the road.

◆ **Next, pull over to the side of the road,** if you're blocking traffic, your car is still mobile, and the police have told you it is okay to do so.

◆ **If it's safe to do so, put out a reflective triangle or a flare** (if you have one …hey, we know many of us Hip Girls don't, but the truth is, we should). Only use a flare if there isn't liquid on the road—it may be gasoline. Move away from the accident and the road.

◆ **Take very specific notes.** Pay close attention to the damages done to all vehicles involved and the people who are obviously injured, as well as those who say they are (but whose injuries aren't apparent). Write down a description of their vehicles. Do this even if there doesn't seem to be anything wrong. You could have extensive underbody damage to your vehicle that's not physically visible. Also, write down the exact location and any circumstances that might have contributed to the accident, such as bad weather conditions or poor visibility.

◆ **Exchange information with the other accident parties.** Specifically, get their names, addresses, and phone, driver's license, and license plate numbers. Ask to see their driver's license and registration—are they current? Be prepared to share yours as well. Most importantly, make sure to exchange insurance information, getting the name of each of the other parties' insurance company, telephone number, and policy number. (You should be able to get this off their insurance card.) Write down their broker's name and direct phone number, if they have it.

◆ **Look for witnesses.** Did anyone see the other driver run the red light? Jot down names, addresses, and phone numbers of anyone who might have seen what happened, including passengers in all vehicles involved. Having someone to corroborate your story might help to settle the dispute between the insurance companies faster (and maybe get you reimbursed more quickly).

◆ **Call your insurance agent as soon as you can.** Give her all the details of the accident and the information you took down.

*Keep your own file. Get a copy of your file from the insurance company because lawsuits can be filed later and you'll want to make sure you have all the information you can.*

**Hip Tip**

◆ **We can't emphasize enough the importance of phoning the police** even if no one is hurt or the damage is minimal. (Uh . . . not for checking out a man in a uniform—although we like the way you think.) Some police departments won't come out to an accident where no one has been hurt. Regardless, ask the authorities on the phone about documenting your call and how, or if, you should go about filing a police report. Make sure you get a copy of any police report when it's completed, and the name and badge number of any investigating officer. Any insurance companies involved will want it for their investigation.

*In most states, it's required by law for the person responsible for an accident, totaling over a specified amount of money, to file a written report with the DMV within a certain amount of time. Typically your insurance agency can file the form for you, but ask to make sure it gets done.*

**Hip Tip**

◆ **Here's an important tip:** Don't sign any documents on the spot unless it's for the police or paramedics. But even then, read it as carefully as possible. Ask questions if the wording is confusing, and inquire if it's okay to sign the form later when you're thinking more clearly. If the authorities require your signature on the spot, make sure to ask for a copy of the signed document. Some people might try to intimidate you, including other people involved in the accident, towing companies, or repair shops, while you're feeling vulnerable. Stay strong. Refuse to give in to any guilt trips or hustle jobs.

◆ **Stay cool.** Don't let yourself get dragged into an argument. Let the police and/or the insurance companies determine whose fault it is. And by memorizing key points in your insurance policy about getting your car fixed, like your right to choose your own mechanic, free towing service, or your car rental limit, you can stand your ground with poise and confidence.

## Uninsured Motorist or Hit-and-Run Victim?

You've heard of it happening to your own friends or family, but it's still hard to believe that someone would have the audacity to drive without insurance, or even worse, hit you and take off like nothing happened. We know you wouldn't do that, but here's what you should do if you're in an accident with one of those people:

◆ **No-insurance motorist.** If you're hit by someone who pulls over but doesn't have insurance, follow all the steps above. But in this situation, it's especially important that you call the cops. You'll want the police report as proof for your insurance claim, besides, driving without insurance is illegal. (No Hip Girl would ever drive without insurance because even if an accident is determined not to be her fault, a person driving without insurance may be charged with a crime and face hefty fines or even lose his or her license to drive.) Then call your insurance agent. Hopefully your insurance policy covers damages caused by uninsured motorists. (See the *Auto Insurance* chapter for more about obtaining uninsured motor coverage.)

◆ **Hit-and-run victim.** If you are sideswiped by a passing motorist who doesn't stop, pull over to the side of the road as soon as it's safe to do so. Do not chase after the vehicle responsible. Now is not the time to reenact your favorite *Buffy The Vampire Slayer's* butt-kicking moments! Following the hit-and-run driver could only endanger your life more. Call 911 and give all the details you remember about the car that hit you—its color, make, model, license plate number and your exact location. With this kind of information, the police just may be able to track the culprit down, turning your status from victim to All-American heroine! Then after all the excitement, call your insurance agent.

◆ **Work the witness angle**. In either case, did anyone witness the accident? Hopefully he or she will have pulled over to let you know. Get their contact information as well.

## What Was That Parked Car Doing There Anyway?

Oops. You could have sworn the red Ferrari parked beside you wasn't quite that close! (Does a sports car really need side mirrors anyway?) As luck would have it, you're running late for your tennis match. But doing the right thing here not only improves your karma, but also helps you comply with the law. So here's what you need to do:

◆ **Stop!** Just as you're required by law to stop if you are involved in an accident where the parties are present, you're required to stop even when the owner of the vehicle or property you hit is not nearby.

◆ **Look around.** Is the owner close by? Ask around. Someone at the coffee shop across the street might know who it belongs to (and might be able to gently break the news to the owner with you). If not, skip to "Nowhere to be found?"

◆ **Found the owner?** Exchange information and follow the procedures noted for accidents above. Particularly note the damages to both cars. You don't want to be wrongfully blamed for the dent that was already in the roof of the other car.

◆ **Nowhere to be found?** Most state or local laws require you to write a note and securely attach it to the car. Give the following information:

- Your name.
- Date and time the accident occurred.
- Your phone number or that of your insurance agent. (We recommend letting your insurance representative deal with the hassle.)
- Your local or state law may require other information as well. A call to the local police department can tell what other information you need to leave.

◆ **Call your insurance agent.** Give all the details to your insurance representative as soon as possible, so as not to be blamed for more than was your fault.

◆ **Call the police.** Depending on where the accident occurred (different states and cities have different requirements), you may be required to call the police and report the accident. If you don't know the law that applies, it makes sense to call them (just to be on the safe side).

## You're Out of Control

If you're driving along and suddenly realize that you don't have control over your car, the most important thing to remember is: Don't panic! OK, that's easy for us to say, but truly, your number one life-saving technique is remaining level-headed. (This is a good approach when entering into heated debates with your roomies too.)

*Hip Tip*    Most cars are "rear wheel" drive, and these instructions are for those cars. If you have "front wheel" drive, check your owner's manual for instructions.

◆ **Skidding**. Skidding is most likely to happen when you change speed or direction, and especially in bad weather. A skid can happen when your foot is on the accelerator and you hit a slick spot, or if you suddenly hit the brakes hard. Just as there are ways to control your wild mane, there, too, are ways to regain control of a car that starts skidding uncontrollably. Here are the basics to remember in this emergency:

☐   Ease up on the accelerator. Letting up on the gas pedal all at once will only cause your car to skid even more. If your skid started when you slammed on the brakes, take your foot off the brake.

☐   For standard transmissions (otherwise known as stick shifts), push in the clutch. This makes the car coast in neutral, and allows you to maintain more control over steering and wheel positioning. Automatic transmission? Put it in neutral.

☐   Steer in the direction of the skid. So, if the back of your car is sliding sideways to the left (causing the front of the car to point right), turn your steering wheel to the left. (You may find it easier to remember that you should steer in the direction you want the front of the car to go.) Your auto should start turning in the opposite direction (your back end swings right). Try straightening the wheel as best you can. Continue this pendulum maneuver (steering into the skid and straightening) until the swings become smaller and you can steer your wheel completely straight. You can cut down on the pendulum action by making smaller turns on the steering wheel.

☐   If you wish to stop, brake slowly, and only when the car is under control. Braking too soon could make you skid again. If you're continuing on after skidding on a slick spot, release the clutch (with a stick shift) or put the car in drive (with an automatic) and slowly accelerate to a safe speed.

◆ **Hydroplaning**. When your car is riding on a cushion of water and road oils, usually in wet weather, it's hydroplaning. Hydroplaning occurs frequently when driving in the first rains after a long dry spell, because there is a lot of oil built up on the road (imagine if you didn't wash your hair for weeks). You know your car is hydroplaning when you lose control of your steering wheel and your car feels like it's sliding. Here are three simple tips to taking charge:

☐ Take your foot off the gas pedal.

☐ Do not hit your brakes. It will only throw you into a skid (and you've already got enough of a headache as it is). If you have to slow down, pump your brakes slowly.

HipTip *Some newer cars have "anti-lock" brakes which should NOT be pumped, but instead be pushed down slowly and steadily and held there until you have stopped. Check your owner's manual to know for sure what kind of brakes you have.*

☐ Once you've regained control, drive slower than you were before you started hydroplaning (no test, meeting, or movie is worth risking your life for again).

◆ **Blown tire.** Whether you're on the freeway, in the country, or within the city limits, blowing a tire while driving can be extremely dangerous. Here's how to handle this scary situation:

☐ Do not slam on the brakes! It will only make the situation worse—braking could cause you to roll your car.

☐ Grab the steering wheel with both hands and steer straight ahead, staying in your lane.

□ Let up on the gas pedal while you're concentrating on your steering.

□ Tap the brakes (or brake slowly if you have anti-lock brakes), but *only* when you have regained control of the car.

□ Steer onto a shoulder or next to a curb where you should brake slowly. *Note: If you have a blowout on the freeway, follow the instructions exactly as above, but make sure to signal before crossing lanes of traffic. Also, avoid braking at all costs until you have successfully made it to the shoulder.*

□ Now flip to the *Tire Trivia* chapter to see how to change your blown tire.

◆ **No steering.** OK, how many times have you been told that if you don't stretch before and after exercising, your muscles will stiffen up? Your steering wheel or engine will do the same without enough power-steering fluid. If suddenly you can barely turn your steering wheel, here's what you should do:

□ Signal to move off the road.

□ Grasp the wheel tightly and angle your car onto the shoulder or next to a curb. We hope you have been doing your workouts—the wheel is going be hard to turn.

□ Brake, but not before you are in a safe place to do so, as steering your car is much easier while it's in motion.

□ Now get to a service station or repair shop and turn to the *Give Me Five for Fluids* chapter to learn how to add power steering fluid.

◆ **No brakes.** Brake failure can be like falling in love. You know you should take things slower, but you just can't stop. But seriously, knowing what to do could save your life, so read up:

□   Pump the brakes hard and fast a few times to see if they will start to operate again. However, *don't* pump if you have anti-lock brakes.

□   Shift down to a lower gear, but *not* neutral.

□   Gradually apply the emergency brake. Do not yank it all at once, otherwise you're likely to skid or spin out. Warning: You may have to release the emergency brake again if you start skidding. If you have an emergency brake operated by hand, you can use the button at the end of the lever to apply and release the brake as needed. Foot emergency brakes are tougher to use.

□   If you're headed for a steep drop-off, focus on steering away from it and head toward safer ground. Bushes will do just fine as a bumper pad!

□   Finally, flash your lights and sound your horn. Alerting others to your trouble could save your life and the lives of others.

◆ **Pedal stuck to the metal.** What do you do if your gas pedal suddenly sticks to the floor? Besides not freaking out, here are the other steps in handling a stuck gas pedal:

□   Shift to neutral. Don't worry about the noise your car makes when you do this—just drive! Whatever you do, don't turn off the ignition at this point because your steering might lock up!

□   Gradually push on the brakes. Stepping on the brakes all at once could cause you to spin out.

□   Flash your lights and honk your horn.

□   Try to steer your car safely off the road.

□   Turn off your car, but only after you no longer need to change directions.

◆ **Stuck in snow or mud**. Not only can bad weather mess up your perfectly coiffed hairdo, it can make you really late to that job interview, that party—that date! If you find yourself in a sticky mess, focus and try this:

- If you have a shovel, try removing as much mud and snow as you can from around the stuck wheels (with the car off).
- Get in, put your car in a low gear, steering straight ahead, and slowly step on the gas pedal.
- Go forward as far as you can. If your wheels start spinning, stop.
- Now put it in reverse and slowly back up as far as you can. Again, refrain from spinning your wheels (it will only dig you in further). Repeat the process of driving slowly forward (in a low gear) and then in reverse, trying to gradually increase the distance each time. Continue until the car is free.
- If you're unable to break out of the rut, turn off the car. Gather tree branches or any boards you may find and put them under the stuck tire or tires. Before moving onto the next step, make sure to get everyone out of the way of the car. What you put under the wheels may come flying out as you accelerate, especially if the wheels start spinning.
- Start the car again and proceed with the backward-forward motion until you've dug your way out of it. If you can't make it out, here's where your membership to AAA comes in handy.

◆ **Animal attraction.** Most everybody loves big, furry animals. But when it comes down to you or them, saving your life is ultimately the most important. Here's what to do when an animal darts out in front of you:

- Take your foot off the gas pedal. Do not slam on your brakes! You could cause your car to spin out or you could go flying through your windshield.

□ Only for a small animal like a skunk, cat, or puppy should you consider steering the car out of the way—and only if you can keep your car under control, on the road, and out of the way of oncoming traffic.

□ If a deer or another large animal is staring you in the face, hitting it head on (as horrible as that sounds) offers your best chance of survival. Swerving your car could cause you to lose control or spin out.

□ As soon as it's safe, pull over to the side of the road.

□ Call 911. In most states, the law requires you to notify the authorities about your accident. Request the police to file a report. The report can later serve as important documentation for your insurance claim.

□ Do not try to rescue an animal from a busy road or freeway. You could get hit by an oncoming car or cross traffic, or be severely injured from a bite. Call the animal control people or the humane society.

—◦◦◦—

Phew! Any accident can send your blood pressure skyrocketing. Stay cool in the heat of the moment and take charge of your future: Virtually memorize this chapter (as you would a new Dave Matthews album) and own the road you're cruising on!

# Financial Fun

*Who says money has to be the root of all evil? Not a Hip Girl, that's for sure! Step up to the plate and take charge of your financial future. What's not fun about planning how to afford a trip to Brazil for sightseeing? (And we're not talking about the cute surfers in their, uh, Speedos. That should be illegal!) Or does your credit card debt have you down? We'll lift your spirits with step-by-step instructions for paying them off without cutting out your manicures. So avoid punching numbers and calculating figures no more. Check out Financial Fun's chapters for the latest and greatest on everything from filing your taxes to what your 401(k) has to offer—and enjoy watching your money grow.*

# Checking Out Checking Accounts:

## Where to Stash Your Cash

—◦◦◦—

*"I wanted a killer tan for the summer so I signed up for a package at a local tanning salon. A few months later, I graduated from college and moved out of the area. But that didn't keep the tanning salon from automatically withdrawing monthly payments from my checking account. And because I never balanced my account, I didn't catch it until a year and $500 later. Worst of all, I didn't even have a tan to show for it!"*

—Patty, 27

## What's a Checking Account Got to Offer?

CHECKING ACCOUNTS ARE NOT ONLY A SAFE PLACE to stash your cash, but they're useful tools for keeping track of your money and for paying bills. You can look back and tally how much you've actually been spending on clothes (not that it's necessarily going to stop you from spending more— hey, you need to look good for your job, right?). Besides money management, opening a checking account is usually the first step in establishing a relationship with  a bank as well. If you like your bank, you may want to go back there later on for a car loan or mortgage.

Each bank offers one or more types of checking accounts with different requirements and benefits. But here are some of the features you should look for when deciding where to open your account: an ATM/debit/check card, free direct deposit, free checks and unlimited check writing, no monthly fee or minimum balance requirements, overdraft protection, and free 24/7 telephone banking and banker access. (Phew! Feeling overloaded? Don't worry, we'll go over each of these below.) If you carry more money in your checking account than you spend each month, be sure to check into an interest-bearing account as well.

*Hip Tip* *No matter which type of account you open, make sure that the bank you are dealing with is insured by the Federal Deposit Insurance Corporation (FDIC), which means your account is insured (up to $100,000) by the federal government if the bank should fail. That's right, you could get your money back.*

Now, as if you were checking out the perks of a new job or school, let's analyze what features suit you:

◆ **ATM/debit/check card.** An ATM card ("ATM" stands for automated teller machine) allows easy access to your cash from just about anywhere in the world. Gotta love that! (Gee, ain't technology groovy?) If your ATM card doubles as a debit/check card, just present the card anywhere that credit cards are accepted and the money will come straight from your account. (If your card can be treated as a credit card as well, please read the *Credit Card Confidence* chapter too.) Try to get a checking account where there are no service charges for using your card, whether at your bank's ATM or another bank's ATM. Most banks will charge you a service fee for using your card at their ATM if you don't have your account with them (the fee can run from between $1 and $3), and your own bank may charge you a small fee as well (for using another bank's ATM—talk about jealous!). So between the fee your bank charges and the fee from the bank where you are drawing the cash, you could end up dumping as much as $6 a shot just for the privilege of withdrawing your own money. (That's a quick meal, a paperback book or, heck, that's almost enough for a movie ticket.) So, know what your rights are when using your ATM card, and if you can find a bank that doesn't penalize you for using another bank's ATM, all the better.

◆ **Direct deposit.** Whether your monthly income comes from your parents or you have a cool, new job in fashion, opt whenever possible for an account that lets your parents or employer deposit your support money or paycheck directly into your account. It'll save you time and frustration in the long run (and you won't have to worry about having those checks stolen or delayed in the mail). Most banks offer this service for free (they get your money faster). Sometimes you can also get another benefit, such as free checking, for agreeing to direct deposit.

Hip Tip *Whenever you make a deposit in person, whether at the bank counter or ATM, you'll get a receipt for it. To protect your money, we recommend that you always check your receipt to make sure it shows the right amount. And copy your checks before you deposit them or keep your check stubs—banks make mistakes too! You will be more likely to win an argument with a bank about a mistake on your deposit if you have copies of the actual checks you gave to the bank or the check stubs that were attached to the checks.*

◆ **Free checking, check writing, and checks.** Consider carefully before choosing a financial institution that requires you to pay a fee for having a checking account. A bank may also want to limit your check writing to a certain number of checks each month and charge you for going over that limit. Try to find a bank that offers the deal that works best for you. If you only write a few checks a month, a check-writing limit may not be a problem.

◆ **Interest-bearing account.** Simply put, in an interest-bearing account, you'll earn money just for having money in the account. Usually, the return on your investment is minimal, but every little bit helps! Ask what requirements there are for these accounts (many banks require a minimum balance—see below). Checking account interest rates are notoriously low. Before agreeing to "trading" a minimum balance for interest on your account, make sure the money isn't better used somewhere else—like paying off a high interest rate credit card.

◆ **Minimum balance.** Do you spend less than you make? Rock on! A Hip Girl knows to save for a rainy day (or for dance lessons to nurture her soul). In that case, consider an account that requires a minimum balance in exchange for waiving certain other fees or getting interest on your account. Minimum balances usually start at $250. But if you're cutting it close every month, be sure to look for a checking account that reflects your peanut-butter-and-jelly-sandwich lifestyle—that means, no minimum balance required.

◆ **Overdraft protection.** That check for the $200 pair of leather pants will be covered by overdraft protection even if you only have $150 available. With overdraft protection your bank will automatically loan you the extra funds (up to your predetermined credit limit), but not without charging you interest (and usually it's pretty hefty). We do recommend having overdraft protection, but only use it as protection in the event you make a mistake in your bank balance, or a check you deposited in your account doesn't clear—not as a long-term financing option.

◆ **Telephone banking and banker**. Pick an account that gives you 24/7 access to your account via the telephone for free, whether it be with their automated account system or with a real-live person.

**Hip Tip** *For more information about different types of checking accounts and what different banks have to offer, take a look at aboutchecking.com and bankrate.com.*

## How to Choose?

Now that you have all the information about several accounts, see which one works for you. You may not be able to get everything that you want, but you can balance out your needs with what is available. For instance, if you use an ATM a lot, focus on getting an account with free ATM use, no matter what bank's ATM you use. Also, if you write only a few checks per month and can get a free account with limited check writing, that may be a good deal for you. That being said, many banks will negotiate in order to get or keep you as a customer, especially if they see you as a Hip Girl whose income is going to grow. Therefore, squeeze as many freebies from the bank as you can. See if you can get them to cover the cost for your actual checks. Asking the bank representative what deals the institution can offer is smart shopping (like bargaining with a sales clerk at a small boutique for a discount). Some banks may bring in new business by offering free stuff or waiving certain fees if you open a new account. After all, banks have sales too! They don't call them that, but they offer special breaks once in a while, so keep your eyes peeled for the best deal.

## Balancing Your Checkbook

To avoid the nightmare stories like the one at the beginning of this chapter, it's important to balance your checkbook monthly. Is it a pain? Absolutely. But once you get good at it, it'll take you no time at all and you can rest easy knowing you're keeping good track of your money.

◆ **What does balancing a checkbook do?** The point of balancing your checkbook is to make sure you and your bank agree about what's in your account, and to tell you how much money you actually have in your account at the time. Remember that the bank statement shows a "snapshot" of your bank balance on a certain day, which may be different from the balance which you actually have on the day you're looking at the statement. Think how much a snapshot of you may not look anything like you a week later—after you had your hair dyed and chopped off! Reading your statement may not be as interesting as *Elle*, but it does make for a handy tool in figuring out if you really have enough money in your account for that fresh, new J-Lo jumpsuit.

**Hip Tip** *Every time you write a check, or use the ATM, record the transaction in your check register right away. Don't forget to note automatic deductions. Keep all your receipts, etc. in one place for when you are ready to balance your checkbook, 'cuz those charges can sneak up on you. And just when you think you've been a good girl, surprise!—you spent more than you intended to.*

◆ **How to do it?** The back of your bank statement will clear up any abbreviations or terms that may seem foreign to you. There also may be a form on the back of your statement for you to follow in balancing your checking account. If there isn't one, go to aboutchecking.com and follow the step-by-step instructions (with video!) on how to balance your checkbook. Your bank likely has a pamphlet that can take you through the same procedure. Try to balance your checkbook right after getting your monthly account statement, when you'll most likely be able to remember details.

◆ **Is there another way?** Hip Girls who are computer-savvy might want to invest in a computer program that does all the calculating for you. (Of course you still need to enter the numbers correctly into the program). Check out Quicken, one popular financial software program, at your local computer store. All you have to do is enter your checks, deposits, and other bank transactions and with a few simple steps—poof! you suddenly have your checkbook balanced. Now that's awesome!

# Protecting Your Checking Account

OK, here's where the real world is a bummer. The fact is, there are a lot of scammers out there who want your money. Help protect yourself by taking good care of your checks. Here are a few tips to do that, but read the *Stolen Identity* chapter too.

◆ **Don't throw away unused checks** from accounts that are no longer open or checks that you have made a mistake on. Somebody may actually go through your garbage and use those checks for you. Hard to believe, but true!

◆ **Likewise if your bank returns your cancelled checks** (the ones that have been processed). If you want to do a little financial house-cleaning, it's best to get rid of cancelled checks, or old unused checks from closed accounts by shredding them whenever possible.

◆ **Keep your checks stored away** where they aren't easily accessible to someone else.

You can protect yourself by being careful when you are filling out the information on your checks as well. Keep in mind the following:

◆ **Always use an ink pen when filling out a check,** so it can't be changed (never a pencil—you're not taking your SATs!).

◆ **If you make your check out to "cash,"** it's for all practical purposes, the *same* as cash. Anyone who has it, can cash it. If you're going to get cash at the bank by writing a check, wait until you get there to fill out and sign the check.

◆ **When filling out the spaces on a check,** start writing as far to the left on each line as possible. That prevents someone from adding additional information to it. For instance, if there is enough room, someone could turn your $25 check into a $125 check. Ouch!

◆ **When there's remaining space on a line,** draw a line through it. This also limits someone from making changes to the check.

◆ **Keep your check register up to date.** That way you know the last check you've written and if any are missing from your checkbook.

When making deposits, take care as well. When you deposit a check—those that are not *directly* deposited for you—you will need to *endorse* it. That just means that you're signing the back of it, which gives the bank permission to cash it. Wait to endorse the checks until you're at the bank. And if you're depositing checks at an ATM, ask your bank how to most safely endorse checks. You will probably write something like "for deposit only" on the back of the check, with your signature under it (some banks may request that you add your bank account number as well). That way, you're telling the bank that it only has your permission to cash the check by depositing it into your account.

## Additional Banking Terms

◆ **Business day.** Monday through Friday, except federal holidays. Any cash dumped into your account on Saturday and Sunday to cover your weekend post-party pizza munchies doesn't get processed until Monday (but then, neither do the checks you wrote for the munchies!).

◆ **Certified and cashier checks.** Certified checks are sometimes used when making legal contracts. For example, when you buy a car and need to give a certified check to the seller, your bank verifies that you have the right amount of the check in your bank and guarantees it by "certifying" the check. A cashier's check is similar, but you don't have to have an account at the bank issuing it: you just give them the cash, pay a service fee and they produce a "cashier's check" for you.

◆ **Check register.** You received your check register with your first box of checks. In it, you keep track of all the money going into your account (credits) and all of the money going out of it (debits). That includes deposits you have made, checks you've written and money you've taken out of the bank through an ATM or for payments pre-approved by you. For each transaction, fill in the form of the check register—if you are writing a check, the number of the check, the date, the person (or payee) that you are writing the check to, and the amount of the check. For a deposit, you would include the date and the amount of the deposit.

◆ **Deposit.** Every time you deposit money in the bank, you'll use a deposit slip of some sort, which lists what checks you're depositing and what amounts they are. You have deposit slips at the back of your checkbook. If you deposit checks through your ATM machine, the "deposit slip" may be the envelope itself, on which you write the deposit information.

◆ **Deposit account.** Any account (like a checking, savings, certificate of deposit (CD), or money market account) you own at a particular banking institution is considered a deposit account.

◆ **On-line banking.** You may not use it now, but one day you may not be able to live without on-line banking. See the *On-Line Banking* chapter for more information.

◆ **Payee.** Individuals or companies you're paying money to are "payees." (You are the "payor.")

◆ **Payment.** By now, you've likely made plenty of these. But officially a "payment" is a transfer of funds to a payee by check or automatic clearing house (ACH).

◆ **User ID, password, PSC (Personal Security Code) or PIN (Personal Identification Number).** These are the names or numbers of the access codes for your account which were either assigned to you or which you selected.

━━━◆━━━

Now that you're in the know of the checking account basics, be resourceful and find an account that fits your spending (and saving) habits. (Don't forget that each bank offers something just a little different; so use your *Hip Girl's Handbook* as a tool for getting the dialogue between you and a bank representative started.)

# Credit Card Confidence:

## Using Credit without Pain

—∞∞—

*"In college, my parents co-signed for a credit card for me—for emergency purposes only! Well, when my friends and I road-tripped to Mexico one year for Spring Break, I realized I'd forgotten a swimsuit. I panicked! I couldn't survive without one. An adorable purple bikini became my first of many 'emergencies.' But because my 'careful' splurging kind of got out of hand, I had to start hocking my personal belongings when I got back to pay off the bill."*

—Linda, 37

## Breaking Down the Fine Print

AHHH, THE ALMIGHTY CREDIT CARD! Your new best friend. Or, your worst enemy. Yep, it's a fine line between love and hate. But just as you diligently choose your friends, you should also carefully pick your credit cards. Make sure you know what to look for before beginning your credit or charge card courtship:

◆ **Is it a charge card or a credit card?** Many people confuse charge cards, such as American Express, with credit cards. While charge cards are also handy pieces of plastic that you can substitute for cash, they are different from credit cards in a significant way—you are required to pay the balance off completely each month. The advantage to the charge card is that you pay no interest while establishing great credit (you pay an annual fee instead). Do we suggest that? Absolutely, in a perfect world. Yet, in a perfect world, you wouldn't be paying the tab! Credit cards, however, such as Visa, MasterCard, Discover, and a slew of department store and gas credit cards, all allow (and encourage) you to make purchases and keep carryover balances from month to month so they can make money off of your purchases (by charging you interest). Interest charges can rack up before you know it. So if you're going to shop until you drop—what are we talking about, *when* you shop until you drop— do it wisely!

◆ **What is the APR (Annual Percentage Rate)?** The APR is the interest rate that credit card companies charge you for loaning you money. The rates usually range anywhere from 10.9 percent to 20.9 percent per year, but can go higher for high-risk cardholders and lower as well (especially for introductory offers to entice you to sign up, and boy are they ever appealing). When considering whether an APR is a good deal, think of it as just the opposite of a 50 percent off shoe sale: For a credit card, the lower the percentage, the better the deal. If you're a college student, check out StudentCredit.com. Be cautious with low introductory rate offers—after the initial period, the rate can skyrocket. (See the "Recovering from Credit Card Abuse" section below for more details on introductory rate offers.)

◆ **Does the card charge an annual fee?** An annual fee is the amount a credit or charge card company charges you once a year just for having their card, whether you use it or not (you know, kind of like your gym membership). Annual fees can range anywhere from $5-95 (or even more!). Should you get a card with an annual fee? Maybe, maybe not. If the card offers an extremely low APR or fantastic reward points (see below), you might want to consider it. However, there are plenty of credit card companies competing for your money, and some who may be willing to waive an annual fee (this probably isn't true of charge cards). As if you were looking for a good, trustworthy mechanic, shop just as vigorously and wisely for a credit card that has both a low APR and no annual fee.

◆ **Is the APR a fixed or a variable rate?** A fixed APR simply means it's an amount that will remain the same (at least until the credit card company forewarns you of a change, which they can do at any time). A variable APR means the interest a company charges can fluctuate. A bank may set its APR to rise and fall with another interest rate that is familiar to the financial world. Reading credit card offers carefully (and that means sometimes having to wade through the fine print) will tell you what factor that bank bases its APR on. For instance, credit cards with a variable APR usually will have an interest rate that reads something like "prime + 6.9 percent." Without boring you with too much detail, a prime rate is simply the base interest rate charged to some corporations, and can be found by checking various credit card websites or financial pages of the newspaper, or by giving your bank a call. So, for example, if the prime rate is 10.9 percent that billing cycle (generally a billing cycle is a month—just like your period) your APR would be 16.9 percent. If you don't want to continuously monitor your credit card interest rates, you should opt for a card that has a fixed APR.

◆ **What is the grace period?** Like the number of days you'll give a date before not returning your call becomes unacceptable, a grace period is the number of days a credit card company gives you to pay your debt before it starts charging you interest on your purchases from that month. Insist on a card with a twenty-five day grace period.

*At the risk of being annoying, we are going to remind you to read* **Hip Tip** *the fine print again. Make sure you understand how the grace period works for a card you are considering. For many cards, there is no grace period if there is ANY balance carried over from the previous month. (Yep, that means racking up interest charges from day one.) This is one of the many reasons to pay off your balance each month! (Wouldn't that be nice to swing!)*

◆ **Are there reward points?** Think Spring Break or a European vacation! Some credit card companies offer reward points just for using the credit card. Rewards can be anything from frequent-flier miles, free Internet service, money toward a new car, or even cash back. Maybe this is your ticket for frolicking overseas! Be careful though—cards with rewards usually charge an annual fee, which may be quite high. Make sure the pay off is worth it.

*Cards that offer rewards, such as airline miles that apply to your* **Hip Tip** *frequent flyer program for dollars charged on your credit card, almost always have an annual fee. Before you decide it's worth it, calculate your "winnings" against the actual charge. If your card charges $75 for an annual fee, and you receive a mile for every dollar you charge, how long is it going to take to earn the 25,000 miles for a "free" ticket? Even if you charge as much as $500 per month on your card, it will take over four years to win a 25,000-mile award. In the meantime, you have spent over $375 in annual fees alone, not to mention the interest you've paid if you've carried any of the credit balance. If you've got a killer job that requires you to spend* your own money for company-related expenses up front, why not slap the charges on a card that earns you frequent flier rewards? As long as you apply your company's reimbursement check to the bill, you just pulled a double-whammy and hooked yourself up with legitimate mileage points for a personal trip. Now that's working the system, girl! Just make sure your company let's you keep the points for yourself first.

## Spending, Spending, Spending

Your father has said it a thousand times: "Use your credit card for emergencies only." But we girls know that Dad's idea of an emergency and our idea of an emergency can be completely different. But do choose your "emergencies" very carefully. A credit card isn't free money. Use cash, check cards, or checks whenever possible so as to not rack up unnecessary debt. Too late? Has your back-to-school or new job spending spree already bitten you in the rear? Let's first go over your credit card statement, then later we'll talk about how you can recover from credit card problems.

A credit card statement is the monthly report sent to you by the credit card company listing your credit status with them (kind of like a report card). Check out these terms on your statement:

◆ **Available credit.** This is the amount of credit you still have for your use. It's calculated by subtracting your balance due from your credit limit. Keep in mind that the actual credit available may be less than reflected on your statement if you've used your credit card after the date on the bill.

◆ **Cash advance.** A cash advance is money a credit card company allows you to borrow directly from it (as opposed to covering your purchases from third parties like The Gap). While not every bank offers you cash advances on a credit, many do, and if you have available credit, you can probably get a cash advance. Oftentimes, cash advances carry much higher interest rates than regular credit charges and you will usually incur a transaction fee on top of that. There's probably *no* grace period, either. You may not be able to use all of your available credit for a cash advance. If you can't get a cash advance however (and that's not necessarily a bad thing!), here's where your loyalty to friends (for all the times they bummed cash for gas) and family (for all the times you covered for your brother when you were kids) may be repaid.

◆ **Interest rate.** Confirm that your interest rate is what you agreed to when you signed up for the card. Banks can change the interest rate at any time (they'll let you know by putting a notice in with your bill— usually on a small slip of paper in very small type). If you use the card after the notice, you have "agreed" to the increase. (Seems a bit tricky, doesn't it? But it's perfectly legal.) Over time, any difference could wipe out what you could have contributed toward your girlfriend's birthday party.

◆ **Balance.** The balance is the amount you owe the credit card company. If you have enough money in your checking account to pay it off, do it, so long as you can cover your rent, makeup needs, groceries . . . you get the picture. If not, pay as much of it as you can. The more you pay now, the less you'll have to pay later (and the less interest you'll pay too).

◆ **Credit limit.** Unlike your career potential, the sky's not the limit when it comes to credit cards. You're given a credit limit, the amount up to which the credit card company has agreed to loan you (either through your purchases or cash advances). They determine that amount from the application you filled out where you noted your income and other bills. *Note: If you pay your bills on time, you may be able to get a credit limit* increase over the phone in an emergency. For instance, if your getaway to Vegas left you a little low in cash flow, and you need more money to get back home, you can call your credit card company and ask them to increase your credit limit. The card company doesn't have to approve your request, but you never know. And if it's a matter of eating or starving, it might be worth it. You decide.

**Hip Tip** Having your credit limit increased isn't necessarily a good thing. It may mean you've already got more debt than you can pay off and now you can go deeper!

◆ **Due date**. Think of it like a video rental. If you return the video late, you're charged an additional amount. The same is true with a credit card payment—the payment has to arrive (not just be mailed) by the due date. Here's a hint: If you think your payment will be late, call your credit card company and try making a check payment over the phone. Occasionally they will let you do it, but usually for a fee running from $10-15. Compare it to the late charge fee to see if it's worth it. Or it might be cheaper to send it overnight.

◆ **Finance charges.** This is the total amount you pay to use credit, including interest, service, and transaction fees.

◆ **Late fee.** If your payment isn't received by the due date, you're charged a late fee. Most late fees run between $25-30. Oops. There goes that haircut you needed. Another hint: On rare occasions, a valued customer can get a late fee reversed—at least once. It doesn't hurt to call up the credit company and request it, but don't count on it. (So don't be booking your hair appointment until you swing the reversal for certain.)

◆ **Minimum amount due.** The amount a credit card company requires you to pay on your balance that month, usually between one-and-a-half to four percent of your outstanding balance. Let's just hope your minimum balance is never more than your rent!

◆ **Over-credit or over-limit fee**. The credit card company charges you an over-credit fee for spending more than your credit limit. This can run as high as $30-50 each time. Ouch! (Check it out: If you're a valued customer and your credit history is good, you can call the credit card company and ask them kindly to remove the charge. Again, they're not required to, but as long as you don't abuse the system regularly, they just might be willing to.)

◆ **Purchases.** Each of your purchases will be listed separately. Check them carefully so you're not overcharged or charged for something you didn't purchase (like that mysterious subscription to *Playboy* magazine). If you were, call your credit card company immediately and dispute the charges. The phone number will be listed on the bill.

◆ **Previous balance**. This is the amount you owed at the end of the last billing cycle. Study it closely. Make sure last month's payment is reflected in this month's balance.

## Making Your Credit Card Work for You

Accentuating your assets (like your wit, charm, kindness, and intelligence) appropriately can increase your chances of getting what you want. Using good judgement when making credit card purchases can also help achieve your financial goals.

◆ **You can build a good credit history.** By charging small amounts (like for gas or groceries) on your card, and paying off the entire balance at the end of the month, you can build an attractive credit history, therefore enticing other lenders to see you as a good, safe bet when you hit them up for another loan (ahhh, you can already picture yourself in that brand new Jeep).

◆ **You can gain credibility with current lenders.** When you pay on time, your value as a customer goes up. You may have more bargaining power when requesting a lower interest rate or asking the credit card company to waive their annual fee (yep, you can do that). Credit card companies trust you more and are likely to raise your credit line. Translation: That means more money at your fingertips for emergencies, of course, but be careful—don't raise those limits without good reason.
◆ **You can get free stuff.** Fun, sun, and surf, here you come. Depending on which credit card you choose, the purchases you charge may accrue frequent flier miles or other rewards. Again, consider "awards" type cards carefully when calculating their true "cost."

## Recovering from Credit Card Abuse

Hey, cheer up. Blowing a ton of money wasn't the smartest thing you could have done. (But we can't deny that it probably sure seemed fun at the time!) Your tenacity in getting your spending under control is what counts now. Start by paying those babies off.

**Hip Tip** *For more "getting out of trouble" suggestions, we recommend you read* DEBT FREE BY 30: PRACTICAL ADVICE FOR THE YOUNG, BROKE, AND UPWARDLY MOBILE, *by Jason Anthony and Karl Cluck.*

◆ **Pay more than the monthly minimum.** Taking longer to repay charges means more cash in the credit card companies' pockets and less in yours. Short on cash? Minimize daily living expenses. Learn to love ramen noodles. Take all that extra lunch money and put it toward your monthly bill. Even a little bit more each month can make a huge difference. See the *Show Me the Money* chapter for more ideas on cutting your expenses.

◆ **Combine and transfer balances**. If you combine all the debt from each credit card and move it to a lower interest rate credit card, you reduce your overall interest expenses and only need to make one monthly payment. Depending on your outstanding balances and interest rates, this can save you big dollars by year's end. Just make sure that balance transfers aren't treated as cash advances (with a higher interest rate) under your new card. And be cautious about doing this too often because transferring balances too many times can reflect poorly on your credit history (a report of your credit transactions that's used by creditors in determining whether to loan you money).

**Hip Tip** *You can easily research available credit cards on the Internet. Try bankrate.com, kiplingers.com, or cardratings.org for information about various cards and rates available. Cardratings.org (soon to be ".com") also contains debt relief information and consumer comments about various credit cards and card offers.*

◆ **Pay attention to low introductory APRs.** Keep an eye out for low introductory APR opportunities. You can transfer your balance to "special-deal" cards. These entice you with very low interest rates on transferred balances for a specific amount of time (usually three to six months), after which the interest rate increases to meet the quoted APR. The fine print on the application will tell you what the future APR will be, and when it switches. Transfer your debt to a card whose APR is still relatively low, even after the increase, and pay down the debt.

**Hip Tip** *Put a note in your day planner or Palm Pilot to alert you when the introductory rate period ends to avoid paying that higher interest rate. You always have the option of transferring your debt again to another card with a lower interest rate after the introductory period is up* *(just keep in mind that transferring credit card balances too often can look bad on your credit report).*

◆ **Renegotiate if you can.** Still behind? (Don't give up. Money management can be tough. But that's when a Hip Girl kicks her tenacity into high gear.) Try renegotiating your terms with your credit company. Most credit card companies hate to lose a customer, and you may be able to lower your rate simply by telling the company that you're thinking about switching to a lower rate card. You can also admit your problem. Owning up to your overspending and asking for help in coming up with a new payment plan might entice a company to give you a break—either by agreeing to stop accruing interest or reducing the amount of debt in exchange for a prompt payment. Most credit-card companies would rather get some of their money back than have you claim bankruptcy and never have a chance at getting their money at all. However, no credit card company is obligated to help you, and you shouldn't count on this.

◆ **Consumer Credit Counselors.** Call up your local Consumer Credit Counseling Service (CCCS), or other nonprofit debt-counseling agency. For a nominal monthly fee (usually $10 a month), the CCCS acts as a liaison between you and your creditors. This agency helps arrange for consolidation of your debt and may negotiate a low or no interest charge with your creditors so that you can repay them in a timely fashion. As part of the procedure, the CCCS calculates a monthly repayment plan for you based on your income. *Note: Your use of CCCS may show up on your credit report.* You can locate your local CCCS office by calling the toll free 800 and 888 phone directory, in the yellow pages of your phone book (usually under "Credit & Debt Counseling Services"), or logging onto the Internet. Just search under "consumer credit counselors," and your state's or region's local agency should be on the list of numerous credit card debt management companies that pop up. CCCS is a reputable organization, but if you use a different one, investigate that organization carefully and choose wisely. Read the fine print and check with your local Better Business Bureau to make sure the company has a credible reputation.

◆ **Cut it up**. Not enough? Last resort: Admit defeat. Bow your head in shame while tear drops roll down your cheek. Own up to your mistake and ask someone you can count on for help. If a friend or family member helps you out of this dilemma, make sure you find a way to pay him or her back. A Hip Girl always pays her debts! Then make the ultimate commitment (and sacrifice) to yourself. We suggest you sit down and brace yourself: Take out the scissors and cut (yes, cut) up your credit cards—at least until you can get your debt, and spending, under control.

## Stolen Credit Cards

We'd be the first to agree that credit cards are convenient to use. However, if you lose them or they are stolen, you're in for some hassles. Make sure you act quickly if you're unlucky enough to find yourself missing a credit card. (See the *Stolen Identity* chapter, too.)

◆ **Having your credit card(s) stolen is serious stuff,** so always keep all your credit card account numbers and emergency numbers (each company has one) in a safe place at home or with a service that takes care of this for you. Call your credit card companies immediately, if your cards are lost or stolen. Only a small amount, usually between $50 and $100, of additional charges incurred after reporting your card lost or stolen is your responsibility. (Your previous outstanding balance remains your responsibility, however. Sorry. Can't have everything.)

◆ **Suddenly you discover you have your own personal Mini-Me?** Cloning identities is another serious risk related to credit cards. Someone may steal your credit card numbers or cards and pass herself off as you (despite that your fabulousness is truly one in a million). You don't even have to have applied for a card for a criminal to steal your identity. When you get a credit card application in the mail that you're not interested in, rip it up, especially your identifying information and offer code. If you don't, someone could copy or steal the info and you could be responsible for an astronomical amount of debt that you didn't even have the pleasure of accruing. Better yet, ask for a shredder for your birthday (also helpful for shredding love letters and pictures from your ex).

◆ **Another precaution to take when preserving your good credit** is to be sure to cancel any credit cards you no longer use. Simply cutting up your cards doesn't protect you from fraud. Officially close out your account by calling the credit card company. You may want to follow up with a letter. Then it's documented and you cannot be held responsible for activity on the card thereafter.

⚊⚊⚊

Girl, we hear ya! Credit cards can be very tempting. But paying off lingering interest for a pair of outrageously priced jeans isn't all that rewarding. Instead, save up the cash for them and donate the money you saved yourself in credit card interest charges to your pet charity.

# On-Line (Not In-Line) Banking:

## Banking in Pajamas

—◦◦◦—

"I picked up a few totally cheesy party favors from the local sex shop for my friend's bachelorette party. I didn't have any cash, so I just used my debit card to cover it. When my monthly bank statement came, the name of the store appeared —twice. Yep, they'd double-charged me. I paid a visit to my bank to settle it. Just my luck, the bank teller was a hottie. Humiliated, I recounted my sex toy purchase ordeal to him. He smirked. I turned red. And when the problem was resolved, I swore to myself that I'd never make that visit to the bank again! I've been banking on-line or by phone ever since."

—Blossom, 30

# Does On-Line Banking Fit Your Style?

CAN'T GET ENOUGH ELEVATOR MUSIC? Then you might enjoy hanging tight on the phone for hours waiting for the next available bank representative. Otherwise, try on-line banking. Accessing your accounts via the computer means you can do it all as fast as your fingers can type. Besides saving time, check out some of the other benefits:

◆ **You have 24/7 access to your accounts.** If you're a night owl, this is really perfect for you.

◆ **For now, it's totally free** (unless you also opt to pay your bills online) and literally at your fingertips. You can check your balance, view all transactions including withdrawals and deposits, and look at past statements. You can even transfer funds between accounts during the day, so you'll have enough cash in your account to cover the check you wrote the night before—after all, somebody had to ante up cheesy party favors for the bachelorette party!

◆ **You can print out your account statement(s),** which comes in handy should you and your financial institution disagree about a specific transaction. Rather than wait to receive your bank statement via snail mail (or stand in line at a local branch office and pay to have the statement printed for you), you can deal with the problem right then and there, instantly!

◆ **Need to know if you have enough cash** to take a spontaneous road trip with your friends? With on-line banking, you don't have to wait a month to get your bank statement. You can simply balance your checking account within minutes.

◆ **With the click of the mouse, you can reorder your checks** and receive them in a matter of days.

# On-line Banking with Bill Payment

◆ **Wait, there's more.** You can also pay your bills through the computer by subscribing to on-line banking with bill payment. Most banks charge a small monthly fee (usually around $5 or so) for this service. With the addition of a bill payment option to your on-line banking service, you can authorize the bank to automatically make payments (either one-time or regularly scheduled) to your creditors. For instance, if you have a car loan, your lender might offer an automatic payment option. If you choose it, your monthly car payment will be withdrawn from your account and paid to your lender for you. Yep. That means one less check to write. And best of all, no more past due charges for sending the payment late because the bill payment service remembers for you.

**Hip Tip** *Some banks operate totally on-line, which means there aren't actually any physical branches to visit. These banks may charge no fee for on-line bill payment. Before you sign up with an Internet-only bank, make sure that it's legitimate.*

◆ **Do you find the monthly bills stacking up unnerving?** If you have on-line banking with bill pay, you may be able to receive some bills on-line as well, which you can review in the same detail as bills sent by mail. Your bank should be able to provide you with a list of creditors who offer the on-line "bill-presentment" option (not all do).

◆ **Planning to travel the world?** With on-line banking and use of a computer, you can access your account and even continue paying your bills on time, all while studying or traveling abroad gorging on Italy's fabulous food or raiding France's fashion boutiques.

◆ **Finally, you can divide your bill payment responsibility from your roommates.** Yeah, sure, you share your clothes with your roommates and your deepest, darkest secrets. But when you cross living with friends and splitting bills together, sometimes it causes disagreements. On-line banking with bill payment lets you log on and pay your portion of a shared bill on time—leaving your roommies to be responsible for their portion and splitting any late charges incurred. (While a Hip Girl is always considerate of others' feelings, she knows that taking care of her own first is smart business.) Keep in mind, however, if a service is in your name, it's your credit on the line. So if a payment is late or the bill doesn't get paid at all, you're the one the company will come after, not your roommates.

## The Downside of On-Line Banking

◆ **Gotta go high tech.** If you don't own a computer, you'll probably have to skip it until you do. Or if your computer is so old-school style that it doesn't have a fast connection or even have an Internet connection at all, don't bother. There are other specific computer equipment requirements you'll need to meet too, and you may have to upgrade your system (or part of it) when the bank updates its system. Read "Logging On" below for some examples.

◆ **You have to stay domestic.** Forget your brainy idea of setting up monthly payments directly to your favorite Italian shoe manufacturer. All banking payments made on-line must have a United States address.

◆ **Beware the hacker.** While most banks take the utmost care setting up their on-line security measures, there's always the slim possibility of a technical genius gaining access to your financial records. (And no matter how little you actually have in your account, this can mean big-time money troubles for you.)

◆ **Make sure you know your bank's liability policy.** A bank's liability for incorrect entries for transactions to and from an account via on-line banking and on-line banking with bill payment is limited and very specific. A bank will most likely not take responsibility for any equipment failures on your end either.

◆ **If you've signed up for on-line banking with bill payment,** you must have enough dough in your account to cover any prescheduled individual, weekly, biweekly, monthly, quarterly, semiannual, or annual payments. Don't forget! Although it's not required to, the bank may still process the transfer even though you don't have enough money in your account. In that case, you may be required to pay the difference and the overdraft fee immediately. And if by chance you accidentally do let it slide, chalk this up to a learning experience and think about picking up a side job (like waitressing or freelance writing) to pay for your goof-up.

◆ **You can't talk to a machine.** There's always the frustrating reality that your computer isn't human. Your computer can freeze up while completing a transaction, you can experience a faulty transmission, or you might not get an immediate response to your e-mail inquiry. With automatic bill payment, most banks will allow you to cancel a payment to a payee on-line, but you might want to double check that the cancellation actually took effect. Some banks may require you to actually speak to a bank representative either by phone or in person to cancel a prearranged payment, while others may want it in writing. Read the fine print for your financial institution's policy on canceling on-line, automatic payments.

## Logging On

◆ **No Hip Girl should be on her own without the essential financial tools.** A checking account, ATM card, and credit card are the first tools in your financial survival kit. The first step in banking on-line is opening your own checking account.

◆ **Accessing your on-line account.** As you know from the *Checking Accounts* chapter, most banks will issue an ATM/check card when you open your checking account, and a PIN (Personal Identification Number) so that no one else can access money from your account with your card. *Note: Ask to customize your PIN. Use a number easy for you to remember but difficult for someone else to guess—like the date of your very first kiss.* You'll probably need your PIN to access your on-line account or you may have to select a different password for the on-line function.

◆ **What do I need?** Your bank will tell you the computer configuration requirements if you want to sign up for on-line banking. Generally, however, you will need the following:

☐ an Internet service provider (a company that hooks you up to the Internet) such as America Online (AOL) and an e-mail address.

☐ browser software with the level of encryption required by the bank (the encryption level corresponds to how safe the information is that you send over the Internet). Currently, the highest level commercially available is 128-bit encryption.

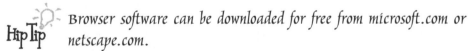 *Browser software can be downloaded for free from microsoft.com or netscape.com.*

☐ a modem, which connects your computer to other computers and manages the information transfer between them (the speed at which the information moves is determined by the "baud" rate). We recommend at least a 9,600 baud modem.

If all this computer mumbo-jumbo is going right over your head—don't feel embarrassed, it's not uncommon—trust us! (We were right there with you until we did some digging ourselves.) Don't be afraid to ask your bank for help. On-line banking makes a bank's job easier and is more cost-effective for their business, so they should be happy to help set you up.

These guidelines should help getting logged on to your bank's on-line banking service a little easier and less intimidating. Empower yourself by reading the details of your bank's guidelines and policies. (You may want to check out the *Checking Out Checking Accounts* chapter for basic bank terminology, too.) Then follow their step-by-step instructions for getting started. Just like if you were dying your own hair fire-red, the instructions are usually pretty simple, but it's still important to not skip a critical step.

━◅◫◖◗◫▻━

Convinced on-line banking will rock your world? Way to flex your Hip Girl courage for tackling the technological world!

# Show Me the Money:

## More Money In, Less Money Out

—∾∾∾—

*"I never seemed to have enough money left over for shopping and partying while I was in college, despite the fact that I worked two part-time jobs. Then I discovered I could make an extra $20 a week donating my plasma. So every Friday, my girlfriends and I lined up one by one to give up body fluid we never even knew we had. It was a total bonus to my fledgling funds, until one day when I passed out while the nurses stuck the needle in my arm. For fear I was too weak, they barred me from ever coming back, and I had to kiss my monthly shopping sprees good-bye."*

—Jennifer, 28

### Budgeting for a Shopping Spree

MONEY'S TIGHT, BUT SO IS THAT RED DRESS. And it'll sure look better on you than on the mannequin. So how are you going to swing it? Budget for it. Budgeting is just balancing what you earn against what you spend—and any Hip Girl knows that sometimes requires creative calculating!

◆ **Income.** The first step in budgeting is figuring out how much money is at your disposal. Only include money you know you can absolutely count on. (Anticipated winnings from the football pool don't count!) Do you have grant or scholarship money coming? How much do you make from your job? Are there any leftover funds from your most recent graduation?

◆ **Total fixed expenses**. Fixed what, you ask? A fixed expense is the money you pay out for something on a regularly scheduled basis. That includes rent, tuition, phone, groceries, auto or renter's insurance, utilities (water, electricity, gas), car payment and gas, and your credit card payments (at least the minimum payments). You'll know it as anything you consistently dish the dough out for because you couldn't maintain your lifestyle without it. (For some of us, getting our eyebrows waxed is at the top of that list.)

◆ **Subtract**. Subtract your fixed expenses from your income (pray on your little black book that your income is higher than what your fixed expenses are each month—or you've got some serious work to do!). If you come out in the hole, talk to someone you trust about getting your living expenses down. It may require that you find a cheaper apartment or take on a roommate. Also, skip to the "Just-Scraping-By Funding" section below to find out how to quickly make a little extra money.

◆ **Discretionary expenses.** Hooray, you have income to spare after your fixed expenses. Here comes the fun part of budgeting, deciding how to spend your extra cash flow! This is known as discretionary (or variable) spending.

*We like the budget sheet and process developed by the authors of* THREE BLACK SKIRTS: ALL YOU NEED TO SURVIVE. *In that book, the authors suggest that if you are having trouble figuring out everything you spend your money on, such as lattes, newspapers, and car washes, ask for a receipt for everything that you spend money on—everything—and put them in the same place every day. After a month, sort your receipts and add them up by type of expense—car, restaurant food, entertainment, etc.—you will have a very clear idea of where your money is sneaking off to! We also have another way to keep track: If you have ever gone on one of those diets that start with keeping a notebook and writing down everything that you eat, including mints, you already know how to do this. Get a small notebook that you keep in your purse or backpack and write down everything you pay for every day (and how much). You may be surprised!—But remember . . . you actually have to do this . . . and no cheating by not including that $3* GLAMOUR *magazine purchase.*

◆ **Make a list of priorities.** Do you get a buzz off investing all your extra money and watching it grow? (That means more dollars, and more fun in the future.) Or does your high come from shopping? (Trust us, you're not alone!) Haircuts, a gym membership, dry cleaning, gifts, partying, and eating out are among many discretionary expenses to consider. Balance is key in figuring out your discretionary spending here. Putting all your extra money into savings with no money for haircuts or occasional dinners out can make you feel deprived and depressed. But spending all your extra cash without saving and investing can make you feel anxious. Pick and choose your priorities wisely!

◆ **Do the math.** Now total up your chosen discretionary expenses and subtract that amount from the cash flow left over from your fixed expenses. Check this formula out again:

*Step one:* Income minus fixed expenses equals extra cash flow!

*Step two:* Extra cash flow minus discretionary expenses equals savings.

◆ **Savings?** No, we didn't mention anything about it before. But don't think of it as a chore. Picture you and your best friend sunbathing on the beach in the south of France. Yep, just you and her, a novel or two, and good girl-talk! If you start saving little by little now, it just might be attainable and could make the perfect vacation for your body and soul! So set a goal for how much you hope to save by the end of the year and make it happen.

◆ **Plan for surprises**. Keep in mind that life occasionally gets in the way of fun (like a blown tire at the start of a road trip). Be prepared to dip into your reserve finances to cover problems instead of relying on your credit cards. Just be smart about taking only what you need. Replace the money as soon as possible. (After all, a French romance could be waiting for you.)

◆ **Bottom line**. Simply, your first goal in managing your money is to not spend more than you make. That includes spending with cash, credit cards, or by check. (Hate to say it, but use your credit cards as a last resort.) The ultimate budgeting accomplishment is when you're out of debt and can accrue a nice little fund for rainy days—because rainy days may call for a little shopping to lift our spirits!

◆ **The great juggling act**. Keep in mind that even if some debt persists, a little nest egg (or fund to help your little sister pursue her dreams of becoming a physician) is nice to have if for no other reason than peace of mind. In other words, pay as much as you can each month against high-interest loans, but also set aside as little as $25 a month for your savings account or to invest in a mutual fund (see "Investment Definitions and Terminology" section later in this chapter). At the end of one year, you'll have at least $300 saved up (and at the end of four years that makes $1,200, not including interest). France, here you come!

# Just-Scraping-By Funding

What if the dollar amount on your bottom line is lower than you thought and you need some quick cash to cover your fun? If you've decided you need extra money to live on or pay off bills, there are two ways to do it—increase your income and/or cut your expenses. Fast cash might be easier to find than you think. Consider the following options for getting yourself out of debt and back in control:

◆ **Part-time job/work-study/paid internship.** The obvious way to make money: Get a job. When money becomes a problem, getting a ten-to-twenty-hour-a-week job just might be the answer to more than money matters. Here are some tips to consider when scoping out your money-making gig:

☐ *Work study.* If you are a student, work-study is a smart option because you can usually make your own schedule. Check with your school advisor, college paper, campus billboards, or administration office to see if you're eligible. Ask your favorite professor if you can assist in researching or organizing materials for studies or books he or she is working on.

**HipTip** *As an alternative, check with your school advisor to see if you can turn your previous real-world work experience into an internship for school credit. Not only will you get through school faster, but many internships come with a stipend. A Hip Girl never passes up a money-making opportunity!*

☐ *Seasonal help.* Working during Christmas and summer breaks, when employers are often looking for extra help, is a perfect way to get more cash without cramping your social schedule too much. Even if you already have a full-time job, you can often do seasonal work in the evenings or on weekends.

□    *Part-time jobs.* As well as enhancing your bank account, working part-time in a field you are interested in can help you figure out your future career path. Who knows? Working as an assistant at a local law firm or as a teacher's aide in a first grade classroom may help you discover a lifetime passion.

□    *Odd Jobs.* Check your school or local paper for unusual, one-time gigs. Some will pay $50-100 for very little of your time. These gigs may include participating in focus groups for advertising agencies (you know, "Can you tell which is Coke and which is Pepsi?"); taking part in research studies (some are innocuous, but steer clear of the drug trials); modeling (for that holiday fashion show at the local department store); or donating plasma and blood (who knows what good you could be doing for someone else?). Or take your shot at stardom: Try out for your favorite television game show. Maybe you'll get fame with your fortune! Check into any venture thoroughly first. Don't respond to any notice that invites you to an isolated place, doesn't indicate who is sponsoring it, or otherwise doesn't ring true.

*Hip Tip*    *Part-time gigs or odd jobs not only provide some welcome extra cash, they also offer a great opportunity for making a new group of friends. Branching out of the comfort zone of your daily routine could expose you to a whole new world of interesting experiences and aspirations. (With your new singing-waitress job, you could rediscover your passion for performing and end up as the new lead singer of a band—or not!)*

Don't be afraid to be inventive. If there is somewhere you'd like to work, just march in and tell them you're willing to do a special project for them whenever they need you. If they like you, it could lead to more steady hours. A Hip Girl is all about creating her own destiny, not waiting for it to happen by way of osmosis!

## Cutting Corners without Cutting Out the Fun

How much you make isn't really the determining factor for how well you live. Nope. It's true. The more important element to living in Hip Girl heaven is how you spend your dough. Dropping that $3 a day on your fancy, fluffy latte can add up to almost $1,100 per year. It's crazy when you look at it like that, isn't it?

Listed below for your consideration are some ways to shave a little off your expenditures. Are we suggesting you completely cut them out? Are you crazy? No way! We're simply saying to give and take a little. Pick and choose wisely when you are thinking about tossing down that eighteen bucks for the new Alicia Keys soundtrack. Perhaps you could find it cheaper somewhere else, and with the savings, save for the CD burner you've been wanting instead. Read on for more options:

◆ **Phone.** Do you still have a honey back at home or is a long distance relationship with a colleague on the opposite coast starting to get hot and heavy? Cutting back on phone expenses can help you get out of debt and gain some independence. Some of the following tips can help you keep your romance hot without digging yourself further into the hole:

   □   E-mail, of course: It's the ultimate communication tool that even college students on a budget can afford. Even if you don't have your own computer, most campuses have some for students' use. Or you may be able to use a friend's, but why not get a sister's back by returning the favor in the form of dishwashing service? (Be cautious about using your computer at work for personal e-mail. Some companies monitor their employees' use.) If you have your own computer—great! An Internet service provider can cost way less than a monthly phone charge (not to mention a late night booty call to your babe back home).

☐ Restrict long distance calls. Have your phone company block long distance from your phone. This is a great way to avoid running up your bill, especially if you have a roommate who's flaky about paying her portion. Plus, if you throw a crazy party in your house, you don't have to worry about random people calling their girlfriends in London on your bill!

☐ Call collect. You're down and out about failing your chemistry exam or getting passed up for that promotion you were sure was yours. Polishing off that box of doughnuts didn't squelch your despair. At any age, sometimes calling Mom and crying on her shoulder is the only way you'll feel better (and she'll be glad you still confide in her). But dial her up by calling collect. She can call you right back and it'll cost less. Or better yet, if your calls to your parents are frequent, suggest that for your next birthday they install an 800 number for your use. That's a gift that keeps on giving!

☐ Prepaid calling cards. Go ahead, recount every detail about your latest date to your best friend living back in your home state. With a prepaid phone card, you'll get cut off when your time and money have run out. You can buy prepaid phone cards in various amounts (like $10, $20 or $30) at most discount stores. They can help you monitor both your money and your marathon phone workouts. Remind family and friends that prepaid calling cards make great presents!

☐ Phone-saver packages. Corporations are constantly marketing their products and services to people with a good income. If you're a college student, companies see your potential earning power as promising (even when you barely have a penny to your name) and often offer deals designed to capture your loyalty as you enter the working world. Check into your long-distance carrier's package options and look for the best price. Flex your business-savvy muscle by letting them know know you've checked with their competition as well. (It's like flirting just enough with other guys to make the guy next door take notice of the little hottie right under his nose!)

☐   Cell phones. Milk the cell phone system as best you can. Getting the cheapest base rate per minute may actually not be the most cost effective. Look for a plan that reflects your phone usage style. For instance, you might get more bang for your buck by paying more per month for your basic plan if you get more free calling time during hours you know you can get your best girlfriend on the phone (like at 2 a.m. when you both are just getting home). Try to use up all the free minutes without going over your limit. Sure, you got the phone for emergency purposes, but if you've got free minutes to kill, why let good, free gab-time go to waste? Call up or text message your big bro with advice on women. You're sure he needs it! But be careful to not go over your allotted time. Between those text message charges and prime-time calling charges, your bill could skyrocket. Why not see if your cell phone carrier offers a service that notifies you or cuts your service off once you've gone over your allotted free time?

◆ **Books, magazines, and newspapers.** A Hip Girl's gotta have her daily fix of fun, sports, and news. Novels, business strategy books, newspapers, fashion magazines, and college texts (and of course *The Hip Girl's Handbook*) provide exactly that, and more! After all, knowledge is a powerful tool. The more well-rounded you are, the more you can bring to the table at work and school, as well as in friendships and relationships. Most importantly, you can nourish your soul. Individually, the cost of these enlightening materials doesn't seem like a whole lot of money. But like your coffee preferences, they can cramp your clothing allowance (not to mention your tuition or investment fund). Here are a few suggestions for spending less money on reading materials:

☐ The good ol' library. Even with all the wonderful technological advances in the world today for finding and reading good stuff on the Internet, there's still something to be said for our old friend, the library. New and timeless books, magazines and even videos are free to take out on loan (just make sure to get them back on time to avoid overdue charges). Plus, libraries make a great place for social engagement. Did you just move to a new neighborhood? The library can be one-stop shopping. While grabbing your reading materials, perhaps you can make a new friend in the historical aisle. This way, you'll know you have something in common, and perhaps a book club or a lifelong friendship will evolve.

☐ Buy used books and shop on-line. If you just have to have that unauthorized Brad Pitt biography or the classic *Pride and Prejudice* for yourself, why not buy it used, either at a used bookstore or on-line (search at ebay.com or by punching in key words "used" and "books")? It just may prove to be less time-consuming, plus there's something wonderful about knowing you've helped save some trees. But put your financial know-how to the test. When buying books on-line, weigh in shipping charges when comparing the cost of just buying them new in the store. Keep in mind that you'll be paying sales tax in the store but not on-line. The Internet is also a good place to try and sell your own used books (but hold onto the ones that you think you might like to have in years to come).

Used bookstores and on-line book websites are a great place to find college texts too. If you're in school, opt for books at the campus bookstore that are already dog-eared and highlighted whenever it's possible. Not only are they cheaper than buying brand spankin' new books, half your reading—and your homework—may already be done for you. (Just make sure you think the last reader had a clue about what he was reading—otherwise just use a different colored highlighter than he did.) When the bookstore is all out of the used texts, try searching on-line before buying new ones. Hop on the Internet and search with the key words "college books" or check out the Barnes & Noble (bn.com) or Varsity Books (varsitybooks.com) websites.

□   If you're taking a class, ask the instructor about cost-cutting possibilities. Sometimes one class requires two books and one workbook. Before going out to get them, try talking with the instructor to make sure you'll absolutely need all three. Don't argue if she says yes. Just explain your position. (It's a great way to break the ice with the person in charge of passing or failing you.)

□   Make a new book friend. Does the bubbly girl in class or in the cubicle next to yours look like someone you'd want to make friends with? Here's your perfect opportunity to introduce yourself. See if she wants to share or swap books and magazines, which will split your costs in half. It could be the start of a lasting friendship, and the two of you can go out on the town with the extra money you saved sharing your materials. And if you're college students, you gain notes privileges and can cover each other on days the other can't stumble out of bed for class.

◆ **Laundry.** You don't have your own washer and dryer? That's a bummer. So, whenever possible, load up your dirty clothes and haul them home or to a girlfriend's house who does (maybe you can do a couple of loads of her laundry in repayment). If you don't go home regularly and none of your closest friends have their own washing machine and dryer, laundromat, here you come. Just make sure you're washing and drying full loads to maximize your quarters! And need we say it? Avoid buying "Dry Clean Only" clothing.

◆ **Food.** Save your steak and lobster meals for dates (and pray chivalry is not dead after all). Instead of eating out, try brown bagging it. Campus food and business district cafes can be outrageously priced. Making your meals at home can stretch that dollar twice as far. And there's always good old-fashioned coupon clipping and grocery discount cards that sometimes can add up enough in savings to hire someone to clean your apartment for you.

HipTip *Keep in mind that healthy eating can be cheap eating as well. A simple meal of cooked vegetables and rice will be inexpensive to prepare, and have far fewer calories and fat than your typical fast food fare.*

◆ **Printing and copying.** Campus printers and copy machines sometimes cost ridiculous amounts. Head off campus for the cheapest deals on printing out your twenty-page paper on why guys who wear biking shorts should be arrested! See if a friend has a printer you can borrow, or check out your city library or other local copy centers.

◆ **Make your job work for you.** What else does your job offer you besides wages? While we don't suggest you abuse any of your privileges, working may offer some unofficial benefits. For instance, your office may not provide triple lattes to start your day, but the regular coffee may be free. If you work at a restaurant, a free meal during your shift may be included in your benefits. Investigate your company's policy on making copies and personal phone calls. What's your boss's take on staying after hours to make a few copies of your Armenian culture report on the office copy machine? Is your work getting rid of any extra supplies? Would they be cool with you snagging some for yourself? Who cares if their folders, spirals and pens advertise awareness of STDs? (Consider it your chance to educate your community while saving yourself money in school supplies.) It never hurts to ask (but it may hurt to *not* ask, so you better do so before assuming you have the right to use office equipment or other business property).

◆ **Be creative.** Save wherever you can. Turn long-distance love calls into romance novels by writing e-mails or letters instead. Actually start that New Year's exercise resolution: Walk instead of wasting gas. Save money on gift-giving by surprising your friend with a unique and thoughtful birthday present: How about actually scrapbooking her precious photos for her?

◆ **Borrow, trade, and buy used.** Make a pact with a girlfriend who is also trying to save money—her clothes are new to you, and vice versa. If you are the same size, agree on a clothes lending program— how many items can you borrow from each other in a week? What items are off-limits? How much notice do you need to give if you want to borrow something? What happens if one of you ruins the other's piece of clothing? While borrowing clothes can test friendships, setting some rules beforehand can cut down on annoyance and hurt feelings, and save you both a lot of money. Because truthfully, how many times does that new sweater really give you a lot of pleasure? Probably just the first few times you wear it. Enjoy it, then put it in the lending program.

Head for a consignment shop and take along the clothes neither you nor your girlfriend wants. At a consignment shop (and this is different from places like the Salvation Army, where you give your clothes away), you get paid part of the money that the shop sells your clothes for. You'll feel virtuous cleaning out your closet, knowing your clothes will get good use, while making a little cash at the same time.

If you are really desperate, you can sell other, more valuable things. But before you sell off your great-aunt's necklace, better come up with a good story if your mom asks you about it later. If you think it would really upset her if she found out, keep it in the family by selling it to your little sister.

## Investing Wisely

Rumor has it your ex just made a killing on the stock market. Your roommate is psyched about her new 401(k) plan at work. Jealous? Of course not! A Hip Girl is smarter than that. She's all about wishing the best for others while hooking herself up. Below are some basic tips, and suggestions for investing your money wisely:

◆ **Start investing as early as you can**. You now know that, ideally, a Hip Girl keeps enough money in her checking account to cover her checks and other withdrawals. If she has extra, she makes sure she has some money for emergencies in an interest-bearing checking or savings account. But a Hip Girl also knows the interest rate is low on these accounts. How can she get a better return? While she wants some "rainy day" money for emergencies kept safe in one of these accounts, she also wants to think of her future and invest some cash where she may gain a higher return. We're not talking about "investing" your spare quarters in Las Vegas slots either. We're talking about investing in the stock market, baby. Well… there and other places where you can earn a higher return on your investment than in regular, old savings and checking accounts. There's a whole world of people out there who are rockin' and rollin' with their dough—all due to their investment know-how. How about you? Do you know how to save and invest for your future, like for a home or when you retire? You're not thinking that far in advance? Why not? You could have the hottest pad amongst all your friends while they keep dumping their $$s into rent.

◆ **A little can go a long way.** Although you may feel like you barely have enough to live on (in fact, you're practically eating ramen noodles every night just to get by), finagle a way to invest even a little each month. The payoff for starting young with even a minimal investment plan is usually much greater than starting out later with a ton more money.

**Hip Tip** *We also recommend reading Suze Orman's book* THE NINE STEPS TO FINANCIAL FREEDOM: PRACTICAL AND SPIRITUAL STEPS SO YOU CAN STOP WORRYING. *Not only does it include more detailed information about managing your money, it gives great basic savings and investment advice. She also takes seriously the emotional costs of financial problems. Consider her amazing example about investing: "If you're age 45 and start putting $100 a month into an account that averages a 10 percent return, you'll have $71,880 by age 65... If you start at 25, you'll have $555,454." Of course, no one can guarantee a 10 percent return on anything, but you see her point—start when you are young and you have a much better chance of an easier retirement!*

◆ **Invest first in your retirement.** Invest your money first where you can get tax benefits from the investment. That includes in retirement plans offered by your employer (see below), and individual retirement accounts (IRAs) if you are not eligible or your company doesn't offer such plans.

◆ **Know what your job offers.** Some companies offer investment opportunities and programs to their employees, sometimes even to part-time workers. Become fast friends with your human resources department and see what employee benefits you're eligible for. Check out any retirement plans first.

◆ **401(k) plans.** Most for-profit companies that offer a retirement plan are offering what is called a 401(k) plan. This type of plan allows you to have income deducted from your paycheck and put into your retirement plan account. That amount you put in the plan is called your "contribution." You choose how your contribution is invested from among the choices offered to you under the plan. The beauty of it is that you don't pay taxes on your contribution (or on any income which comes from investing your contribution, such as interest or dividends) while the money stays in the retirement plan.

While one company's 401(k) plan may differ from another's, here are a few more details on how a 401(k) retirement fund generally works: Your company determines the maximum percentage of your wages you can contribute (usually it is anywhere from 5-15 percent). Whatever the percentage, the government puts another cap on the dollar amount you can contribute in any year (in 2002, it is $11,000). Your contribution is then taken from your paycheck *before* the "taxman" (see Uncle Sam from the *Taxes* chapter) gets any of it, and is deposited into your 401(k) account. You then choose how the dollars in your account are invested from among several investment options that the company has already selected. These investment options usually vary in risk, and may include mutual funds, bonds, or your company's stock (or, if you're lucky, those of other companies, too). The plan administrator then invests your money as you directed. You pay no taxes on this money (either on contributions or the income you make on those contributions) until you withdraw funds from your account (see more on that below). If the tax advantages of this type of plan aren't enough to tempt you, the kicker is that many companies will match your contributions to your account (that could be as much as 50 percent of your contribution, depending on your company's policy). Can you say "free money"? Now that rocks!

Does the 401(k) sound lovely? It is, unless you take out money prior to turning 59½ years of age (who knows why the half-year makes a difference). Because the tax benefits of a 401(k) were meant to encourage you to put away money for your retirement, you are punished if you take the money out earlier. After 59½ years, you can take out the money, which is when you pay tax on it, just like with a paycheck. If you take it out before then, however, you'll face a 10 percent federal tax penalty on that money, a state tax penalty (the amount depends on the state you are a resident of), and you'll pay ordinary income tax on the money. Ouch! You can say that again. OK, it's our book, so we will. Ouch! So, yep, it's probably in your best interest not to withdraw money from your 401(k) plan whenever there is an alternative. Investigate thoroughly with your human resources representative for all exceptions to these rules (and benefits).

◆ **Other company retirement plans.** A nonprofit organization, such as a university, hospital, research or charitable company, is not allowed to offer a 401(k) plan, but may offer a similar 403(b) retirement plan. Generally, this plan follows the same guidelines as the 401(k) retirement plan. Smaller companies (with one hundred or fewer employees and that meet a few other requirements) may offer a SIMPLE retirement plan, otherwise known as the Savings Incentive Match Plan for Employees. These other plans are similar to the 401(k) plan, in that there are ceilings on the amount of dollars you can contribute each year (for 403(b) plans, it is $11,000 in 2002 per year; for SIMPLE plans, it is less), and there are nasty penalties for early withdrawal. Because of the stakes involved, and because the plans differ from company to company, make sure you check with your company's benefits coordinator or human resources department for all the details on investing your funds in their retirement plan.

◆ **How much should you invest in a retirement plan?** Generally, investment counselors will tell you to invest all that you can afford in a company retirement plan, and definitely as much as the company matches (if it does). It's relatively easy (the company and the plan administrator do a whole lot of the work for you), relatively painless (after you make your choices, the money is automatically withheld from your paycheck so you aren't tempted to blow it on a new stereo), offers great tax benefits (you don't pay taxes until withdrawal in your retirement, when you're probably in a lower tax bracket), and your employer may match part of your contribution (talk about a good deal). However, if your company's retirement plan requires you to invest all or most of your contribution in its own stock, be careful. You would be putting all your retirement eggs in one basket, and if your company fails, you're not only out of a job, you've probably lost your retirement fund as well. Your retirement plan is much safer if you have several choices about where you can invest your hard-earned cash.

◆ **No retirement plan available?** Not all companies offer retirement plans (they aren't required to), and if they do, they have certain requirements for participating. You may have to work a minimum number of hours or have worked there several years before you are eligible. If you aren't working at a company that offers a retirement plan, or are not eligible for a plan, not all is lost! You can invest for your retirement in another way—through an IRA. IRA stands for Individual Retirement Account. There are two distinct kinds—the Roth IRA and the traditional IRA. Basically, with an IRA, you take part of your income and put it into an account and then decide what you want that money invested in. (It's like a fancy piggy bank that allows you to allocate your money to different investment opportunities, or different parts of the piggy bank, if you will excuse our analogy.) The big deal with IRAs is that, like 401(k) or other retirement plans, the government is trying to encourage you to put money away for retirement, and it does that by allowing you to avoid paying some taxes on your income in exchange for putting some of your money away for later. An IRA account can be opened with a bank, a credit union, or a stock brokerage firm, depending on what kinds of investments you want to make with your IRA money.

◆ **Roth IRA.** You can tell the type of IRA by the tax benefits that go along with it. With a Roth IRA, the money that you put in—your contribution—is money that you have already paid tax on. However, once deposited in the Roth IRA account, any income you make from investing that contribution is tax-free, even when you take it out of the IRA account, so long as the money earned has been in there for five years and you are at least 59½ years old (there's that weird age again). And the beauty is that you can take out your contributions (but *not* the income) at any time without taxes or penalties (as long as your contribution wasn't "rolled over" from another IRA). What's the snag you ask? See how smart you are already! Well, starting in 2002, the government only allows you to put up to $3000 into your Roth IRA account each year, and you may not be able to open a Roth IRA at all if your income is really good (a single person's eligibility starts phasing out when her income reaches $95,000).

Are there exceptions for early withdrawal of the income if you need the cash? Happily, yes, there are a couple of loopholes. You may be able to withdraw up to $10,000 of that money early to buy your first home, so long as you meet all the requirements. For instance, say you turn thirty and get the urge to buy your dream home in the Hamptons. (Okay, so Hip Girls think large and in charge. Aspirations are instrumental to living well, after all.) There are some other exceptions, too.

◆ **Traditional IRA.** These are called "traditional" because they were around before Roth IRAs (not because they have traditional values). Like the Roth IRA, the income you make off money you put into a traditional IRA is tax-free so long as it remains in the IRA, but unlike the Roth, when you take it out after age 59½ years, you pay taxes on it. However, also unlike the Roth, the contribution you make to the traditional IRA may be tax-deductible in the year you make the contribution. (It depends on the income you make and whether you are already participating in another retirement plan, such as a 401(k) plan at work.) What's the catch? Same as in a Roth IRA, the government only allows you to contribute up to $3,000 into your traditional account each year— until you turn 59½ when you have to stop contributing. And you have to start withdrawing your IRA funds (and paying tax on the withdrawals) by age 70 . . . and a half. (These contribution and withdrawal restrictions do not apply to Roth IRAs.)

What about withdrawal of any of your hard-earned cash? Well, in most cases, you can't withdraw the money prior to, you guessed it, that magical number of 59½ years of age without paying taxes and a 10 percent penalty on the amount you take out. Surprise! There are exceptions to that rule also, like for first-time home buyers. You can withdraw up to $10,000 to get the home of your dreams—or at least a cute quaint one within your means.

Okay, so those are your basic retirement plan options. There are some more, but that is enough to get you started. We know that is a lot of detail, but this is important—it's your future and well-being at stake. Aren't you worth it? So take your time and read the section as many times as you need to get a basic understanding of retirement options. Then get your questions ready—it's time to choose a financial planner or consultant. But let's take a look at something else before you meet with an advisor—what kind of investor are you?

## Investment Attitude

◆ **Know your investment personality.** There are generally three types of investors: conservative, moderate, and aggressive. Read below to discover which you are before you decide what you'll invest your money in:

☐ *Conservative.* You're not much of a gambler. In fact, when you go to Las Vegas with your girlfriends, you'd rather hang out poolside, people-watching and getting a great tan. Growth on your investment, no matter how little, is most important to you. And like your dating style, you invest your time in stock that has little risk of failure.

☐ *Moderate.* You like your cake and you want to eat it, too. In other words, you like the comfort of a steady boyfriend, but when you're out with the girls, you want to play the field a bit. When it comes to investing your money, you like the security of knowing that some of your investments will always be growing—no matter how slowly. But, you like to dabble on the wild side and play the stock market from time to time. You have a fair understanding of what the investment game is all about and would only consider selling some of your stocks and other investments for real emergencies.

☐ *Aggressive.* The stakes are high and your adrenaline is pumped. Watch out rookies, a high roller is in the house. Chances are, you're no serial monogamist. Relationships are about the thrill of the chase for you. You're a risk taker financially, too. So you lose a match every now and then. You're certain your stock will rise again.

◆ **Rule of investing.** Generally, most investment advisors will tell you that if you like the risky business of investing aggressively, do it while you're still young. This theory assumes that you're investing for the long haul, and have plenty of time to make up any money lost. (It's kind of like dating around for fun while you're young, because you have plenty of time—and lots of growing to do yourself—before getting serious with just one person.) As you get older, your investment style may become more conservative (more security may become more attractive). Your priorities will be different, and all of a sudden retirement isn't as far off as it used to be.

◆ **Know your goals.** Think about what you want to accomplish with your money. Do you want to be able to purchase a house in five years? Pay off your student loans early? Start your own business? Create a reasonable plan for retirement? Knowing what you want is the first step to getting it. Your work with an investment advisor or planner will be more effective if you can start listing what you want to accomplish when you start. Hey, that doesn't mean that your priorities won't change! But just take a little time and jot down some ideas before you go.

# The Investment Advisor Hunt

◆ **Seek out a financial advisor**. If you are participating in a retirement plan at work, or are opening up an IRA, you will likely have someone (or a group of people) who is available to answer questions about your account and the options you have for investing. But, you'll want someone else, too, who can help you start investing some of your other dough besides what you're already allocating to your retirement accounts. That person can help you look at your whole financial picture and develop a plan that meets your investment needs and goals. Think of him or her as the person who can help you get what you want in life! —or at least the dreams with monetary value.

◆ **How to find an advisor**? The best way to find a financial advisor is through word of mouth—and doing your homework. (Yes, homework will follow you even post-graduation.) See who your or your friends' parents use, or who your work colleagues trust. Give them a call, but feel free to add some others to the list, too. Talk to several, ask lots of questions, and then choose the one you trust and are most comfortable with. Also, try checking the yellow pages under "financial consultants" or log onto the Internet and punch in the key words "financial investment." Make sure you meet the person whose going to be handling your hard-earned money.

◆ **Know what to ask**. There are many different types of financial advisors out there, each with different licensing and testing requirements. (Think of it like trying to find just the right personal trainer. Either way, you're entrusting someone with two of your most precious commodities—your health and your money.) "Financial advisor" is a general term, which includes stockbrokers, registered investment advisors, accountants, certified financial planners, and insurance brokers, among others. Like most things in life, what kind of financial planner you choose will depend on what you need him or her for. Each type may provide a different service (for instance, investment advisors can only advise you about securities, while stockbrokers can buy them on your behalf). Also important to remember: Each type of financial planner may earn their money a different way (for instance, a stockbroker is usually paid by commissions on the products you buy and sell through him or her, whereas an investment advisor may charge you a flat fee).

Try meeting with a few different types of financial planners to learn more about how they can help you. (You wouldn't hire a trainer who didn't fit your "no pain, no gain" workout mentality. It's just as important to find a financial planner who fits your investing personality.) He or she may offer a free introductory meeting to help you figure out what they do and the kind of services you want.

The Securities and Exchange Commission, the federal agency which monitors the sale of securities (that's the general name for stocks, bonds and mutual funds) and those who work in the securities industry, offers a list of questions which any investor should ask a potential financial professional. Go to sec.gov/investor/pubs/invadvisors.htm for the list and a longer explanation of what you are looking for. The list includes questions about an advisor's background, how he or she makes their money, if they are restricted in the type of investments they sell you and why, and whether there are any government investigations against the advisor. The website also tells you how to check up on your candidate with the agencies that regulate him or her. We recommend you visit this site and browse around—there are a lot of free publications on the site that can help you become one investment-savvy Hip Girl!

*If you see the term Certified Financial Planner™, or CFP™ after a planner's name, it means that the financial advisor has had a certain amount of training and years of experience, has voluntarily taken (and passed) an exam administered by the Certified Financial Planner Board of Standards, and is subject to continuing education requirements and a code of ethics. According to the CFP Board's website, Certified Financial Planners are purported to be trained in a wide range of financial planning services. You may want to start your search for a financial planner with a meeting with a CFP. Check out the CFP website for more information at cfp-board. org and to find out whether someone who says they are a Certified Financial Planner really is one.*

◆ **Another bottom line.** When financial advisor shopping: Window shop until you find the one who fits all your money management requirements. Whoever you choose should make you feel comfortable, be attentive and available either via phone or for in-person meetings to discuss your financial status, and should not make you feel stupid or talk over your head. This is especially important if you don't have much experience in investing. After all, this is your money and they're making money off you!

## Investment Definitions and Terminology

A simple overview of some terms and definitions you might want to know before heading to your financial planner follows. Don't worry if you are still confused. Some things in life are a little complicated and take practice! A Hip Girl isn't afraid to ask for help if she needs it.

◆ **Bonds.** When you buy bonds, you're making a loan to the company that is selling them. Just as if you were loaning money to friends, consider carefully to whom you're willing to lend money. Bonds carry a wide range of risk and profit potential. "Junk bonds" are high risk (i.e., there's a higher chance you'll lose your money). But junk bonds pay a higher rate of interest (companies have to offer more interest in order to tempt investors to buy). Some bonds, such as U.S. government bonds, are guaranteed—the federal government guarantees that you will not lose your money. However, the interest rate on these bonds are low. Generally, the higher the risk, the higher the interest rate.

Bonds vary in "term" as well. The term is the time period before the company has to pay the loan back to you. (Think of it like when you were little and made your sister pay back the money she owed you by the next allowance pay-out.) Some are short term (90 days) and some have terms of many years. The term also has an effect on the interest rate, depending on what's happening with other interest rates in the economy. As you can see, investing in bonds can be a complicated deal. Make sure that your financial advisor explains to your satisfaction the characteristics of the bond, and the risks and benefits to you.

◆ **Diversification.** Your CD collection may include a variety of rock, rap, pop, and country music. So should your investments. Don't let all your money ride on one investment. Instead, diversify your portfolio (your collection of stocks, bonds, and other investments.) That way, if one stock "tanks," you haven't lost everything!

◆ **Inflation.** Inflation is an increase in the supply of dollars or available credit, relative to the availability of goods and services. Say what? Say you and a friend both have $50 to spend and you both desperately want the same $50 sweater (but there's only one of them left). If all of a sudden you both get handed another $25 each, guess what? You're both going to bid up the price for the sweater because you're both thinking, "I know it's going to look better on me than on you." Your competing demand for the sweater (there's still only one) just caused inflation. And inflation's end result is higher prices.

◆ **Maturity date.** No, it's not the date when guys hit their sexual peak. A maturity date is the day a bond or other loan is supposed to be paid.

◆ **Mutual funds.** Remember diversification? Safety in numbers is the bottom line in mutual funds investment. To put it simply, a mutual fund is just a collection of investments in stocks or bonds. Your investment in a mutual fund buys a piece of that collection. While your return on your investment can vary (depending on the fund and the market), you at least have spread some of your risk over investments in many companies.

Confused? Relax. This can be tough, but read it as many times as necessary to get it. Think of it like this: Would you feel safer fashion-wise (and more hip) if you had one really expensive Gucci belt? Or would a bunch of less costly Nine West belts—even that neon green one—that you could pull from for any season, outfit or fashion trend make your wardrobe the best of all your friends? While that one belt could be great, you could also be out of luck if you happen to lose it. Same with investments—one stock may be really great for a while, but if you lose it, too bad.

Remember, though, that different mutual funds also have different levels of risk. Some may be invested completely in one industry (like high tech). So if something happens to that industry, you will be affected too. There's no guarantee you won't lose money. Your risk is just more diversified. Just do your homework and pick a mutual fund that matches your investment style.

Hip Tip *If you buy mutual funds, make sure you know what fees are involved, and if there are restrictions on selling the mutual fund* shares. Some charge a hefty penalty if you sell before holding it for a certain period—sometimes many years. And again, find out how a broker makes his or her money on a sale of these securities to you!

◆ **Stocks.** When you buy stocks (also known as equities), you are buying a piece of a company. Stock prices can be very different from one another and can shift dramatically (up *and* down). You can make a lot of profit, but you also can lose your entire investment. For this reason, if you want to invest in stocks, most advisors will suggest you buy stock in several companies. That way, if one or more of them doesn't do so well—the loss is "spread out" over several stocks. This is really where you want to follow the old adage of "don't put all your eggs in one basket." You wouldn't interview for just one position and turn down all the others when you're job hunting, would you?

—————

Money…more money…less money… No matter what your story, spending money wisely isn't always easy. Now that you know the basics, seek out more specialized investment resources and read up on how to set yourself up comfortably.

# Stolen Identity:
## When Someone Else Is Having More Fun as You than You Are

"In college, someone walked into our house and stole my wallet right off the coffee table, where I'd left it sitting after a late night out. Flash forward to a couple of years later when I discovered that that very same thief stole my identity and had been living like a fat cow off of my name—and at my credit's expense. I felt violated! Getting it resolved has been one of the biggest nightmares I've ever had to face!"

—Nicole, 26

## Proactive Measures to Protect Yourself from Identity Thieves

EVER DREAM OF BEING ONE OF CHARLIE'S ANGELS—a smart, pretty, independent woman living on the edge as a crime fighter? Protecting your identity from being stolen is the perfect real-life opportunity for playing the part. Identity theft is rapidly becoming more common, and considering all the damage an identity robber can do, needs to be taken seriously. Identity thieves can get loans in your name, buy a car or home, run up your credit card and phone bills, or use your name when they get arrested (so suddenly, you have a rap sheet). Or how's this one: An identity thief opens new accounts using your name and social security number, has all the bills sent to her address, then declares bankruptcy in your name—all of which you don't find out about until you are refused a car loan? Horrible? You bet, but these are all examples of identity theft. What can you do to prevent it from happening to you? Actually, you can do a lot, although it may still happen. Unfortunately, your personal information is available in a lot of places—your personnel files at work, on every credit card or loan application you've ever filled out, as well as on school and club applications. But, here are some simple things you can do to protect yourself:

◆ **Make sure your mail—outgoing and incoming—is safe.** Sending your completed application for your very first credit card? Don't just set it out in the open where anyone can grab it. Drop it in a mailbox or take it directly to the post office. And leaving your daily mail delivery sitting in an unlocked box is an open invitation for scams. Even if you're glued to the all-day *Sex and the City* marathon, taking a break to pick up your mail from your mailbox just might save you a ton of hassle later on.

◆ **Keep track of monthly statements.** Part of being a good crime fighter is being aware and noticing any changes in normal routines. Pay attention to when you receive your bills and bank statements. (They should be as regular as your menstrual cycle.) Are you missing any of these? If so, an identity thief may have changed the address to where the account statement is sent. That way, she can rack up new charges on the bill or make withdrawals from your bank account without you noticing it—at least until you figure out you're not getting all your mail. Also, if you're not getting *any* mail, check with the post office—the thief may have filed a change of address form in your name, diverting all of your mail to her!

◆ **Request unusual passwords be put on your credit, bank, and phone accounts.** Don't use a password that your ex could guess. Instead create a unique code that you can remember off the top of your head like the name of your first pet, Kristy Fish, or your fifth grade teacher who inspired you to achieve your best.

◆ **Don't haul three credit cards with you everywhere you go.** Not only does it create too much temptation to redecorate your bedroom, it also provides too much access to your credit. Just carry one credit card so that you limit the possibility of others stealing your identity—and if it's stolen, you'll easily remember which one it was.

**Hip Tip** *List all the account information for all your credit cards and bank accounts, with phone numbers to call if cards are lost or stolen, and put that list in a safe deposit box. There are also account listing services which will hang on to this information for you. If you lose your wallet, you call the service and it cancels all your cards for you. Your bank or credit card company may provide this service to you for free or with a small charge. It doesn't mean your cards won't be stolen, but it makes your life easier if they are and you're feeling freaked out at the loss!*

◆ **Tear up or shred forms that show identifying information.** We advise keeping some information, such as bank statements, cancelled checks and credit card statements, which will help you when filing your taxes, or later if you have questions from the tax people. But anything you throw away, such as charge receipts, credit card applications, insurance forms, unused bank checks, and expired credit cards should be torn up, cut up or shredded before you put them in the garbage or recycling bin. Remember to cut through account numbers and other identifying information on the statements or cards. We don't want to make you paranoid, but if someone wants to become you, they won't be above going through your trash.

◆ **Be careful where you leave your things, even in "your" space.** Don't leave purses, wallets, or identifying information in your car or trunk. And to avoid what happened in the story at the beginning of this chapter, be cautious where you put your IDs, credit cards, and checks— even in your home. Create a routine of dropping your purse in an out-of-sight, safe place each night so that even when you get home from a late night out, you automatically put your purse in that spot. Keep your personal identity information (bills, wallets, bank statements) tucked away if a serviceperson is coming over to clean, fix, or install something (like cable or phone) in your home. We're not saying they can't be trusted, but it only takes one dishonest person to make you feel violated and your life miserable.

◆ **Be smart about who you dole your personal identification information out to** (like your social security number, birth date, mother's maiden name, credit card information, driver's license number, income information, address, etc.), especially if it's over the phone, via the Internet, or the mail. Also, investigate exactly how your information will be used and who will have access to it before you divulge it. You do have the right to refuse to give out your personal information if someone asks for it. However, if you have made the contact or know who you are dealing with, then sharing your info may be necessary to get the service you want. Loan institutions and credit card companies are just two of several places that might require your social security number before considering your request for money (and if you want that new Toyota, OK, you just might have to spill it). But make sure the company you want to do business with really needs the information—it doesn't hurt to ask.

◆ **Be especially smart about not carrying your social security card around.** It provides instant access to anything anyone could ever want to know about you. Don't keep your birth certificate or passport in your purse either (unless you are traveling).

◆ **Change your checks.** If you have your social security or driver's license number printed on your checks, have new ones printed without it (and shred the old ones). Otherwise, you're giving an identity thief plenty of information to open up any number of accounts.

◆ **Review your credit reports.** A credit report contains all your private information, including your home and work addresses, your credit accounts, how promptly you pay your bills, and whether you've been sued (whether you were or weren't found liable), or have filed for bankruptcy, and may even list any arrests. (How's that for exposing all the skeletons in your closet—at least it doesn't list all your old boyfriends!) Your credit report is what car dealers, credit card companies, and landlords request when considering you for a loan or credit card, or as a renter. Keep an identity thief from silently living on your good name by ordering a copy of your own credit reports every year from the three major credit reporting agencies. Each will cost you less than $10, and trust us, you'll get more bang for your buck than spending it on another college sweatshirt or a pedicure. You can check mistakes and discover fraud before your finances are jeopardized for life. (See the end of this chapter for the credit bureaus' phone numbers and addresses.)

◆ **Finally, take your name, address and phone number off marketing lists.** They include customer information that a company you've ordered from sells to other companies so they can send you catalogs and offers of their own. (Just go shopping at the mall instead. And pay cash whenever you can to keep more companies from adding your name to their lists.) Opt out of receiving prescreened credit card offers, which can be stolen from your mailbox or recycling bin. (Call 888-5OPTOUT or 888-567-8688.) We know it may seem like you're really roughing it, but aside from protecting your credit reputation, minimizing your credit offers will remove the temptation to sign up for more cards. To get your name off other marketing lists, contact the Experian Credit Bureau (800-407-1088) to request your name be removed from its lists (the other two credit bureaus do not offer this service) and the Direct Marketing Association (DMA) to protect your phone, e-mail, and mailing address from going to every Tom, Dick, and Bloomingdale's. (See the end of this chapter for the DMA contact information.)

## What to Do if You've Been Scammed

You work hard to be good and to build a good reputation for yourself (including volunteering, paying your bills, going to church or temple, and biting your tongue when your mother calls to snoop in your business). You're devastated that someone can come along and simply swipe away all your financial trustworthiness by stealing your identity.

You did nothing wrong, so don't be ashamed if, despite all your safety measures, your name and identity gets stolen. Instead, stand up and fight. Show the heartless criminal you're in charge of your life, and that she is not going to get away with her crime.

The Federal Trade Commission (the FTC), which is the federal government agency that collects and distributes information about identity theft, publishes a free report called "ID Theft: When Bad Things Happen to Your Good Name." We've included many of their recommended steps here, but if you're a victim, you may want to order a copy for more details. The FTC contact information is at the end of the chapter.

◆ **First, take a deep breath.** If your identity has been stolen, you're going to feel violated. Having to spend hours fixing it is going to make you feel angry and frustrated. Just know that you can do this! Get a pad of paper and pen and start keeping track of every call you make, with details of whom you talked to, what you talked about, the phone number, date, and time. The FTC created a phone log you can download from their website to use for this purpose, if you wish. For simplicity, keep copies of all correspondence you send and receive about your case in one place.

◆ **Breathing again? Immediately call the fraud departments of each of the three major credit bureaus** (see the last section of this chapter for contact information). Tell them you're the victim of identity theft. Request that a "fraud alert" be placed in your file, as well as a "victim's statement" asking that creditors call you at a specific phone number before opening new accounts or making changes on any that already exist.

◆ **While on the line with the credit bureaus, ask them for copies of your credit reports.** They are required by law to give you a free copy if you have alerted them to possible fraud. Inspect the reports carefully, checking for additional fraudulent accounts opened in your name or for any unauthorized changes and charges made to legitimate accounts.

◆ **Next, file a report with the police in the community in which you live or where the identity theft took place (if you know).** Request a copy of the report as proof to your creditors that a crime occurred. Until you receive the report, make sure you have the case file number, the name of the officer making the report or any officers working on your case, and the name and phone number of the police department.

*Don't be surprised if you get a lackluster response from law enforce-*
**HipTip** *ment. Many police departments don't know how to deal with these cases, which may not have even occurred in their jurisdiction. Unfortunately, it's up to you to clear your name.*

◆ **Then immediately call the fraud or security department of all your creditors** (including credit card, phone and utility companies, banks, and any other lenders). Tell them your dilemma and immediately close accounts that have been tampered with. (Yes, sorry, that may mean no shoe shopping until your account is cleared.) Open new accounts using new, unusual PINs and passwords.

*Get your nail polish, because you'll be waiting on the phone for a*
**HipTip** *while when calling creditors. First, you may have to go through phone trees and sit on hold for someone in the general billing department. Once you make contact, tell the person your dilemma. He or she will likely switch you to the fraud department. Once you've made contact with the right person, make sure you get his or her name and direct phone number for follow-up.*

◆ **Make sure to follow up with a letter to each of the creditors that mistakenly extended credit to someone else.** Writing a letter protects you by law according to the Fair Credit Billing Act. In the letter, include what transactions you dispute—your name and address, account number, the nature of the billing error, and the amounts and date of the error—and, if possible, provide copies of police reports, and other documents that support your complaints. (The FTC website has sample letters you can use as models.) Send the letter by certified mail and request a return receipt so you can prove when the creditor received your letter. Keep copies and detailed notes of all correspondence. Just a heads up: Each creditor will likely have an additional form for you to fill out as well. (Yes, this is time-consuming and a pain, but resolving it the right way from the beginning will be less agony in the end.) You may have to have each statement notarized. (Ask around, someone in your office might be able to do that for you, or look under "Notary Public" in the yellow pages of your local phone book.)

**Tip Tip** *A notary public is a person who is licensed to "certify" that certain documents have actually been signed by you. You sign documents in front of him or her, show your ID, and enter your signature and thumbprint in the notary public's log. You'll be required to pay a small fee.*

◆ **Follow up with a letter and all pertinent documentation to the three credit bureaus previously mentioned.** Follow the same letter-writing guidelines mentioned above in the letter to your creditors (send certified mail with a return receipt requested). Copy the credit bureaus on the letters you send to creditors.

What should you expect from the credit bureaus? When their investigation is complete, each credit bureau must send you the results of its investigation in writing and a free copy of your report if the investigation results in a change to it. If you request it, the credit bureau must send notices of corrections to your credit report to anyone who has received it in the previous six months.

◆ **Finally, file a complaint with the FTC via their identity theft hotline, mail, or e-mail.** (See contact information at the end of this chapter.)

Stealing your identity is a federal crime and carries a prison sentence of up to fifteen years, plus a fine. While the FTC doesn't actually enforce this law, it shares the information with enforcement agencies—your information may be helpful in discovering the identity thief.

We realize it's a lot of work, but following each of these steps will help you to completely resolve the issue, and allow you to get back to shopping for that great pair of faux diamond earrings you deserve as a reward for all your troubles!

## Handling Various Types of Identity Crimes

There are many ways a thief can steal your identity or get goods and services in your name. Depending on how your identity was stolen (or how you think it was stolen), you may need to take some additional steps as well.

◆ **Mail theft**. Visit your local postal inspector service office if your mail has been stolen. Check if an identity robber has filled out a change of address form and has rerouted new credit cards, bank and credit card checks and statements, prescreened credit offers, and tax information to his or her home.

Hip Tip *To find the phone and address of of the nearest postal inspector office, look in the yellow pages, check usps.gov/websites/depart/inspect, or call information.*

If it's easy to steal mail from your mailbox, consider getting a post office box or having all your important financial mail sent to you at work (if the mailroom is more secure there). You can also talk to the post office about getting a locked box at home.

◆ **Phone usage fraud**. Did your former roommate dump all her psychic friends' hotline charges on your bill? Or did an identity thief open a brand new cell phone account in your name? Call your service provider and immediately cancel the account and/or calling card. *Note: If you are having difficulty getting fraudulent phone charges removed, contact your state's Public Utility Commission or the Federal Communications Commission for long distance services at 888-CALL-FCC or fcc.gov/complaints. html.*

◆ **Check theft**. Were your checks stolen? Make sure to call your bank immediately and place a stop payment on any stolen checks. If you have overdraft protection, cancel it. Ask your bank to notify the check verification services with which it does business of the theft and to request that they notify retailers using their databases not to accept those checks. You can also contact these check verification services yourself—there are several, but here are three major ones (your bank can give you any others): Telecheck (800-710-9898), International Check (800-631-9656), and Equifax (800-437-5120). No federal law limits your financial responsibility on check fraud. However, most state laws hold your bank responsible for accepting forgery, as long as you have acted responsibly and reported the loss right away.

◆ **ATM/debit cards and electronic transfers fraud**. Call your bank immediately to report any mysterious electronic transfers from your account or if your ATM/debit or check card has been stolen. Follow it up with a certified letter, return receipt requested. How quickly you notify the bank limits your financial responsibility. Federal law states that if you report it within two business days from when you discover your card missing, your losses are limited to $50. After two business days and up to sixty business days, you can be liable for as much as $500 of what a thief transfers or withdraws. Waiting until after sixty days could leave you accountable for loss of the entire amount. After notifying your financial institution about an error on your statement, they can take as much as forty-five days to investigate. In the meantime, close your old account and open up a brand new one with an entirely different PIN number.

◆ **Credit card rip-off**. The Fair Credit Billing Act was a law passed to set up procedures in getting billing errors resolved and usually limits your liability to $50 for unauthorized credit card charges. If someone has stolen your card or is making unauthorized charges on it, call the credit card company and the three credit bureaus listed at the end of this chapter. Again, follow up with a letter of proof to all of them, including all the same information as discussed under "What to Do If You've Been Scammed." You should send your letter to the "billing inquiries" address listed on your bill. (Don't send it to the address where you send your payments.)

**Hip Tip** *If you've discovered credit card fraud or any kind of mistake on your credit card statement, your letter about it to the creditor has to reach the creditor within sixty days after you received the first bill containing the error. The creditor is required by law to acknowledge your complaint in writing within thirty days after receiving it, unless the problem has already been resolved. The creditor must then have your complaint resolved within ninety days of receiving your letter.*

◆ **Social security fraud**. Have you been dying to open an account at Marshall Fields or Macy's department store, but have been valiantly resisting? Brave girl! Think how you'll feel when you find out someone using your social security number has opened one in your name for you (and to top it off, you are in debt for her great home accessories and furnishings). Report a social security thief to the Social Security Administration (SSA) fraud hotline at 800-269-0271. Or what if a criminal is using your social security number to hide her identity while she applies for a job? Call SSA at 800-772-1213 to request a copy of your social security statement so you can verify its accuracy on the jobs you've actually held and what you've earned.

*If your social security number or card has been stolen, the government does not suggest getting a new social security number as it may cause even more problems, especially considering that you lose any good credit history you've already built up. The bad news here is that, if someone has your social security number, she has probably opened many more than one account. Get on the phone to the credit bureaus and get your reports right away.*

◆ **Bankruptcy scammer**. So broke that you can't imagine anyone wanting to use you as a financial haven? Think again. Even the poorest of college students make perfect targets for bankruptcy robbers. Thieves can rack up all kinds of loans and bills in your name and then file bankruptcy in your name as well (all without you realizing it). So before you've even scored your first big career break, you've already got a bad credit history staring you in the face. If you suspect someone has filed for bankruptcy using your name and social security number, write the U.S. Trustee in the region you think the crime took place. Log onto usdoj.gov/ust or check the blue pages of the telephone book under U.S. Government—Bankruptcy Administration.

◆ **False rap sheet**. You may have had your share of speeding and parking tickets, but you swear that's the extent of your criminal offenses (except that itty, bitty TPing arrest). Sometimes an imposter might give your name when being arrested. So if your boyfriend has a psychotic ex, don't be surprised if sometime you find out there's a warrant out for your arrest. If you've got a rap sheet that doesn't belong to you, unfortunately you might have to hire an attorney to clear up the mess. The important thing is to take immediate action if you find you are in this situation.

## Contact Information

◆ **Credit Bureau Information**

*Note: If you are reporting fraud, call* and *write to each credit bureau.*

☐ **Equifax** (equifax.com)

To order your report:

*Call:* 800-685-1111

*Write:* P.O. Box 740241
Atlanta, GA 30374-0241

To report fraud:

*Call:* 800-525-6285

*Write:* P.O. Box 740241
Atlanta, GA 30374-0241

☐ **Experian** (experian.com)

To order your report:

*Call:* 888-EXPERIAN (397-3742)

*Write:* P.O. Box 2104
Allen, TX 75013

To report fraud:

*Call:* 888-EXPERIAN (397-3742)

*Write:* P.O. Box 9532
Allen, TX 75013

☐ **Trans Union** (TUC.com)

To order your report:

*Call:* 800-916-8800

*Write:* P.O. Box 1000
Chester, PA 19022

To report fraud:

Call: 800-680-7289

Write: Fraud Victim Assistance Division
P.O. Box 6790
Fullerton, CA 92634

## ◆ Direct Marketing Association

- □ To remove your name from national mailing lists:

Write: Direct Marketing Association
P.O. Box 9008
Farmingdale, NY 11735-9014

- □ To remove your e-mail address from Internet marketing lists:

Visit: e-mps.org

- □ To stop unwanted phone solicitors, send your name, address, and phone number to:

DMA Telephone Preference Service
P.O. Box 9014
Farmingdale, NY 11735-9014

## ◆ Federal Trade Commission

Call: 877-IDTHEFT (438-4338)

Write: Identity Theft Clearinghouse
Federal Trade Commission
600 Pennsylvania Avenue, NW
Washington, DC 20580

Visit: consumer.gov/idtheft

We know this whole process is somewhat infuriating, but protecting your good name is important. Show you won't be a victim. Stand up for your rights and don't budge from your convictions!

# Taxes:

## Say Hello to Your Uncle Sam

—◦◦◦—

*"I had a crazy boss at my first job out of school and jumped at a new job when it came along. At the end of the year, I'd forgotten about my first little stint and filed my taxes without a W-2 form from that company. Big mistake! An even bigger hassle ensued when the government wouldn't give me my refund check until I amended my taxes. Let me tell you, reading the instructions for the amendment process was like reading a foreign language. Thankfully my brother-in-law knew what to do!"*

—Mary, 25

### Maneuvering through Tax Season Mania

TAXES ARE NEVER ANYONE'S FAVORITE TOPIC (unless you're an accountant, that is). Feeling overwhelmed, frustrated, or ill every time tax season comes around is a normal reaction—not unlike your feelings when you PMS each cycle. At least tax time is just once a year! Once you understand better how taxes work, however, filing your taxes can become a manageable stress.

# Quick-Fix Tax Questions

Basically, when you file tax returns, you are submitting a form to the federal government and, depending on where you live, the state and local government as well. These tax forms lay out your income and help you calculate any tax you owe for the prior year or $$ you get in return. The "prior year" is the calendar year (January 1 to December 31) that has most recently ended. We are talking about federal requirements in this chapter, but many of the same rules apply to state forms. Check with your state government. Here are a few things to get you started:

◆ **Are you required to file taxes?** Generally speaking, as of 2001, if you are single, made $750 or more in a year and your parents claim you as a dependent, congratulations! You probably have to file a tax return with Uncle Sam (he's an old friend of the family that you're going to get to know really well). The same is true if Mom and Dad aren't claiming you as a dependent, but you made $7,450 or more in a year. If you do not meet either of these standards, you'd still better check with the Internal Revenue Service (IRS) or a tax professional, as there are some situations which may require you to file a return anyway.

HipTip *The IRS is the federal agency which handles collecting taxes and processing tax returns. You can call an IRS representative at 800-829-1040 with tax questions. They won't interpret the tax laws for you, but they will tell you what they are.*

If not—skip this chapter for another year, and spend your spare time partying with your friends!

◆ **How do parents factor into your tax equation?** Before you file your taxes, check with your parents to see if they're claiming you on their own tax return as a dependent. They probably are if you're a student under twenty-four years of age, and they're funding your education and living expenses (even though they may not be funding your social activities). If they claim you as a dependent, they pay less tax. You didn't know you were a tax break, did you? Proceed with caution: If your parents claim you as a dependent and you file as an independent, this discrepancy could cause the government to investigate both your and your parents' tax returns. It's likely one of you will end up paying a penalty and interest on any taxes that weren't paid because of the mess-up.

◆ **Who do you owe a tax return to?** Plain and simple, the federal and state government. Don't just file one or the other: you need to file both. That is, unless you live in one of the states with no state income tax.

*HipTip*   *These states don't have personal income tax: Alaska, Florida, Nevada, South Dakota, Texas, Washington, and Wyoming.*

You may also be one of the unlucky people who is required to file a local tax return (county or city). You can call the finance or treasury department of the city, county, and state where you live to find out. You can also simply call a local tax service like H&R Block (listed in the yellow pages) and ask to speak to an agent. Of course, that means $$s.

◆ **When do you file?** April 15th! We'll explain: You file a tax return by April 15th of every year for the tax year which ended on the December 31st preceding it. Say what? If you have to file a tax return for the year 2002, you must do so by April 15, 2003. Sounds like a long time, right? Time flies. Don't procrastinate like you might on your Geology thesis or business proposal. Get started early. If you're running late, you can file for an extension to file your tax return until August 15th, but you're still required to pay the amount of tax you think you owe by April 15th. If you later find you underestimated by more than 10 percent, you pay a penalty. Oy! Save yourself the hassle: Just get your taxes done by the April 15th deadline!

◆ **Where do I find the tax forms?** You may receive your forms in the mail. However, if you haven't filed tax returns before or changed addresses since you last filed, those forms may not make it to you. Not a problem—there are tons of places to find forms. You can find them in IRS offices and often in your local post office or bank. For federal forms and publications that help explain them, you can also download directly off the Internet by going to irs.gov and selecting "Forms and Pubs." To find your state tax forms and information, search using your state's name and "tax." If you are hiring a tax preparer, they will have forms to use.

◆ **How can you get your tax refund quickly (if you're getting one)?** One of the greatest gifts of technology is the ability to get our tax refund more quickly (that and researching your history paper or job classifieds with bed head and last night's makeup still on). Electronic filing is quick, painless, and lets you get your money much faster (that is, if you played your cards right all year and are getting a refund) than filing the old-fashioned way (through snail mail). Check out the "Tax Filing Options" section later in this chapter for ways to submit your taxes electronically, or to actually calculate them on-line.

## Prepping for Your Tax-Filing Experience

Before you decide how you'll file, arm yourself, and if you're using one, your tax preparer, with all the information needed to get as much money back from the government as possible. Basically, the tax form is to help you calculate how much money you owe (or what the government owes you). With a Form 1040, here's how it works: You add up all your income, and make adjustments to the income as directed by the tax rules, to reach your "adjusted gross income." From your adjusted gross income, you deduct certain expenses (which the tax rules say are deductible), to reach your "taxable income." You calculate the tax owed on that amount. If you qualify for a "credit," then you can deduct, dollar for dollar, the amount of the credit from the tax you owe.

Phew! Complicated, isn't it? Don't worry, you'll get the hang of it after doing it a couple of times. Let's go over this again, along with the kind of information that you'll need to gather up for filling out your tax return. Some of the documents and information listed below may or may not apply to you. Either way, don't sweat it! Just dig up those that are applicable.

◆ **Income.** Gather all the forms or other proof showing how much money was paid to you during the year. While this is not an exhaustive list, some common types of income you must include are:

  □   Wages from work. Your employer should have sent you a form called a W-2, which is a statement of wages earned, and shows how much tax was already paid to the government. Look over your W-2 when you get it to make sure that the information is correct. Your employer also sends a copy of the W-2 to the government when it sends it out to you, so if the information is wrong, you may end up paying more or less tax than you should. If the W-2 is incorrect, take it to your employer right away and straighten it out.

Hip Tip   *Make sure to collect all W-2 forms from multiple employers before filing to avoid a major hassle with the IRS.*

Your employer must send these forms out by January 31st, so if you haven't received them by mid-February, give them a call. If they are willing, they can even just fax or e-mail you a copy for speedy processing purposes until you get the originals in the mail. Keep in mind, however, you should file original W-2s with your tax return.

□ Tips. Did your girl-next-door charm help you rake in a bundle as this summer's most likeable golf course beverage-cart driver? Also include income records from odd jobs (like tutoring, writing, or baby-sitting)—your "records" may simply be copies of the checks you received.

□ "1099" income. So called because it's reported to you on different types of Form 1099.

□ Interest. This may be earned from bank accounts or elsewhere. (Girl, way to get the biggest bang for your buck!) The bank will let you know how much this is on a "Form 1099-INT." The first bank statement you receive after the first of the year may also be the Form 1099-INT, so check it out.

□ Dividends. Basically a dividend is a portion of a company's profits that is distributed to its owners, or shareholders. (Confused? We were too. But unless you've already invested in stocks or mutual funds, don't sweat it. Skip it and go to the investment section of the *Show Me the Money* chapter to get started.) If you're ahead of the game and invested in the stock market, any dividends you have earned from your stock is considered taxable income. Your financial adviser, stockbroker, or the companies they work with will tell you this amount too—on Form 1099-DIV.

□ Rent, royalties, or partnerships. If you already have income from any of these, you rock! You're off to a great financial start. This income amount will come to you from whoever paid it to you—on Form 1099-MISC. This form would also show payment or any special, one-time projects you were paid for, such as painting your neighbor's house. Other information you'll need:

☐ Short-term or long-term taxable gains or losses. (Toss this phrase out at a few parties and see how many people you can confuse—or impress!) This is any money you may have gained or lost from selling stocks, bonds, mutual funds or other securities within a twelve-month (short-term) period of purchasing them, or when they were sold after holding them for more than twelve months (long-term).

☐ State or local tax refunds from the prior year.

☐ Any other income from any source. This can be alimony received, disability, pension, or social security income (some of which is taxable, and some of which isn't).

☐ Business income or loss from any business you own. See also under "Deductions" below.

All of that information will help you calculate your income. The next step is figuring your adjustments.

◆ **Adjustments.** These are items which the IRS treats as a subtraction from your income. They include, among others, such things as IRA, 401(k), or other tax-deferred retirement plan contributions. (See the *Show Me the Money* chapter for more about retirement plans.) Adjustments may also include student loan interest, scholarships and grants, and alimony payments. Your income, plus or minus the adjustments which apply to you, equals your adjusted gross income.

◆ **Deductions.** Deductions are items which the IRS allows you to deduct from your adjusted gross income. The "standard" deduction for a single person is $4,550, which means you can deduct that number from your adjusted gross income without any calculations or receipts to prove the deduction. Total your "itemized" deductions, which are particular deductions you need backup for, such as the interest you paid on your mortgage or your charitable contribution you made to VH1's Save the Music initiative. Are your itemized deductions, all added up, more than the standard $4,550 deduction? If so, then claim your itemized total. If it's less, than opt for the standard deduction instead. Check with your tax preparer or your tax return form for a complete list of possible deductions, but here are a few to consider:

☐ Medical expenses. Did you get hurt snowboarding? Yikes. If your medical bills are high enough compared to your income, you may be able to deduct them.

☐ Mortgage payments on your home. Do you own your own condo? You're a rock star! A mortgage payment deduction equals the amount of interest you pay on a loan, and the fee, or "points," a lender may charge you for the original loan (otherwise known as an origination fee) or to refinance an existing loan.

☐ Charitable contributions. A Hip Girl gives back to her community—if not with time, then with money. Just be sure your contributions are to organizations which the IRS recognizes as eligible for tax-deductible donations. Non-cash contributions count, too.

☐ Business expenses. Own a side business like making jewelry or typing term papers? Right on with your fierce initiative. You might be able to file as self-employed and deduct your business expenses. Your taxes can get more complicated when you have a business on the side—we strongly recommend you get some tax advice before deducting any of these expenses. But go ahead and save all those dinner receipts with potential clients; discussing your business proposal over a glass of wine might be a write-off on your taxes!

Once you've figured out your deductions, you subtract the total from your adjusted gross income. The result is your taxable income, which you multiply by the tax rate that applies to you. (Read this again

if you didn't quite get it the first time around. We didn't, but if you did, then rock on!) But wait! You may get a credit against that amount:

◆ **Credits.** A credit is basically the government's way of encouraging or easing a life situation like raising children or getting an education. There are lots more, but here are a few to look out for:

☐ Dependent care credit (child care). Sorry, taking care of your mooching roommate doesn't count!

☐ Student credits. (See "Student-Specific Tax Information" later in this chapter.)

☐ Environment friendly credits (for using clean fuel or solar energy . . . way to think about your future!).

☐ Other credits. Your tax preparer should be well read on other federal or state-specific credits. (Or take the power into your own hands and read up for yourself.) You might be surprised at how much you can save (and later spend on an apartment of your own with no more mooching roommate). For instance, some states offer renter's credit, which can work in your favor when computing your state taxes. Read the instructions carefully, however, as there are always restrictions.

## Tax Filing Options

What? Please! The most you may have ever cared about taxes in the past is how much extra money is tacked onto your purchases at your favorite clothing store. Really, balancing your checkbook is about all you can bear, so why on earth would you want to even try to comprehend the whole federal and state tax system? But from one Hip Girl to another, and take it from us—beefing up on how the tax process works may help save you money in the long run—even if you use a tax preparer. Having a general idea of how the system works will allow you to identify more deductions, or "write-offs," for hopes of a fat refund. It will also help you identify tax write-offs all year long, and hopefully increase your refund at tax time. So get with the program. Read below about the different routes you can take in filing your taxes:

◆ **Good ol' Mom and Dad.** If your parents are claiming you as a dependent, they may want to file your tax return for you. If so, let them; but hang tight with them while they do, and let them show you how the pros do it. It's your parents way of showing they love you, and you wouldn't want to hurt their feelings, would you? Besides, it's a great way to pick up some key tools for when you have to file taxes for yourself.

◆ **On the Internet, by a tax professional.** In today's technology age, figuring out your tax situation can be pretty simple—too bad the same can't be said for the rules of dating! When you choose to use a professional tax filing service on the Internet, all you do is organize your information, answer some simple questions, and poof! Tax professionals take care of the rest for you. Advice and tips about how to work your mojo with the new tax laws are usually also included on any professional tax filing website and via chat rooms. Most professional tax services on the Internet charge a low fee, but the convenience and peace of mind that comes with professional help can be worth it. Log on to the Internet and search for key words such as "taxes" or "tax preparation." Just make sure you use a site that's credible—remember that you're giving them all your personal information (including your social security number) and we've seen in the *Stolen Identity* chapter what can happen if the wrong person gets hold of that! Check the yellow pages for tax preparation businesses you recognize or with your local Better Business Bureau, and see if those recommended are among the websites available to you.

◆ **Do-it-yourself on the Internet.** Up for a little challenge? We say go with your bad self! And once you've learned how to do it, teach it to all your girlfriends! For as little as $20, all you do is answer simple questions and the on-line tax program calculates the rest for you. Some sites offer access to live professional help (an additional fee might apply) and electronic filing (for a faster refund) at little or no additional charge. Best of all, besides the comfort of filing your taxes in your pajamas, you can do them in your own time, at your own speed. (Wouldn't it be nice if professors offered test-taking like this?) Just follow the simple steps from beginning to end and watch it magically compute everything for you. Log on and search "taxes" or "tax preparation" for the right site for you. Just make sure it's accredited and one you trust. (Check with the IRS or the Certified Public Accountant (CPA) Society, which can be found by logging onto the Internet or by calling telephone directory assistance for a toll-free number.) Here again, you don't want to send off your social security number and other financial information to an identity scam artist! If you really want to go to the source, you can go directly to the IRS website to fill out your tax return on-line (irs.org).

◆ **Take-charge techie.** Are you a computer whiz? Consider purchasing your own tax software to calculate your taxes. (You can purchase it for as little as $30.) The software can be sent to you by snail mail, you can download it from a credible tax website, or you can purchase it in a computer or business supply store.

*TurboTax and Kiplinger Tax Cut are both highly-regarded tax preparation software. They each provide federal and state forms and will file electronically for free.*

Often, customer service is available for a low additional cost. *Note: Electronic filing requires a credit card for payment and Internet access capability.*

◆ **Pay a visit to your tax woman.** Sometimes the comfort of working with a human is worth the extra money required for hiring a professional to compute and file your taxes for you, especially if you are a tax-filing virgin. While it can be more time-consuming, you can learn a lot, and the face-to-face time and exchange of money-saving ideas just may be what you desire. Get referrals and estimates. If you have a fairly simple return, you may want to try one of the national tax preparation chains, such as H&R Block. If your tax situation is more complicated— you've gotten married, divorced, had kids, bought property, or started a new business—make sure the person you select is accredited by the IRS as an "enrolled agent" or is a CPA (CPAs have had to pass some very difficult exams). The CPA Society website or the Department of Consumer Affairs in your area should be able to tell you if your accountant is licensed as a CPA.

*An enrolled agent is subject to a background check and must take a tough exam—both administered by the IRS. Check out their website: naea.org.*

◆ **Do-it-yourself old school style**. No computer access or you've decided you'd rather have that new purse than pay to have your taxes done? No problem. A girl does have her priorities to worry about after all. After you have gathered all your tax materials, your next step is to hunt down federal and state tax forms. The federal tax form that you use is a variation of the Form 1040: 1040EZ, 1040A, and the 1040 (with, you guessed it, the 1040EZ being the "easiest," the 1040A being slightly more detailed, and the 1040 being the most complicated).

The 1040EZ is usually sufficient for college students living off free food samples at Costco or Sam's Club. Why would you ever use the more complicated forms? Two reasons. One, you may *have* to. Generally, if you earn more than $50,000 in any year, you cannot use the 1040EZ or the 1040A. Two, you may be able to pay less tax by using the more complicated form, which allows you to itemize deductions rather than take a standardized deduction (which you must do with a 1040EZ). The requirements for each form are contained in the instructions that come with it.

**Tip Tip** *If you are eligible to use more than one return, you may want to "try out" each one to see which one you end up paying less tax under.*

Simply follow the directions right on the tax forms. Finally, treat yourself to a night out—you deserve it! Hopefully you'll be getting enough money back from the government to pay for it.

## Student-Specific Tax Information

The information below is meant to give you more background knowledge (not a headache) when asking your tax preparer about tax-saving options that might apply to your situation. Don't let it overwhelm you. There is no worry about a pop quiz at the end of this section. It's merely meant for your information.

◆ **The Hope Credit**. The Hope Credit (hope all you want, but it's not a free college credit for hoping you'll pass your Anatomy exam) is to help students pay for the first two years of college. That means you can only get the Hope Credit twice in your life—your freshman and sophomore years of a four-year school or for a two-year junior college program—and no, they don't have to be consecutive years. The credit covers up to $1,500 credit per student. Remember it's a credit, not a deduction, so the whole amount is taken against your total tax bill. And make sure your parents aren't claiming you, because they get the credit if that's so. Your eligibility for this credit "phases out" after you start earning $40,000. Here is a list of qualifications for the Hope Credit:

☐ You must be enrolled in a program that leads to a degree, a certificate, or some other recognized educational credential. (Sorry, just taking that bowling credit won't cut it.)

☐ You must be at least a half-time student for at least a semester, quarter, or other academic period beginning in the year.

☐ You must not have any felony drug convictions.

◆ **The Lifetime Learning Credit.** The Lifetime Learning Credit involves less money than the Hope Credit, but has fewer restrictions. This credit is for up to $1,000 for post-secondary education (as of 2003 that amount can be up to $2,000). OK, what does that mean exactly? Simply, you can get a tax credit for continuing your education every year. But hold up. Before you start spending that refund, note that once your yearly income increases to $40,000, you may no longer be eligible to receive the credit (or all of it anyway). Here are the benefits of the Lifetime Learning Credit:

☐ It covers any courses you take (including scuba diving) so long as it's part of an undergraduate or professional degree program, or is taken to acquire or improve your job skills.

□   Take the credit as many years as you like because it has no limitations on the number of times a person can claim it.

◆ **Student loan interest adjustment.** You can subtract from your income any interest, of up to $2,500 per year, that you paid on a student loan in the tax year. As you make more money (let's hope your acting career pans out), the adjustment decreases and starts being eliminated once you make $40,000 ($50,000 starting in tax year 2002).

◆ **Scholarships.** Surprise! That free money might not be exactly free. It may be taxable, even if you don't receive a W-2 form for it. As a general rule, the entire scholarship is taxable if you aren't earning a degree (which is reason enough to get a higher education). However, if you are earning a degree, certain costs covered by your scholarship can be excluded from your scholarship income:

□   Tuition and fees for enrollment or attendance.

□   Fees, books, supplies, and equipment required for courses.

That leaves any money you received for room, board, transportation, or the performance of services as income.

◆ **Employer education assistance benefits and tax deduction.** Are you working full-time to put yourself through night school? Hopefully your employer is helping to support your educational goal! If you get educational assistance benefits from your employer, currently, up to $5,250 of that is tax-free. Restrictions? Of course, aren't there always?

□   Legitimate coursework. While a degree in frisbee-golf isn't going to cut it (sports, games, and hobbies have to be reasonably related to your employer's business or be required as part of a degree program), classes don't have to be job-related (although your employer may require it to be in order for you to qualify for its company-paid education assistance).

□   In the past, the courses had to be undergraduate level. Expenses relating to graduate courses starting in 2002 are now eligible for this exclusion from income.

□   Your employer must have a written education assistance plan and meet certain other requirements in order for you to qualify.

□   Educational assistance covers payments for tuition, fees, books, and equipment. Deductions do not include educational assistance expenses for meals, rent, transportation, tools, or supplies (other than textbooks) that you keep after finishing the course (yes, that means you get to keep that human sexuality textbook).

□   If your employer pays more than $5,250, the extra amount is taxable and will be included on your W-2.

◆ **Grants.** Not Hugh Grant! Ha-ha! A grant is funding provided by the government or other source and given to an individual or group for various reasons, such as supporting research efforts in a certain field or promoting the arts. Generally, individual grants are for people with special talents or interests (like that genius that sat alone in the back row of your science class, and is now a Nobel Prize recipient), or students who have few financial resources. Depending on the type of grant you have, it may or may not be taxable. The payer of the grant will usually provide you with a W-2 or a Form 1099 showing what is taxable. If it doesn't, this would be a good time to hire a tax preparer.

—◄▓▓◊▓▓►—

Uncle Sam's the man…for good or bad. Educate yourself on all the tax laws that might apply to you and help you get money back. (Oh, and don't forget to share your Hip Tips with a friend.)

# Owning your Hipness

A S YOU CAN SEE, YOU DON'T WALK ALONE on your path of struggles and triumphs to independence. It's a journey paved by many other women who unknowingly built strength, courage, and character by braving the obstacles set before them. Embrace your own dilemmas along the way. Soon, there won't be anything in life you can't handle.

But why stop with home, car, & money stuff? Amplify your tenacity and go-get-it spirit to all you do! Then watch in amazement how far it will take you. After all, a woman who is self-sufficient exudes a special aura. It's in all that she does: her walk, her talk, and just the way she carries herself. Take a look around—we bet you can spot it in other women yourself. Your sister, mom, friend, boss, or even a total stranger may be able to walk into a room and command respect without uttering a word. Employers, family members, and even friends often count on her "in-control" and calm demeanor to take charge of a crisis situation.

Our guy friends tell us most men can sense this confidence in women right away, too. Among other qualities, a guy is often drawn to a girl possessing a little gumption and initiative. If he isn't, chances are he's not worthy of you.

But every Hip Girl knows it's nice to be pampered every now and then. So let a date practice a little chivalry instead. After all, there's a huge difference between knowing how to change a tire while allowing your date to do the dirty work, and helplessly relying on him to take care of you. By the way, don't discount the chance that your guy won't know what to do. Perhaps he will even have to rely on you!

# Bibliography

## Household Hijinks

Davidson, Tom, and Lorna Gentry. *The Complete Idiot's Guide to Home Security.* Indianapolis, IN: Alpha Books, 2001.

Gookin, Dan and Sandra Hardin. *PCs for Dummies: Quick References.* New York: Hungry Minds, Inc., 2000.

Lagatree, Kirsten M. *Checklists for Life: 104 Lists to Help You Get Organized, Save Time, and Unclutter Your Life.* New York: Random House, 2001.

Raichlen, Steve. *The Barbecue! Bible.* New York: Workman Publishing, 1998.

Reader's Digest. *Ask the Family Handyman.* Edited by Julie Trelstad. Pleasantville, NY: Reader's Digest, 1999.

Werner, Kitty. *The Savvy Woman's Guide to Owning a Home.* Waitsfield, VT: RSB Press, 2002.

Worthington, Diane. *The California Cook.* New York: Bantam Books, 1993.

Al's Home Improvement Center website; www.alsnetbiz.com/homeimprovement/htseries/drains.html.

Apartment Living and Rental website; www.apartments.about.com.

Association for Women in Computing website; www.awc-hq.org/livewire/199608.html.

*Barbecue'n On The Internet* website; www.barbecuen.com.

Better Homes and Gardens website; www.bhg.com

California Energy Commission website: www.energy.ca.gov.

Chicago Software Association website; www.csa.org.

DoItYourself.com website; http://doityourself.com.

Edmonds website; www.edmonds.com.

homestore.com™ website; homestore.com.

homestore.com™ website; imove.com.

iVillage website; www.iVillage.com.

National Crime Prevention Council website; www.ncpc.org.

National Safety Council website; www.nsc.org.

Orange County REMC website; www.orangecountyremc.org.

Realty Times website; www.realtytimes.com

Repair Clinic.com website; RepairClinic.com.

roommatelocator.com website; www.roommatelocator.com.

Roto-Rooter website; www.plumber.com.

Soyouwanna.com website;
www.soyouwanna.com/site/syws/bbq/bbq.html.

The Princeton Review, Inc. "Choosing a Computer that is Right for You."
The Embark website;
www.embark.com/articles/getready/Choosing_Computer_Ugrad.asp.

The Princeton Review, Inc. "The Basics of Laptop vs. Desktop." The Embark
website; www.embark.com/articles/getready/Laptops_Vs_Desktops.asp.

tipsofallsorts.com website; www.tipsofallsorts.com.

theplumber.com website; www.theplumber.com.

Watermolen, Eric. "Buying a Personal Computer System";
http://cogsci.used.edu/~batali/pcbuy.html.

United States Environmental Protection Agency website; www.epa.gov.

University of Cincinnati website;
www.uc.edu/gradfamily housing/look.htm.

## Automotive Antics

Howell, Donna. *The Unofficial Guide to Buying or Leasing a Car.*
New York: MacMillan General Reference, 1998.

Jackson, Mary. *Car Smarts: An Easy-to-Use Guide To Understanding Your Car &
Communicating With Your Mechanic.* Santa Fe, NM: John Muir Publications,
1998.

Leon, Burke and Stephanie. *The Insider's Guide to Buying a New or Used Car.*
Cincinnati, OH: F&W Publications Inc., 2000.

Ross, James R. *How to Buy a Car.* New York: St. Martin's Press, 2001.

Volpe, Ren. The Lady Mechanic's Total Car Care for the Clueless:
A Manual for Car Owners. New York: St. Martin's Griffin, 1998.

American Automobile Association website; www.aaa.com.

Auto.com website; www.auto.com.

AutoEducation.com website; www.autoeducation.com.

Automobile Club of Southern California website; www.aaa-calif.com.

California Department of Motor Vehicles 2001 brochures.

ConsumerReports.org website; www.consumerreports.org.
Department of Motor Vehicles website; www.dmv.ca.gov.
Free Advice website; www.accident-law.freeadvice.com.
Free Travel Tips.com website;
   www.freetraveltips.com/RoadTrip/Road01.htm.
HerAuto.com website; www.herauto.com.
Insurance Information Institute website; www.iii.org.
Learn2website; www.learn2.com.
List Organizer website; www.listorganizer.com/emergauto1.htm.
Mindconnection website; www.mindconnection.com/library/auto/
   emergencykit.htm.
Motorist Assurance Program (in collaboration with Car Care Council)
   website; www.motorist.org/e1.htm.
North Carolina Department of Transportation, Division of Motor Vehicles
   website; www.dmv.dot.state.nc.us.
Samarin's.com website; samarins.com.
State Farm Insurance website; www.statefarm.com.
Sympatico.com website; www.sympatico.ca.
Woman Motorist website; www.womanmotorist.com.

## Financial Fun

Anthony, Jason and Karl Cluck. 2000. *Debt Free by 30: Practical Advice for
   Young, Broke, & Upwardly Mobile*. New York: Dutton/Plume, 2000.
Johnson, Anna. *Three Black Skirts: All You Need to Survive*. New York:
   Workman Publishing, 2000.
Orman, Suze. *The 9 Steps to Financial Freedom: Practical and Spiritual Steps So
   You Can Stop Worrying*. New York: Crown Books, 2000.
Edward Jones Investment 2001 brochures
Viacom Employee Benefits 2001 brochures.
Aboutchecking.com website; www.aboutchecking.com.
Bank Branch online website; www.bankbranchonline.com.
Bankrate.com website; www.bankrate.com.
Certified Financial Planner Board of Standards website; www.cfp-
   board.org/cons_wysc.html.

CNN Money website; http://money.cnn.com

DeGregori, Gormsen & Ringer, LLP website; www.dgr-cpas.com.

Edgar Snyder & Associates website; www.edgarsnyder.com.

Excite.com website; www.excite.com.

Federal Reserve Bank of Atlanta website; www.frbatlanta.org.

Federal Trade Commission website; www.consumer.gov/idtheft.

Franchise Tax Board website; www.ftb.ca.gov

GovSpot of the StartSpot website; www.govspot.com.

H&R Block website; www.HRBlock.com.

insure.com website; www.insure.com.

Internal Revenue Service Department of the Treasury website;
    www.irs.ustreas.gov.

MasterCard website; www.mastercard.com.

National Association of Student Financial Aid Administrators website;
    www.NASFAA.org.

Northwest Networks website; www.nwnetworks.com/sands.htm.

Stolen-Identity.com website; www.stolen-identity.com.

StudentCredit.com website; www.studentcredit.com.

Tax Planet®.com website; www.taxplanet.com

The Internal Revenue Service Department of the Treasury website;
    www.irs.gov.

U.S. Department of Education, Office of Postsecondary Education website;
    www.ed.gov/inits/hope.

U.S. Federal Trade Commission website; www.ftc.gov.

U.S. Federal Trade Commission website; www.ftc.gov. ID Theft. Pamphlet,
    February 2000.

Washington Mutual® website;
    www.wamu.com/servlet/wamu/online/eng/pages/terms.html.

Woman's Institute for Financial Education website; www.wife.org.

Washington Mutual, Inc® website; www.washingtonmutual.com.

# More Wildcat Canyon Press Titles

**girlfriends get together: Food, Frolic and Fun Times!**
The ultimate party planner from the best-selling authors of the *girlfriends*
series. Includes fabulous recipes and theme party ideas.

CARMEN RENEE BERRY, TAMARA TRAEDER, AND JANET HAZEN
$19.95 Paper over boards

**girlfriends: Invisible Bonds, Enduring Ties**
Filled with true stories of ordinary women and extraordinary friendships,
*girlfriends* has become a gift of love among women everywhere.

CARMEN RENEE BERRY AND TAMARA TRAEDER
$12.95 Paperback

**The girlfriends Keepsake Book: The Story of our Friendship**
A unique way to celebrate the bond of friendship, whether it is decades old
or just beginning. Includes pages for writing memories and placing photos.

CARMEN RENEE BERRY AND TAMARA TRAEDER
$19.95 Paper over boards/Full-color photographs

**girlfriends for life: Friendships Worth Keeping Forever**
A collection of true stories sure to warm hearts, tickle funny bones,
and strike a chord with women everywhere.

CARMEN RENEE BERRY AND TAMARA TRAEDER
$13.95 Paperback

**Straight Women, Gay Men: Absolutely Fabulous Friendships**
It's not just Will and Grace! Real women talk candidly about their
fabulous friendships with gay men.

ROBERT H. HOPCKE AND LAURA RAFATY
$15.95 Paperback

**The Worrywart's Companion: Twenty-one Ways to Soothe Yourself and Worry Smart**
The perfect gift for anyone who lies awake at night worrying.

DR. BEVERLY POTTER
$12.95 Paperback

**Aunties: Our Older, Cooler, Wiser Friends**
An affectionate tribute to the unique and wonderful women we call "Auntie."

JULIENNE BENNETT AND TAMARA TRAEDER
$12.95 Paperback

**Teen girlfriends: Celebrating the Good Times, Getting through the Hard Times**
A celebration of and tribute to teen friendships.

JULIA DEVILLERS
INTRODUCTION BY CARMEN RENEE BERRY AND TAMARA TRAEDER
$13.95 Paperback

Available at bookstores and fine retailers nationwide.
To order any of these titles, just call us toll free at: 1-888-774-7595